"COMPANION TO THE FRENCH REVOLUTION,"

John Paxton

Facts On File Publications
New York, New York ● Oxford, England

Library of Congress Cataloging in Publication Data

Paxton, John.
    Companion to the French Revolution.

        1. France—History—Revolution, 1789–1799—
Dictionaries. I. Title.
DC147.P38   1986   944.04   84-21489
ISBN 0-8160-1116-8 (hc)
ISBN 0-8160-1937-1 (pb)

Printed in the United States of America

10 9 8 7 6 5 4 3 2 1

For Jonathy, Marian, Nicholas and Steven

CONTENTS

PREFACE

Two hundred years ago storm clouds were gathering over France for what was to be a decade of violent change. It also proved to be a great watershed in European history and, as a result, no one studying modern history today can ignore the French Revolution of 1789. The aim of this book is much the same as that of an earlier volume in this series, *Companion to Russian History*. It does not attempt to break new ground or give new interpretations of historical events but acts as a guide to the inquirer and helps the reader to further study.

The Revolution has been the subject of a vast literary output, particularly in France, and has also been the subject of historical reinterpretation in this century—for instance, at one period Danton was the hero and Robespierre the villain but at another the roles have been reversed. For many people the knowledge of the Revolution is small and is limited to *A Tale of Two Cities*, the guillotine, *The Scarlet Pimpernel* or the storming of the Bastille. It is for those who would like to make a deeper study that this book is aimed. It contains a who's who, gazetteer, dictionary, chronology and bibliography of the period, and also includes some pertinent maps and diagrams.

The 100 years or so before the outbreak of the French Revolution was one of the most crucial and formative periods of modern European history, but the Revolution in France was not the first to benefit the middle class at the expense of the feudal system— England and America had already gone through the revolutionary process. As 1789 approached, France had become exhausted by the wars of Louis. Prussia was growing in strength, as was Russia, where Peter the Great had extended his hold on the Baltic. The influence and power of France was declining and in the Seven Years' War (1756-63), Britain, siding with Prussia, captured French Canada.

Most people know 1789 as the year the Revolution began, but when did it end? Historians' views differ, but for this *Companion* there are entries up to the date when Napoleon Bonaparte was crowned emperor in 1804. Where to start? A revolution does not just happen without cause, and this is why the *Companion* contains entries dealing with people and events before the well-known date of 1789. This will help readers to understand why France, an extremely prosperous country in the 18th century, was financially bankrupt and the Revolution was, in fact, an attempt to put into practice what enlightened French citizens believed. Many attempts at financial reform were undertaken to stave off national bankruptcy, but in the end Louis XVI was forced to call the Estates-General, the first time this had happened since 1614.

They met in May 1789 and immediately the Third Estate demanded that the three orders should meet together. By June they had adopted the title of "National Assembly" and swore to draft a new constitution.

The shifts and changes during the

decade of the Revolution cause some confusion to students, but it does fall into eight uneven phases starting with the bankruptcy of the social, political and economic systems of the ancien régime from 1787 to 1789. This is followed by the political revolution at Versailles and the storming of the Bastille in the summer and early autumn of 1789. Then followed, from 1789 to 1791, the period spent searching for a suitable constitution and the dramatic changes in political, social and religious life that led to the growth of republicanism in the spring of 1791 until September 1792, when the monarchy was abolished.

The conflict between Girondins and Jacobins followed between 1792 and 1793. Robespierre dominated the scene from November 1793 until his assassination in July 1794, and his reign was followed by a period of moderate republicanism until the Directory was formed in October 1795.

With the coup d'état of Brumaire in November 1799, Napoleon Bonaparte became first consul and a new chapter in French history began.

To compile this *Companion* I have read several hundred works on the Revolution and readers may wish to know of one general history which I have found outstanding: *The French Revolution* by J. M. Thompson, published by Basil Blackwell in 1943 and reprinted many times since.

I've received considerable help in the research for the book from Stuart Chubb and I am very grateful to him. Sheila Fairfield and Dione Daffin came to my aid on several occasions. The staff of the London Library were as helpful as ever and my good friend Penny White, who has typed millions of words for me over the years, did it yet again.

John Paxton
Bruton, Somerset,
England

COMPANION
TO THE
FRENCH
REVOLUTION

A

ABBAYE. Prison built by Gamart between 1631-35. Originally an abbey prison of the monastery of St. Germain des Prés, Paris, it was converted into a military prison and was one of the sites of the massacres of September 2-5, 1792 (*q.v.*). It was demolished in 1857.

ABBEYS. *L'Almanach Royal* of 1789 reported that there were 993 abbeys and these included 253 for females. A law of February 17, 1790 suppressed orders and corporations and refused to recognize monastic vows, but exceptions were made for abbeys where members took care of the sick or gave instruction in colleges. On August 18, 1790, however, a new decree caused the closure of all religious communities without exception.

ABERCROMBY, SIR RALPH (1734-1801). Scottish general who served in the Seven Years' War. Retired from the army because he agreed with the views of the American colonists, he soon resumed his military career and fought against France in 1793. He had command of the expedition to the West Indies and gained the French colonies of St. Lucia, St. Vincent and Trinidad for Britain. In 1800 he was sent to the Mediterranean with an expeditionary force intended to eject the French from Egypt. Abercromby's army, 18,000 strong, landed at Aboukir Bay and defeated the French, under General Menou, in a night battle between Aboukir and Alexandria on March 21, 1801. During the battle he was mortally wounded. (*See* **Nile, Battle of the.**)

ABOLITION, LETTERS OF. The letters had been used by kings to remit punishment and were abolished in 1791, along with the *lettres de grâce* and those of the commutation of punishment or pain. They had superceded any judgments handed down by the courts, but both Louis XV and XVI had abused this privilege.

ABOLITION OF ROYALTY. On September 21, 1792 at the first sessions of the Convention (*q.v.*) under the presidency of Jérôme Pétion de Villeneuve (*q.v.*), a proposal for the abolition of the monarchy was carried.

ABOLITION OF THE CATHOLIC CULT. Part of the movement against the Catholic religion by the Convention. The Paris Commune (Commune de Paris, *q.v.*), directed by Hébert and Chaumette (*qq.v.*), took the initiative against the church. On October 14, 1793 all religious signs, statues of saints, madonnas and crosses in the streets were removed, replaced by busts of Marat and Lepelletier de Saint Fargeau (qq.v.). New funeral ceremonies were instituted that did not require priests. All churches were considered to be national property and the "Catholic Cult" was officially replaced by the "Cult of Reason."

ABONNEMENT. Agreement worked out between a provincial assembly and the crown for a total amount of taxes, fixed in advance, to be collected from the province, town or corporation and apportioned by the local assembly. It had the advantage of being an immediate definite sum due to the treasury instead of what could have been a larger sum but which would take time and expense to collect.

Mousnier, Roland, *The Institutions of France under the Absolute Monarchy*, 1979.

ABOUKIR. Site of two battles fought on July 25, 1799 and March 21, 1801. (For Battle of Aboukir Bay, July 31, 1798, *see* **Nile, Battle of the.**)

In 1799 the battle was fought between the French expeditionary army under Bonaparte, who was the victor, against Said Mustapha of Turkey. The castle surrendered on August 2 with severe Turkish losses.

In 1801 the French, commanded by General Menou, were finally defeated by an expeditionary force under the command of Sir Ralph Abercromby (*q.v.*).

ABOUKIR BAY, BATTLE OF. *See* **Nile, Battle of the.**

ABOYEUR. Sellers of revolutionary newspapers and pamphlets who were scattered along the boulevards and principal streets of the cities. They used smooth talking and sharp comments to attract the attention of prospective buyers. Royalist newspapers had their own sellers who did not operate without risk in the streets, but the "patriot" criers were always supported by the crowds.

ACADÉMIE DES SCIENCES, L'. Founded in 1666 under the direction of Colbert, who had the idea of giving it official status. An informal scientific club had met for 30 years prior to its foundation. Chemists, physicians, anatomists and mathematicians formed the nucleus of the club. It was originally a laboratory and observatory, rather than an academy. Louis XIV provided each member with a pension. Members included Laplace, Buffon, Lagrange, D'Alembert (*q.v.*) and Lavoisier (*q.v.*). It was suppressed with its sister academies on April 8, 1793. In 1795 the Convention decided to form an Institut National to replace the academies. In 1816 the original title was reconstituted as a branch of the Institut.

ACADÉMIE FRANÇAISE, L'. The first of the academies in France, based at the Louvre and confirmed by letters patent in 1635 under the influence of Richelieu. It was designed to protect the regularity and purity of the French language, emphasizing the study of language, grammar and literature. The number of members was fixed at 40. Its *Dictionary of the French Language* was undertaken in 1639 and completed in 1694, with later editions as appropriate. Suppressed with other literary societies patented by the ancien régime, it formed, under the Republic and Empire, the second class of the Institut—*Langage et Littérature française*—and regained its original name in 1816.

ACADÉMIE ROYALE DE PEINTURE ET DE SCULPTURE, L'.
Established in 1648 by Jules Mazarin (1602-61) as the Académie des Beaux Arts, to which was later added the Académie d'Architecture which was founded in 1671. It was composed of painters, sculptors, architects, engravers and musical composers. It was suppressed in 1793 and later became part of the Institut National (*q.v.*).

ACCAPAPEURS.
Speculators, who bought up cereals and flour in the markets in order to fix higher prices. These speculations caused scarcity during the period preceding the Revolution. The Constituent Assembly (Assembly, National, *q.v.*) decreed that speculation was a capital crime, but it still continued, aided by antirevolutionary profiteers and the *pacte de famine (q.v.)*.

ACCUSATEUR PUBLIC, L'.
One of the most influential journals of the counterrevolutionary reaction. It was published 1795-97. Founded by Richer-Sérisy, a Paris attorney and denouncer of the Austrian Committee. He was suspected by Robespierre (*q.v.*) because of his connections with Danton and Camille Desmoulins and imprisoned on their deaths. On release, Richer-Sérisy became an ardent Royalist, was repeatedly denounced, and was accused of being involved in the Insurrection of 13 Vendemiaire *(q.v.)* but without culpable intention. He died in England in 1803.

ACCUSATEUR PUBLIC, L'.
A temporary tribunal established December 1, 1790, for the judgment of criminal affairs. The judges were nominated by the people, but the nomination of the magistrate charged with pursuing the accusation was the prerogative of the king. In 1791 the Assembly determined the qualifications of the public accuser, and in addition he was to be responsible for the police. On March 10, 1793 a Revolutionary Tribunal was instituted. There was confusion at the beginning of the Revolution, relating to the relative jurisdictions and powers of the king's commissioners and the public accusers. The Constitution of Frimaire (*q.v.*), Year VIII, gave the government the sole right of naming the magistrate.

ACQUITS AU COMPTANT.
Notes signed by the king ordering the treasury to pay the bearer. The notes did not have either a signature of the drawer, or the sum therein inscribed. The nature of the expenditure was never adequately explained, but the *comptants* issued in 1792 by Louis XVI are specific as to the amount and for what reason they were being paid. In eight years the king signed away 850 million livres by these notes.

ACRE.
Ancient port now situated in Israel, 9 miles northeast of Haifa on the Mediterranean Sea. Strategically placed, it changed hands many times until it was taken by the Turks in 1517. It was defended by Djezzar

Pasha against Napoleon until relieved by Sir Sidney Smith, who resisted twelve attempts by the French between March 9 and May 20, 1799, when Napoleon retreated. Napoleon's withdrawal was hastened by bubonic plague spreading through his army.

ACTES DES APÔTRES, LES (THE ACTS OF THE APOSTLES). Founded in November 1789 by the strongly Royalist Joseph Peltier, this newspaper consisted mainly of sarcastic epigrams and pointed satires against the Revolution and its apologists. It caused so much anger and bad feeling that it was closed down by the king in October 1791.

ADDINGTON, HENRY, FIRST VISCOUNT SIDMOUTH (1757-1844). English statesman, speaker of the House of Commons (1789-1801) and prime minister (1801-04) on Pitt's retirement. He concluded the Treaty of Amiens *(q.v.)* in March 1802. Pitt withdrew his support of the government when it became apparent that no preparations were being made for the renewal of war with France (May 1803).
Ziegler, Philip, *Addington,* 1965.

ADÉLAIDE, MADAME MARIE (1732-1800). The eldest daughter of Louis XV she left France in 1791 with Madame Victoire, her sister. They were refugees in Rome, Naples and then Trieste, where Adélaide died. They had been arrested at Arnay-le-Duc in the Côte d'Or and the Assembly forced them to return to Paris, but they were helped by Mirabeau *(q.v.)* and released.

ADIGE RIVER, BATTLES OF. River that rises in the Tyrolean Alps and flows south and then east to the Adriatic Sea. The second largest river in Italy, it was the scene of many battles. In 1794 the French army under the minister of war, Schérer, defeated the Austrians here and near it the Austrians defeated the French in 1799.

AÉROPOREISTE. Revolutionary aeronauts (balloonists). *See* **Aérostats and Aérostiers, Compagnie des.**

AÉROSTATS. The Montgolfier brothers (Jacques Etienne [1745-1799] and Joseph Michel [1740-1810]) demonstrated the first public example of ballooning in 1782 near Annonay.
Gillispie, Charles C., *The Montgolfier Brothers and the Invention of Aviation, 1783-84,* 1983.

AÉROSTIERS, COMPAGNIE DES. Company of soldiers responsible for directing balloon ascents for the army. The first company was formed in Year II (*see* **Calendar, Revolutionary**) and saw service at the Battle of Fleurus (June 26, 1794, *q.v.*) where a balloon kept observation for nine hours. They were also used at Maubeuge and before Charleroi for reconnaissance and defense. After the successful use at Fleurus, balloons were much in use. The Committee of Public Safety *(q.v.)* formed the Compagnie. A second was formed shortly thereafter to work with the Armée du Rhin while the first was attached to the Armée de Sambre-et-Meuse, and their service continued until the corps was disbanded in Year VII. Gaspard

Monge (1746-1818, *q.v.*) was the first to suggest the potential usefulness of balloons in Year II.

AGRICULTURE, FÊTE DE L'. The Fête de l'Agriculture was one of the major festivities during the 36 *décades* (*q.v.*) under Robespierre (*q.v.*). A second fête occurred in Year IV, following the law of 3 Brumaire (*see* **Calendar, Revolutionary**), which instituted seven grand fêtes a year. These were celebrated with enthusiasm, participants meeting before patriotic altars, where a plough decorated with flowers and leaves and drawn by cattle or horses was placed. It was preceded by 24 of the most respected local laborers, and they were followed by their wives and children, who carried in one hand flowers, in the other samples of the tools of their trades. The name of the most meritorious person was proclaimed. Tools were exchanged for rifles, and the procession went to the patriotic altar, covering it with flowers to the sound of music. In Paris the fête was at the Champ de la Réunion (Champ de Mars). The last celebration was on June 20, 1799.

AIDES. Excise taxes, chiefly on wines and spirits, this was the principal indirect tax. (*See* **Taxes**).

AIGUILLON, ARMAND VIGNE-RON DUPLESSIS RICHELIEU, DUC D' (1761-1800). Commandant of the King's Light Horse, he was elected to the Estates-General (*q.v.*) by the nobility of Anjou. A liberal, he helped to lead the secession to the Third Estate (*q.v*) on June 25, 1789. On August 4 he was the second noble to move the abolition of all feudal rights and privileges, "in the name of sound philosophy and of the regeneration of the state." He died as an exile in Hamburg.

AINESSE, DROIT D'. Under the ancien régime the eldest son inherited all the landed property of his parents. Younger brothers, unless their elder brothers were generous, generally had to fend for themselves, and many sisters went into convents. *Droit d'Ainesse* was abolished by the constituent laws in 1790.

AIX-LA-CHAPELLE (AACHEN). Here Charlemagne was born (742) and died (814), having built the minster (796-804). The city was taken by the French in December 1792, retaken by the Austrians in March 1793 and by the French, September 1794. It became part of Prussia after the Congress of Vienna (1815).

AJACCIO, CORSICA, FRANCE. Town and port on the Gulf of Ajaccio. Napoleon was born on the Via Malerba in 1769, living here for ten years. Corsica became part of France in 1768.

À LA LANTERNE. Part of "Ça ira" (*q.v.*), the revolutionary rallying-cry, calling for the hanging of aristocrats on a lamp post: *Ah! ça ira, ça ira! Les aristocrates à la lanterne!*

ALARMISTES, LES. False-news carriers, a name given to Royalists and counterrevolutionaries. They were thought to foment troubles within the country, and alarm citizens. They were said to falsify the meaning of new laws, spread news of the victories of the enemies, usually totally contrary to the truth. Barère *(q.v.)* pushed for a decree of deportation against false-news carriers, but it was rejected.

ALEMBERT, JEAN LE ROND, D' **(1717-83).** Mathematician and philosopher and one of the Encyclopedists. He was educated at the Collège des Quatre-Nations in Paris, became a nonpracticing law advocate, then studied medicine and, finally, mathematics. He was elected to the Academy of Sciences. Until about 1757 he collaborated with Denis Diderot *(q.v.)* in the founding and editing of the *Encyclopédie (q.v.)* and his *Discours préliminaire* to this (1751) added to his reputation as a man of letters, as well as a scientist. He was admitted to the French Academy, and became secretary in 1772. He declined invitations from Frederick II of Prussia to become president of the Academy of Berlin, and from Catherine II of Russia to tutor her son.
Grimsey, J., *Jean d'Alembert*, 1963.

ALEXANDRIA, BATTLES OF. Napoleon occupied Alexandria, Egypt on July 2, 1798 immediately before his victory at the Battle of the Pyramids (July 21, *q.v.*), which made him master of Egypt. An English army under Abercromby *(q.v.)* defeated the French, commanded by General Menou, at Alexandria September 2, 1801.

ALKMAAR, CONVENTION OF (October 18, 1799). Agreement by which General Brune of the French

army agreed that the Allies could evacuate Holland, provided that they repatriated all French prisoners. This was achieved by the beginning of November 1799. Withdrawal was encouraged by news that the Allies *(q.v.)* were not to receive help from the Austrians, the growth of disease within the army and the military setbacks at Bergen (September 19) and at Castricum (October 6).

ALLIES. Attempts by Austria and Prussia to influence France fomented revolutionary activity, and in April 1792 the Girondins *(q.v.)* forced Louis XVI to declare war on Austria. After a disastrous initial attack on the Austrian Netherlands, Danton's *(q.v.)* professional organization of national defense led to the check of the Allies at Valmy *(q.v.)* on September 20. Following this, Dumouriez *(q.v.)* led the French to victory at Jemappes; the Netherlands were captured and Custine *(q.v.)* cleared the Middle Rhine, while Montesquieu and Anselme occupied Savoy and Nice. With the execution of the king in 1793 and the occupation of Belgium, Britain came into the war.

Pitt's *(q.v.)* First Coalition, consisting of Britain, Austria, Prussia, Holland, Spain and Sardinia, had some success: Belgium was cleared after the Battle of Neerwinden; Dunkirk was besieged; and Toulon was occupied under Admiral Hood. With the rise of the Jacobins, however (and Carnot's reorganization of the army, which emphasized massed troops attacking single, vital points), the balance changed. The Allies retreated across the Rhine, Bonaparte forced Hood from Toulon *(q.v.)* and in 1794 Jourdan's victory at Fleurus *(q.v.)* saw the reoccupation of Belgium. France captured Holland in the following year; Prussia left the war and the Coalition was thereby ended.

In 1796 the French movement to Vienna was defeated by Archduke Charles, who routed Moreau (q.v.) on the Main and Jourdan on the Danube. However, Bonaparte (in command of the Army of Italy), having forced Sardinia to a peace which ceded Savoy and Nice to France, took the Bridge of Lodi and entered Milan on May 16; control was taken, of all Lombardy, except Mantua. Bonaparte defeated Austrian efforts to relieve Mantua at Brescia and Castiglione (in August), Arcola (in November) and Rivoli (in January 1797). Venice was then occupied. Northern Italy was organized into the Cisalpine and Ligurian Republics (q.v.), and the Peace of Campo Formio was dictated to Austria. Britain, the one remaining enemy, had had a series of naval victories and had captured colonies. Bonaparte landed an army in Egypt and won the Battle of the Pyramids, but the destruction of his fleet at the Battle of the Nile (q.v.) by Nelson in August 1798 and the failure at Acre of his plan to attack Turkey caused a major change of plans. Bonaparte returned to Paris, accomplishing a coup d'état, which made him the master of France on November 9. A new coalition developed, consisting of Britain, Russia, Austria, Turkey, Naples and Portugal. The French were successful in southern Italy, but initially in trouble on the Rhine, in Switzerland and in northern Italy, where Russian Marshal Suvaroff's lightning campaign climaxed at the River Trebia in June 1799. In September, however, Massena defeated the Russians at Zurich, Bonaparte won the Battle of Marengo in June 1800, while Moreau was the victor at Hohenlinden in December. Austria then signed the Treaty of Lunéville in February 1801. Russia had left the coalition but her "Armed Neutrality of the North" was decisively broken by Nelson's victory at Copenhagen in April.

Following Abercromby's (q.v.) defeat of the French at Alexandria, peace was signed with Britain at Amiens in March 1802. France agreed to evacuate southern Italy and Egypt, while Britain returned her conquests, except for Ceylon and Trinidad.

ALLOBROGES, SOCIÉTÉ DES. Founded in 1792 by Savoyards who had lived in Paris for many years, the Society kept up close relations with its compatriots and was influential in pressing for Savoy's demands to become part of the Republic. The Society disappeared with Savoy's union with France (1794), but it still sent a deputation to the Paris Commune (Commune de Paris, q.v.).

ALMANACH ROYALE, L'. First published 1679, with primitive predictions, the phases of the moon, the departure of messengers, palace fêtes, the major fairs and so forth. From 1689, Laurent Houry, bookseller and printer in Paris and the *Almanach's* editor, added notices, statistics, and the list of the royal family and the principal dignitaries and officials of the state. Louis XIV renewed the right of publication. At the Revolution, the name was changed to *Almanach National.* The volumes for 1789 and 1793 are rare, and that for year IV is virtually unobtainable.

ALSACE. Region in the northeast of France situated on the western side of the River Rhine Valley and the eastern slopes of Vosges. Chief towns are Strasbourg, Mulhouse, Colmar and Belfort. Alsace has long been a disputed territory. It was once part of Germany but in 1648 much of it was ceded to France, and additional territory later. After the Franco-Prussian War, all Alsace except Belfort was incorporated into Germany to form, with part of Lorraine, the territory of Alsace-Lorraine. The Treaty of Versailles returned Lorraine to France, and Alsace became the departments of Haut-Rhin and Bas-Rhin.

ALTENKIRCHEN, BATTLE OF. Altenkirchen, situated in the Rhine Basin, was the scene of a decisive defeat of the Austrian army, under the command of the duke of Württemburg, by the French army, under the orders of Jourdan, on June 4, 1796. On September 19, 1796 the French were defeated and their general, Marceau, killed.

ALTORFF, BATTLES OF. Swiss village in the canton of Uri, first taken by Bernadotte (*[q.v.]* August 27, 1796) and then by the Armée d'Helvétie (August 13, 1799).

AMALGAME. Part of the wholesale compulsory enlistment (*levée en masse*) in the army, which replaced the earlier voluntary enlistment. In 1789 Dubois-Crancé had pressed for a universal short-term service, with a regular small army. Carnot's Decree was passed by the Convention in August 1793 and 543 battalions were to be raised by conscription, distributed among eleven in the field. Men between eighteen and twenty-five, the first class of "requisitionnaires," provided over 400,000 conscripts. In the spring of 1794 the total, including

volunteers, ran to 750,000 men under arms. The amalgamation consisted of merging the remnants of the old army with the new, replacing the earlier voluntary recruitment by universal conscription.

AMBERG, BATTLE OF. Amberg, Bavaria, on the Vils River, the capital of the Upper Palatinate until 1810. On August 24, 1796, during the War of the First Coalition (*q.v.*), the French under Jourdan were defeated here by Archduke Charles of Austria.

AMBIGU-COMIQUE, THÉÂTRE DE L'. It was constructed by Audinot in 1769 and was situated in the Boulevard du Temple. A marionette theater, it staged a number of puppet-spectaculars such as "Testament de Polichinelle" (1772) and "Dorothée" (1792), a pantomine which massed religious figures and furniture on the stage in a riot, creating both protest and applause.

AMBULANCES VOLANTES. Invented by Dominique Jean Larrey (1766-1842), a military surgeon, the flying ambulances were developed in 1791 to transport wounded soldiers from the battlefield to military hospitals where they could be treated quickly.

AMENDE HONORABLE. Ancient punishment requiring a person to undergo a degrading public ritual as a sign of his guilt for crimes that included sacrilege, blasphemy, incest, sodomy, usury and, in certain instances, adultery, or which were against the security of the state or crown. It was abolished in 1791.

AMERICAN REVOLUTIONARY WAR. French sympathies were, from the outset, with the American colonists, partly as a result of the humiliations arising from the Seven Years' War, partly from a concern with England's commercial and economic power, as expressed both within the country and abroad, and partly with the need to somehow pull England down a peg or two.

On April 6, 1776 the Americans opened their ports to all except Great Britain. On May 2, 1776 the French foreign minister, the comte de Vergennes, persuaded Louis XVI to give the colonists one million livres in munitions through a fictitious company headed by Beaumarchais (q.v.). On March 12, 1777 Congress reconvened in Philadelphia and reconstituted the "Committee for Secret Correspondence" as the "Committee for Foreign Affairs," appointing several commissioners to represent the United States abroad. Foreign officers aiding the American cause included Major-General the marquis de Lafayette (q.v.) and "Baron" Jean de Kalb; their commissions were dated July 31 and September 15, respectively.

The Franco-American Alliance of February 6, 1778 occurred as the result of French fears that the new British peace proposals would strike them adversely. These proposals were brought forward after General John Burgoyne's defeat at Saratoga (his men laid down their arms on October 17, 1777). The French finally recognized American independence in two treaties: the first was of amity and commerce and the second of alliance. The latter treaty set forth war objectives and provided a general agreement not to make a separate peace. Conrad Gerard became the French minister to the United States in March 1778, and Congress ratified the treaties on May 4, appointing Benjamin Franklin (q.v.) as the minister to France on September 14.

The French provided various forms of military assistance to the Americans. The French fleet, under the comte d'Estaing, arrived on July 29, 1778 to support the Franco-American attack on Newport, Rhode Island. The appearance of Admiral Howe's ships on August 10, however, prevented an attack, and a storm on August 11 scattered both fleets. In October 1779 d'Estaing and General Benjamin Lincoln joined forces in an abortive attack on Savannah, Georgia (October 9). On July 10, 1780 the comte de Rochambeau reached Newport with 6,000 troops.

In order to carry out the American peace negotiations, Congress appointed John Jay, Franklin, Henry Laurens and Thomas Jefferson on June 14, 1781 to assist John Adams in their dealings. This delegation was to be advised by the French minister, the chevalier de la Luzerne. By June 15 Congress had reduced its essential demands to independence and sovereignty, and instructed the commissioners not to act without French consent.

In July 1781, Rochambeau's force left Newport, joined up with Washington's on the Hudson and marched south. The Yorktown Campaign of August 1781 spelled the end of English power in the country. Admiral de Grasse engaged Admiral Thomas Graves's fleet on August 5, which retired to New York on August 10 after the arrival of the comte de Barras's squadron to reinforce de Grasse. On August 30, de Grasse landed 3,000 troops to join Lafayette near Yorktown. French ships fetched Washington's and Rochambeau's soldiers in September at Williamsburg, from where they approached

Yorktown on September 28. Cornwallis capitulated on October 19 and the war was, for all intents and purposes, over.

AMI DES HOMMES, L'. *Ami des Hommes, ou traité de la population* ("The Friend of Man, or Treatise on Population"), published in 1756-58, was the work of Victor Riqueti, marquis de Mirabeau *(q.v.),* political economist and physiocrat. His major work, highly regarded by Rousseau *(q.v.),* it was written before *Théorie de l'Impôt,*

AMI DU PEUPLE, L'. Widely read newspaper edited and written by Jean Paul Marat *(q.v.),* whose nickname it was, with a complicated printing history and variety of names. It was published from September 12, 1789 to July 14, 1793 (Marat was assassinated by Charlotte Corday *[q.v.]* on July 13), with several breaks in between (Marat fled to England in July 1790 and December 1791). It was known initially as *Le Publiciste Parisien,* changing with the sixth issue (September 16, 1789) to *L'Ami du Peuple, ou Le Publiciste Parisien;* this ran to issue 685 (September 21, 1792). At the declaration of the republic, *L'Ami* was closed, and on September 24 the *Journal de la Républic française* was started, running for 143 issues (September 24, 1792-March 9, 1793). After March 11, 1793 the newspaper became *Publiciste de la République française, ou Observations aux Française,* from March 14-July 14, 1793. Finally, under J. Roux, the paper ran 260 issues with the title *Publiciste de la République française, par l'Ombre de Marat, L'Ami du Peuple.*

AMI DU ROI, L'. *L'Ami du Roi, des Français, de l'Ordre et surtout de la Verité, par les Continuateurs de Fréron,* a violently antirevolutionary, Royalist newspaper which took over when *Année Litteraire (q.v.)* was no longer published. It ran, in two editions, between June 1790 and May 1792, one published by Galart de Montjoye (1746-1816) and the other by Thomas Royou (1741-92). It was condemned by the Legislative Assembly in 1792.

AMIENS. City and capital of the Somme department in Picardy, on the Somme River 80 miles north of Paris. It was the capital of Picardy until 1790. On March 27, 1802 it was the scene of the signing of the Anglo-French treaty, at the Hotel de Ville, ending the War of the Second Coalition *(q.v.).*

AMIENS, PEACE OF. *See* **Peace of Amiens.**

AMIS DE LA CONSTITUTION, SOCIÉTÉ DES. The most famous of the revolutionary political clubs. It had its origin in the Club Breton, established at Versailles shortly after the opening of the Estates-General *(q.v.)* in 1789. Initially only deputies from Brittany were members; later it was joined by others from various parts of France. Mirabeau, Sieyès, Barnave, Pétion, Robespierre *(qq.v.),* the duc d'Aiguillon, the Abbé Grigoire, and Charles and Alexandre Lameth *(qq.v.)* were early members.

The club, which was still composed entirely of deputies, followed the National Assembly to Paris after the march on Versailles of October 5 and

6, 1789. There it rented the refectory of the monastery of the Jacobins in the Rue St. Honoré, near the seat of the Assembly. "Jacobins," the name given to the Dominicans in France because their first Paris house was in the Rue St. Jacques, was applied to the club, in ridicule, by its enemies.

The rules in February 1790 were to discuss in advance the questions to be decided by the National Assembly, to work for the establishment and the strengthening of the constitution, in accordance with the spirit of its preamble (that is, of respect for fully constituted authority, and the Rights of Man [q.v.]), to correspond with other societies of the same kind, which should be found throughout the country. Importantly it was decided that any member who, by word or action, showed that his principles were contrary to the constitution and the Rights of Man was to be expelled; this later made it much easier to "purify" the Society, by the expulsion (and execution) of its more moderate members. The seventh article specified that the club should contact, as associates, similar societies in other parts of France, and maintain a regular correspondence with them. By the end of 1791 the Jacobins had branches all over France, giving the club a widely-spaced and yet highly centralized organization, with considerable power.

After the promulgation of the constitution of 1791 the club adopted the title of the "Société des Amis de la Constitution séants aux Jacobins à Paris. This was changed after the fall of the monarchy, on September 21, 1792, to "Société des Jacobins, Amis de la Liberté et de l'Égalité." The Society occupied, in succession, the refectory, the library and the chapel of the monastery. See Jacobins.

AMIS DE LA PAIX. A great number of clubs founded in Paris and the departments were given this name by the Société des Amis de la Constitution Monarchique.

AMIS DE LA PATRIE, SECTION DES. Formerly the Trinité district, then the Ponceau section, becoming the quarter of the Porte Saint-Denis in 1795 (VIe arrondissement). It demanded the departure from Paris of all professional soldiers and the punishment of all those who criticized the popular societies.

AMIS DES DROITS DE L'HOMME ET DU CITOYEN, SOCIÉTÉ DES. *See* **Cordeliers.**

AMIS ET AMIES DE LA VERITÉ, SOCIÉTÉ DES (CERCLE SOCIAL, CLUB DU). The "Cercle Social" was, at first, a freemason's lodge, which worked to create social reforms. It proposed to become the center and direction of all freemasons' lodges, to organize a universal confederation of its followers. The abbé Fauchet, who had pronounced the funeral oration over those who had fallen at the taking of the Bastille, was its most influential member. Its publication was the *Bouche-de-Fer*, edited by Fauchet. Meetings were held in the Palais-Royal, where 12,000 people could listen to the theories of Fauchet, Condorcet, Sieyès (qq.v.) and others. Women joined as "Amies."

AMSTERDAM, OCCUPATION OF. Principal city of the Kingdom of Holland at the mouth of the Amstel River. It was seized, with only slight resistance, by the French, who were welcomed as liberators, under the command of Pichegru *(q.v.)* on January 19, 1795. The French were expelled in November 1813 by the inhabitants and the former government was restored.

ANABAPTISTS. Members of a sect, founded in 1529 by Nicholas Stork, a disciple of Luther, which demanded the abolition of feudal privileges. Persecuted, Anabaptists settled in Holland and along the banks of the Rhine. Many accepted revolutionary ideas, in spite of their religion's interdiction against the swearing of oaths or bearing arms. In August 1793 they demanded to be considered as French citizens.

ANARCHISTS. Individuals who, according to the Jacobins *(q.v.)*, took advantage of troubles and arguments between different political groups during the Revolution, to band together to create social and political disorder. On September 2, 1790 a band of anarchists threatened members of the Constituent Assembly with death. The elections of Years VI and VII were annulled by the government, because of the terror-threats provoked by anarchists.

ANCIEN RÉGIME (OLD RÉGIME/ ORDER). The social and political structure existing in France prior to the Revolution. Its main characteristic was the rigid division of society into three orders: the aristocracy, the church and the third estate. Above these orders was an absolute monarchy, based on the divine right of kings.
Behrens, C. B. A., *The Ancien Régime,* 1967.

ANGERS. Capital of Anjou and by 1790 the chief town of the department of Maine-et-Loire. It was one of the most important centers for republican operations against the Vendéan rebels *(see* **Vendéan Rebellion***)*. The city was taken by the rebels on June 24, 1793, but the republicans later regained it, repulsing the Vendéan army in December, 1793. The guillotine occupied a permanent position in the Place du Ralliement, and those condemned were either beheaded or shot en masse. Famine during the Revolution killed many of Anger's citizens

ANGOULÊME, MARIE THÉRÈSE CHARLOTTE DE FRANCE, DUCHESSE D' (1778-1851) (known also as **Madame Royale**). Born at Versailles, eldest daughter of Louis XVI and Marie Antoinette, she married Louis Antoine de Bourbon, duc d' Angoulême (1775-1844), the last dauphin of France, elder son of the Comte d'Artois (afterwards, Charles X), and of Marie Thérèse of Savoy. She was imprisoned (1792-95) with the royal family in the Temple *(q.v.)*, then released in exchange for members of the National Convention, who had been handed over to the Austrians by General Charles Dumouriez. In 1814 she returned to France with Louis XVIII and in March 1815 after Napoleon had entered Paris, she was able to maintain the loyalty of Bordeaux to the royal family for ten days. She died in Austria.

ANNALES PATRIOTIQUES ET LITTÉRAIRES, LES. Newspaper published October 1789-June 1797 under the direction of Louis Sébastien Mercier (1740-1814, *q.v.*) and Jean Louis Carra (1743-93). It gave good coverage of commerce, literature and politics. Mercier was a staunch conservative. Author of the extremely popular *Tableaux de Paris* (1789) he stood, as a journalist, in the middle ground between the Jacobins and Royalists. A political moderate, as a deputy to the Convention he voted against the death penalty for Louis XVI. He was imprisoned but was released on the death of Robespierre (*q.v.*).

ANNALES PHILOSOPHIQUES, LES. First published 1788 as the fortnightly *Journal de la Réligion et du Culte catholique* and edited by D. Ricard (1741-1803). It changed titles several times (with publication breaks), *Annales réligieuses, politiques et littéraires, Annales catholiques, Annales philosophiques, morales, et littéraires,* ending as *L'Ami de la Religion et du Roi, Journal ecclésiastique, politique, et littéraire* (1814-59). Edited for most of the period by the abbé E. A. de Boulogne (1747-1825) and the abbé M. N. S. Guillon (1760-1847). (Conservative, traditionalist Guillon [who became Dean of Sorbonne] also served Napoleon, the Bourbons and Orléanists.) After 1859 it became a general daily newspaper.

ANNALES POLITIQUES, CIVILES ET LITTÉRAIRES DU DIX-HUITIÈME SIÈCLE, LES. Newspaper of literary, political and economic interest which was published 1777-1792 and edited by Simon Nicolas Henri Linguet (1736-94, *q.v.*), journalist and advocate. Linguet was a believer in the principles of absolutism, and a violent attacker of whatever was modern or enlightened. Anti-philosophe, he quarrelled with d'Alembert (*q.v.*), wrote pamphlets against Mirabeau (*q.v.*) and in defense of Louis XVI, and was supported by Marie Antoinette. He was guillotined "For having flattered the despots of Vienna and London." The *Annales* was published in London 1777-1780, in Geneva 1780-83, London 1783-1790 and Paris 1790-92.

ANNATES. Right of the pope to receive or collect the first year the revenues of a benefice, or of all the benefices, of a diocese. *Annates* were abolished on August 11, 1789.

ANNÉE LITTÉRAIRE, L'. Newspaper started by Elie Catherine Fréron (1719-76) and others in 1754. It supported the church and the monarchy. After Fréron's death, the paper was taken over by his son, Louis Marie Stanislas Fréron (1754-1802, *q.v.*), G. M. Royou, J. L. Geoffroy and others, and it was published until 1790.

ANTI-CLERICALISM. In France the Enlightenment (*q.v.*) provided the basis for hostility towards the influence of the church in society and the state. Joseph II of Austria and other Catholic rulers brought the church closely under the control of the state and by 1773 the Jesuits had been expelled from all Catholic countries. During the Reformation this control had been largely achieved in Protestant states. Anti-clericalism tended, therefore, to affect primarily the Catholic Church.

ANTI-JACOBIN. Whig satirical newspaper, also known as the *Weekly Examiner*, was published from November 20, 1797 to July 9, 1798 by George Canning (1770-1827), George Ellis (1753-1815) and William Gifford (1756-1826). It was directed against the English "Radicals" of the period.

The term "Jacobin" has been generally applied to all promulgators of extreme revolution.

ANTRAIN, BATTLE OF. Battle, taking place at Antrain, Ille-et-Vilaine department, 15 miles west-northwest of Fougères on the Couesnon River, resulting in the victory of the Vendéans over the republicans on November 20, 1793.

AOSTA, BATTLE OF THE VALL' D'. Battle fought at the opening of the Great and Little Saint Bernard roads, and the scene of the victory of the Armée des Alpes, commanded by General Alexandre Dumas, over the Piedmontese in 1794.

APANAGES. Provinces, seigneuries, châteaux or lands given by the kings of France to their younger sons. These apanages reverted to the crown after the death of the recipients. On December 20, 1790 the Constituent Assembly supplied apanages to royal children and decreed that they should be a charge on the Civil List until they reached the age of 25. With the end of the monarchy apanages were abolished but were reinstituted by Napoleon for the benefit of his children.

ARBRES DE LA LIBERTÉ, LES. Trees planted at the beginning of the Revolution to symbolize liberty and fraternity. By 1792 they numbered about 60,000. There were, in addition, "Arbres de la Fraternité," which were planted at the Place du Carrousel in Paris.

ARCHIVES, NATIONAL. During the course of the Revolution, many archives which had been held in monasteries and religious houses or châteaux were lost or destroyed, mainly through the suppression and dispersal of old foundations.

On August 14, 1789 the National Assembly ruled that minutes of its acts and rulings be brought together to form the particular archives of the Assembly.

Laws of September 4-7 and September 7-12, 1790 regulated the organization of National Archives, which were to consist of all acts that established the constitution of the state, its public rights, and its laws. Later decrees brought to Paris all appropriate materials held in the departments, to be centralized and controlled at the Hôtel de Soubise.

ARCOLA, BATTLE OF. Battle fought at this village in Verona province on the Alpone River, 16 miles east-southeast of Verona. From November 15-17, 1796 during Napoleon's First Italian Campaign, the French won an important victory here over the Austrians, under Field Marshal Alvinczy. Casualties were 7,000 Austrians and 4,500 French.

ARGONNE, BATTLE OF. Region in the northeast of wooded hills extending from Aisne to Meuse rivers, it had been of strategic importance as a barrier between Lorraine and Champagne and it was the scene of a campaign that ended on September 20, 1792 when the French defeated the Prussians at Valmy.

ARISTOCRATES, CLUB DES (1789). Founded in 1789 it held its meetings at the Grands-Augustins. The club was not long-lasting but a portion of its membership reunited as the "Club des Impartiaux." At its Palais-Royal meetings, the members amused themselves by giving the principal leaders burlesque names: "Archbishop of Paris," "aristocrosse," the "comte de Artois," "Aristocrane," etc.

"ARISTOS." Name given towards the end of the Revolution to a section of the former privileged classes who engaged in obstructionism, propaganda and general agitation following the passage of major reforms in the Assembly.

ARMED NEUTRALITY, LEAGUE OF. In the summer of 1778, the outbreak of hostilities between Britain and France brought the issue of neutral rights to a head. Requiring naval stores, French diplomats tried to cultivate the neutrals using the liberal doctrine of "Free Ships, Free Goods." Catherine II of Russia moved to lead a league of neutrals in 1780, and to champion their rights. Russia, Denmark, Sweden, Portugal and, eventually, the Dutch Republic, joined the league. The principle was anti-British in effect, leading to war between the Dutch and Britain at the end of 1780. In December 1800 French diplomacy, and resentment among the neutrals at Britain's interpretation of maritime law, led to a second league, which joined Denmark, Sweden and Russia. Baltic and German markets were briefly cut off, but after Nelson (*q.v.*) bombarded Copenhagen (April 2, 1801) the league collapsed.

ARMÉE DES EMIGRÉES, L'. Army formed in 1791 (also known as

l'Armée des Princes) by French princes of the blood who had left France; later, commoner émigrés joined. The commander was the comte de Provence (later Louis XVIII), brother of Louis XVI. While the forces were being organized, they were concentrated mainly at Worms, the headquarters of the prince de Condé. In 1792 its three forces were attached to the coalition: First, the Armée du Centre of about 10,000 was defeated at Valmy and disbanded. It was led by the comte de Provence and the comte d'Artois (later, Charles X). The second, the most successful force, the Armée du Condé of about 5,000, it existed from 1793 to 1801 and was disbanded after the Treaty of Lunéville (1801). It fought extensively, in Alsace, Austria, Russia, Bavaria and in the Rhine War (1793-96). The third force, numbering about 4-5,000, was led by the duc de Bourbon under the Austrians. It was disbanded after Jemappes (November 1792).

ARMES D'HONNEUR. From the early years of the Revolution, rifles, pistols and sabres, known as *Armes d'Honneur*, were given to soldiers who had distinguished themselves through their heroism or bravery.

ARMIES. The army in the early years of the Revolution was undisciplined, there was mutiny and little leadership. Nearly 600 generals had left the army in the 18 months preceding July 1792. Since 1789 over half the officers had left the service. In 1789 there were 160,000 regular volunteer soldiers and 110,000 militia. In 1792 there were about 50,000 soldiers capable of waging war. By early 1793 the number had risen to 140,000—all volunteers. In February a *levée* of

300,000 was decreed and on August 23, 1793 the Committee of Public Safety conscripted the whole male population in the *levée en masse*. The decree stated that "until the enemies have been driven from the territories of the Republic, the French people are permanently available for army service. National buildings shall be converted into barracks; public places into armament workshops; the soil of cellars shall be washed in lye to extract saltpeter. Guns shall be turned over exclusively to those who march against the enemy. Saddle horses are called for to complete the cavalry corps; draught horses, other than those employed in agriculture, shall haul artillery and provisions. Unmarried citizens or childless widowers, from eighteen to twenty-five years, shall go first; they shall meet without delay, at the chief town of their districts, where they shall practice manual exercise daily, while awaiting the hour of departure. The battalion organized in each district shall be united under a banner bearing the inscription: 'The French people risen against tyrants'."

The nine armies in 1793 were the Armées du Nord, des Ardennes, de la Moselle, du Rhin, des Alpes, d'Italie, des Pyrenees, des Côtes, and de Reserve.

Glover, Michael, *The Napoleonic Wars: 1792-1815*, 1979.

Phipps, R. W., *The Armies of the First French Republic*. 4 vols. 1926-39.

Wilkinson, S., *The French Army before Napoleon*, 1915.

ARMOIRE DE FER, L'. A concealed cupboard with an iron door, built by one Gamain under the instructions of Louis XVI, hidden in a corridor at the Tuileries. After the Flight to Varennes (*q.v.*), and subsequent searches of the royal quarters at the Tuileries for sensitive documents, the king had decided to conceal his private papers and correspondence, and those of his wife, where they could not be located. Gamain, however, told Roland (*q.v.*), minister of the interior, of the existence of the cupboard, and with Louis held at the Temple, a search was made in August 1792. Severely compromising documents were found, some of which centered on secret correspondence with the Paris Austrian Committee which had, in turn, been in direct contact with the émigrés.

ARMS, COMMISSION FOR. The commission was established on 13 Pluviose (*q.v.*), Year II. The Convention (*q.v.*) named three members of the Committee of Public Safety and charged them to direct the various establishments, manufactures, foundries and workshops making weapons. The commission oversaw every aspect of the manufacture and distribution of every type of weapon, land and sea, and had at their control a sum of 40 million francs, voted by the Convention.

ARMS MANUFACTURE. In 1791 a first priority of the military committee was to create new arms factories at Autun, Moulins and Paris. By November 1793 Paris was manufacturing 1,000 rifles a day. Cannons were produced at the Luxembourg and the Place de l'Indivisibilité and there were over 600 weapon-making firms. Paris held magazines for the storage of charcoal, iron, acid and tools.

On 19 Messidor (*q.v*), Year III, the Committee of Public Safety (*q.v.*)

ruled that all the weapon-makers, aged from 18 to 25, were subject to military conscription, and were to remain at their jobs.

ARRAS. In 1790 Arras was the chief place of the département of the Pas-de-Calais, the scene of a massive fête on October 10, 1793, celebrating the revolutionary calendar (q.v.). About 20,000 people were involved in the festivities. It was the home of the notorious Joseph Lebon (1764-95) of the Comité de Sûreté générale, who caused the deaths of Royalists and "suspects" in particularly ruthless ways. The birthplace of Robespierre (q.v.).

ARRÊT. A decree usually having the force of law.

ARRONDISSEMENT. A district consisting of 100 communes. Three or four arrondissements made a département. The structure was formalized by Bonaparte on February 17, 1800.

ARSENAL, THE. Founded in Paris by François I in 1533 to serve as an artillery forge. It blew up in 1562 and was later rebuilt. It became the residence of the Great Masters of the Artillery. During the Revolution it was a depot for powder and saltpeter and a source of some worry to the locals. Counterrevolutionaries tried several times to seize the Arsenal, but failed.

ARTILLERY. At the outbreak of the Revolution the artillery was not as important as during the following war years. It was composed of twelve regiments, six companies of miners and nine companies of artisans, totaling 11,005 men. Gribeauval (q.v.), who later perfected the horse artillery, was commander-in-chief and first inspector of the artillery. In 1792 Louis XVI proposed the creation of nine horse artillery companies. The Battle of Valmy saw them in action for the first time, and in 1793 it decided the victory of Arlon. A school of artillery was established at Châlons in 1791.

ARTISTS. Artists, including sculptors and architects, were given, in 1790, gratuities and pensions, which were dispensed equally among the young to help them in their studies and to perfect their crafts. In case of death, their wives and children were accorded the same privileges and protection as the wives and children of citizens who had died in the service of the state. In 1794 the Convention (q.v.) released artists who were in detention, and allowed a sum of 100,000 écus to be distributed to artists.

ARTOIS. Comte d'Artois was a title held by royal princes but best remembered by the brother of Louis XVI, Charles-Philippe, later Charles X (see below).

ARTOIS, CHARLES PHILIPPE DE BOURBON, COMTE D' (1757-1836). Fourth child of the dauphin, son of Louis XV and of Marie Josephe of Saxony, brother of Louis XVI and later King Charles X. At the outbreak of the Revolution he was, with the queen, the chief of the court reactionaries. He left France in July 1789, became leader of the émigrés, and attempted to enlist support for the Royalist cause. In 1795 he tried to help at the Royalist rising of La Vendée but returned to England, returning to France in 1814. (*See* **Vendéan Rebellion.**) He reigned as Charles X (1824-30) until his abdication, replaced by Louis Philippe, duc d'Orleans. An unpopular man, Charles adhered to the anachronistic principle of ruling by divine right and refused to accept any reforms.

ASSEMBLY, CONSTITUENT. *See* Assembly, National.

ASSEMBLY, NATIONAL. On June 17, 1789 the third estate (*q.v.*), joined by reformers from the nobility and clergy, declared itself to be a "National Assembly" and on June 20 it swore never to dissolve until France had a constitution. These declarations were nullified by the crown on June 23, and the National Assembly was ordered to rearrange itself into the original three estates, which it refused to do. On July 9, 1789 the Assembly proclaimed itself the "National Constituent Assembly," which devised the constitution of December 22, 1789. According to its provisions, franchise was to be on the basis of taxation; political rights were to be given to groups of citizens according to whether those groups were active in primary assemblies or electoral assemblies eligible for the Legislative Assembly. Suffrage was to be granted to adult males over 25 with tax and residence qualifications, who were not domestic servants; these "active" citizens were to elect local councils for a reorganized administrative system of cantons; they also chose delegates to elect departmental councillors and departmental deputies in the Legislative Assembly. Delegates were eligible on property qualifications. The Assembly was given 745 deputies (for France; there were colonial deputies later), and these were allotted to the departments according to area, population and revenue. This body sat until September 30, 1791.

Campbell, Peter, *French Electoral Systems*, 1965.

Thompson, E., *Popular Sovereignty and the French Constituent Assembly, 1789-1791*, 1952.

ASSEMBLY OF NOTABLES. This assembly was called on February 22, 1787. Calonne (*q.v.*) had urged the king to call this consultative gathering, consisting of 144 members, all of whom were to be nominated by the crown, in order to push through radically needed reforms based on the massive fiscal and economic problems of the country. Calonne's remedy was to tax all lands without attention to privileges, establish provincial assemblies and to allow free trade within the country. By calling together magistrates, the great nobles and princes of the blood, councillors and intendents, clerical members, municipal officers and representatives of the provincial estates, it was hoped to avoid conflicts with the magistracy and demands for the convening of the old Estates-General (*q.v.*). By November 6, 1788 the notables refused to sanction any changes in their privileges, drove Calonne from office (he retired to England), and had Necker (*q.v.*) banished from Paris. As a result the crown called the Estates-General to meet for the first time since 1614.

ASSEMBLY OF THE KNOWN AND VERIFIED REPRESENTATIVE OF THE FRENCH NATION. On June 15, 1789 Sieyès (q.v.) moved that the Third Estate (q.v.) should, for the last time, invite the First and Second Estates (qq.v.) to join them in forming a national assembly but in the event of refusal they would continue regardless. On June 13 a few clergy, followed by others, joined the Third Estate. Sieyès suggested that a new title be adopted, as the members present could no longer style themselves the Third Estate, but withdrew his submission of "Assembly of the Known and Verified Representative of the French Nation" when Jérome Legrand, a deputy from Berry, suggested the title "National Assembly" (q.v.).

ASSIGNATS. A forced paper currency meaning first mortgage on land, issued in France 1789-96 to support public credit during the Revolution. *Assignats* were first to be paid to creditors of the state who could then purchase national lands. If land was not wanted, the holders could obtain the face-value from those who wanted land. Purchase-money *assignats* were returned to the state and cancelled, and the issue would disappear as the national lands were distributed. Assignats were over-issued by the treasury and together with Royalist forgeries, caused depreciation of value and inflation. Coinage became the preferred medium of exchange. Assignats were superseded by *mandats* (q.v.) in 1796.
Harris, S. E., *The Assignats*, 1930.

ASSOCIATION OF THE FRIENDS OF THE PEOPLE, THE. A reforming society with members including the Whigs Sir Philip Francis (1740-1818), Charles Grey, second earl Grey (1764-1845), and adherents of Charles James Fox (1749-1806), although he was not a member. The society was committed to constitutional reforms within Great Britain, mainly though not exclusively in Parliament itself, and was influenced by the writings of Paine, Priestley and the news of the revolution in France. It was founded in April 1792 and had little if any influence in promoting reforms, apart from alienating many Whigs from Fox.

ASSOCIÉS, THÉATRE DES. It was constructed in 1774 on the Boulevard du Temple, and was first directed by the actor Beauvisage. At the beginning of the Revolution the name was changed to "Théâtre patriotique" and in 1795 to "Théâtre sans prétention." It closed, and in 1807 became the "Café d'Apollon."

ATELIERS DE CHARITÉ, L'. Public workshops of a charitable nature, set up to absorb and employ the out-of-work. Established on a national basis in 1789, they were closed in June 1791 by the constituents, because of growing fears of the numbers of unemployed, the threat to public order and the ruinous cost of supporting them.

AUBAINE. Right of the French kings, whereby they claimed the property of every foreigner who died having lived in France for a year and a day without having been naturalized. It was abolished by the National Assembly in 1790-91, reestablished by Napoleon in 1804 and finally annulled July 14, 1819.

AUBRY, MLLE. Celebrated dancer of the Opéra, a remarkable beauty. Represented "Reason" at the fête held near Notre Dame in 1793. On leaving the fête, she was taken to the Convention (*q.v.*), where the president led the applause. (*See* **Fête de la Raison.**)

AUGEREAU, PIERRE FRANÇOIS CHARLES, DUC DE CASTIGLIO-NE (1755-1816). Marshal of France. A general of division in 1793, he served honorably under Napoleon in Italy and was instrumental in gaining the victories at Lodi (May 10, 1796) and at Castiglione. Augereau and his troops pushed through the coup d'état of 18 Fructidor (*q.v.*). He was not involved in the coup d'état of Brumaire (*q.v.*). He fell out of favor with Napoleon, serving Louis XVIII until the Hundred Days, when Napoleon accused him of being a traitor.

AUSTRIA. Austria in 1789 included the provinces of Bohemia, Moravia, Galicia, Slovakia, Transylvania, Bukovina, Croatia-Slavonia, Carniola, Gorizia, Istria, Dalmatia, Lombardy and Venetia, and the Kingdom of Hungary. The sovereign of Austria ruled as king (or queen) of Austria and Hungary until 1804, when the king of Austria, who was also Holy Roman Emperor, took the title of emperor of Austria; he remained king of Hungary.

Marie Antoinette (*q.v.*) was a sister of Emperor Joseph II (1765-90), who visited France but had limited sympathy for his sister's fears of an impending disaster. He was succeeded by his brother, Emperor Leopold II (1790-92), who was obliged to back the interests of the émigré princes threatened by the decrees of the French Constituent Assembly, and who, in turn, was succeeded by Marie Antoinette's nephew, Francis II (1792-1835).

In 1789 the Austrian Netherlands had declared its independence. Prussia, England and the United Provinces of the Netherlands had initially recognized the new state, but the Agreement of Reichenbach (1790) and a fear that France might conquer Belgium, led these states to reconsider their position. Leopold's Circular of Padua of July 1791 called on the European powers to assist the French king. Austria was willing to take a leading role in fighting the dangers of republicanism. At the Declaration of Pillnitz in August 1791, there was a temporary understanding between Austria and Prussia. It called for the maintenance of the monarchy in France and for collective action against the republic by European powers if the French king and his subjects failed to reach an agreement. Pillnitz, however, strengthened the hand of the French war party. In January 1792, a provocative note from France was sent that gave an ultimatum to Austria, and in February 1792 Austria and Prussia constructed a defensive alliance. Leopold offered to protect all "right-minded" Frenchmen against the republic. The fourth French ultimatum arrived on March 27 and the French declared war on April 20. By a decree of January 25, 1792 the legislature had demanded that the emperor categorically renounce all treaties against the security and the sovereignty of the French nation. The Austrians responded by demanding that the French monarchy must be reestablished on the lines of the bases fixed by the royal declaration of June 23, 1789 and Alsace was to be returned to the princes of the Empire. As a result Louis XVI was forced to declare war against Austria. Austria was at war with France six times from 1792 to 1815.

AUTEL DE LA PATRIE, L'. From the beginning of the Revolution, "Altars of the Fatherland" were raised spontaneously at various places by the citizens, as symbols of a new cult of Country, Law, Philosophy, Liberty, Equality of Classes. On July 6, 1792 the Legislative Assembly gave instructions for the erection of an altar in each commune, where people would bring their children, where young husbands and wives would come to be united, and where births, marriages and deaths would be recorded. In July 1790 the enormous Autel de la Patrie was raised in the middle of the Champ de Mars in Paris, ceremoniously marking the anniversary of the fall of the Bastille (*q.v.*). On August 10, 1793 the Fête de la Reunion marked the acceptance of the constitution of Year I. All of the altars disappeared under the Consulate (*q.v.*).

AUTEURS DRAMATIQUES, SOCIÉTÉ DES. In February 1794 dramatists founded a central bureau in Paris, to correspond with different theaters throughout the country, dealing with the individual directors. Its purpose was to act as a "performing rights" center, to receive payments for the public performance of their works, wherever they might take place, and to act on behalf of individuals within the membership as an agent.

AUTRICHIENNE, L'. The "Austrian dog" or "bitch." Extremely rude and pointed term of abuse used against Marie Antoinette (*q.v.*). It came into being at the time when she was engaged to Louis XVI, then dauphin. The term was widely used by the people at large, and when war against Austria was declared (April 20, 1792), "A bas l'Autrichienne!" was heard in the streets.

AUTUN, BISHOP OF. *See* **Talleyrand.**

AVIGNON. Town on the Rhône River 55 miles north-northwest of Marseille. It was captured by Louis VIII in 1226 and was bought for the papacy by Clement VI in 1348. In August 1789 economic discontent and dislike of papal rule caused a revolt and on October 27, 1790 the government began to take steps to annex Avignon by sending troops. The pope condemned the ecclesiastical reforms of the National Assembly in March and April of 1791 and Avignon became the scene of vicious battles. In 1793 Avignon became part of the department of Vaucluse.

AVRANCHES. Capital of the Avranchin. After the crossing of the Loire by the Vendéan army, the Royalists seized the town, without resistance, on November 12, 1793. The republicans withdrew. The next day the Royalists marched to Granville from where they were repulsed, retreating to Avranches. Attacked by the republicans, they retreated, fleeing from Avranches.

B

BABEUF (BABOEUF), **FRANCOIS NOEL** (CALLED 'GRACCHUS') (1760-97). A radical journalist who wished for an egalitarian revolution. Babeuf's paper, *Le Tribun du peuple*, denounced the constitution of 1795 as a violation of the plebiscite, which had approved the democratic Montagnard constitution of 1793. Babeuf demanded an insurrection, a return to revolutionary government and the removal of the Directors. Later he repudiated the entire social order and called for its destruction. In doing so, private property, the source of oppression and injustice, would be eliminated, democratic freedoms and equality established. The Directory (*q.v.*) ordered Babeuf's arrest, but he escaped. His movement was known as the "Conspiracy of the Equals." They were betrayed to the Directory and arrested on May 10, 1796. Babeuf saw and felt the popular misery and was critical of the 1793-94 economic controls. He was interested in the distribution of food, not its production.

Babeuf and the six or seven men who formed the Secret Committee had worked out the idea of a popular dictatorship. Although the Equals (*q.v.*) accepted the sovereignty of the people, they felt very strongly that they would have to take it under their charge until their opponents were eliminated and the people had become "enlightened." Skilled in their use of agents and propaganda, these ideas were carried through to the revolutions of the 1830's, and into revolutionary history.

The trial of Babeuf and his associates took place in 1797; 65 people were indicted, but only 47 were present. Babeuf gave a superb self-defense and convinced his judges that no one had done any more than publish acceptable opinions. He and all of his companions were acquitted of conspiracy but the government had the charge altered at the last moment. They were accused of advocating the return of the 1793 constitution. Seven of the accused were sentenced to deportation, including Filippo Michele Buonarroti (1761-1837), author of the *Conspiration pour l'Égalité dite de Babeuf* (1828) and a major figure in Paris during the 1830 revolution. Babeuf and Augustin Alexandre Darthé (1769-97) were sentenced to death. Both attempted suicide but were guillotined on May 27, 1797.

Rose, R. B., *Gracchus Babeuf: The First Revolutionary Communist*, 1979.
Thomson, D., *The Baboeuf Plot*, 1947.

BAGATELLE, CHÂTEAU DE. Constructed on the edge of the Bois de Boulogne not far from the Seine by the comte d'Artois (*q.v.*) in 1779, it was confiscated during the Revolution and fêtes publiques were held there.

BAILLIAGE, SÉNÉCHAUSSÉE. Court whose judges acted in the name of the king's *bailli* (bailiffs) and also the administrative division under their jurisdiction. These divisions were called *bailliages* in the north of France, but the term *sénéchaussée* was used mostly in the south.

BAILLY, JEAN SYLVAIN (1736-93). Astronomer born in Paris. From art he turned to literature and then to astronomy, writing his great five-volume *Histoire de l'astronomie* (1775-87). He was elected a member of three academies. In 1789 he was president of the National Assembly *(q.v.)* and mayor of Paris. He became unpopular because he allowed the National Guard *(q.v.)* to fire on crowds that were demanding the abolition of the monarchy. Later, he was arrested, tried and guillotined.

BAISER LAMOURETTE. *See* **Lamourette's Kiss.**

BAKER, THE. Name given to King Louis XVI, who gave bread to starving men on October 6, 1789.

BAKER'S WIFE, THE. Name given to Queen Marie Antoinette.

BALLINAMUCK. *See* **Killala.**

BANALITÉS. Monopolies which gave to seigneurs the exclusive right to ovens, mills, presses, slaughterhouses and the bull to service the heifers. Peasants had to purchase these essential services and it was a source of great revenue to the monopoly holders. *Banalités* were abolished in 1789.

BANNERS. Considerable use of banners was made during the revolutionary period. On the day of the great Federation of 1790, the 83 departmental banners were distributed to the deputies. Each banner formed a large white square, on which was painted an oak-garland and the name of the department. The oldest in each deputation had the honor of carrying the banner. Tricolor banners featured in all of the revolutionary fêtes.

BANQUE DE FRANCE (BANK OF FRANCE). On December 14, 1796 a group of deputies met in Paris to establish a bank, but the project was opposed by the Directory *(q.v.)*. The idea was renewed in 1797, and in 1800 Bonaparte established the Bank of France by transforming the Caisse des compte courants, which was founded in 1796. The prime aim was not to solicit commercial business but to act as the state bank.

BANQUE DE LONDRES (BANK OF LONDON). Paris branch of the Bank of London, it was regarded with suspicion in the early stages of the Revolution. The Assembly *(q.v.)* seized on a declaration by Georges Couthon *(q.v.)*, put forward as a decree and sustained by Danton *(q.v.)*, which declared that all French citizens who had placed funds in the bank were condemned to a fine equal to the sum deposited but, in fact, the fine was not subsequently imposed.

BANQUE SAINT CHARLES. Spanish bank in Paris, a branch of the Bank San Carlos, founded in Madrid in 1785 by the French banker Cabarrus. When the Convention (q.v.) ordered the arrest of the bankers and the demand, under seals, of all their assets, a sum of two million livres which belonged to the Spanish government was put under sequestration.

BARBAROUX, CHARLES JEAN MARIE (1767-94). French revolutionary born at Marseilles, one of the leading Girondins (q.v.). He was guillotined at Bordeaux.

BARBÉ DE MARBOIS, FRANÇOIS (1745-1837). Minister of the public treasury. He began in the foreign service in 1768 and from 1786 to 1790 he was the intendant-general in the Windward Islands. He returned to France, then went to Germany on diplomatic business. Eventually he was charged by the Directory (q.v.) for being pro-Royalist, and in 1797 he was transported.

He returned to France in 1800, reestablished himself and played an important part in the Louisiana Purchase, being joint-signatory with James Monroe of the subsequent treaty. He served Louis XVIII (q.v.) and also held office under Louis Philippe (q.v.).

BARBETS, LES. Marauders who caused havoc in the countryside and who dogged the army of Italy. They were led by a chief named Contin, who was captured in July 1798.

BARÈRE DE VIEUZAC, BERTRAND (1755-1841). Lawyer who served in the Parlement (q.v.) of Toulouse (1770), member of the National Assembly in 1789 and the Convention (qq.v.), where he was president. In voting for the death of the king he said "The tree of liberty could not grow were it not watered with the blood of kings." His newspaper, *Point du Jour*, reported the debates in the National Assembly. Originally he was a constitutional monarchist but he lacked the courage to carry his convictions forward.

He was named the "Anacreon of the Guillotine." A flowery, brilliant speaker, he first attacked Robespierre (q.v.) and then flattered him. He voted for the deaths of the Girondins (q.v.) and worked to maintain the support of the Mountain (q.v.). On July 27, 1794 he drew up the report outlawing Robespierre. However, he was accused, with Collot d'Herbois and Billaud-Varenne (qq.v.) for the Terror. He escaped and hid. Although elected to the Council of 500, he was not allowed to take his seat.

Later he acted as an agent for Napoleon. He was exiled (1815-30), and from 1832-40 he held an administrative post in his department of Hautes-Pyrénées. He died as the last survivor of the original membership of the Committee of Public Safety.
Gershoy, L., *Barère de Vieuzac: Reluctant Terrorist*, 1962.

BARNAVE, ANTOINE (1761-93). French revolutionary who was born at Grenoble. He was responsible for bringing the royal family back from Varennes (q.v.). He advocated more liberal courses to advance the Revolution and was subsequently executed.
Bradby, E. D., *Barnave*, 1915.

BARRAS, PAUL JEAN FRANÇOIS NICOLAS, VICOMTE DE (1755-1829). French aristocrat and revolutionary, born at Var. He served in the army against the British in India. After returning to France he took advantage of the political situation to restore his fortunes and became an original member of the Jacobin Club. (*See* **Jacobins**.) He represented Var in the National Convention and voted for the king's execution. He was capable of great cruelty, as was seen in Toulon (*q.v.*) after its recapture from the British in 1793. He was disliked by and played a leading part in the downfall of Robespierre (*q.v.*), and as a result he was appointed a near dictator by the Convention. He invited Bonaparte to quell a Royalist uprising on October 5, 1795. Later Barras became one of the five members of the Directory (*q.v.*). He was corrupt, extravagant and immoral, and eventually, at the coup of 18 Brumaire (November 9, 1799, *q.v.*), he agreed to resign from the Directory on Bonaparte becoming First Consul.

BARRICADES. Hastily improvised street obstructions made from paving stones, vehicles and barrels (the word comes from the French word for barrel). "Aux barricades" became the rallying cry in all French revolutions.

BARRIÈRES. Customs posts in the Paris wall, which was being constructed to encircle the suburbs. Many were burnt down on the night of July 13, 1789 because the citizens felt that customs taxes were responsible for the high price of bread.

BARRUEL-BAUVERT, ANTOINE-JOSEPH, ABBÉ (1756-1817). Editor of *Actes des Apôtres* (1795). A champion of religious orthodoxy, he offered surety for the king at the time of his arrest.

BARRY, MARIE JEANNE GOMARD DE VAUBERNIER, COMTESSE DU (1741-93). Daughter of a dressmaker, in 1769, as Mademoiselle Lange, she was noticed by Louis XV, who married her to Comte Guillaume du Barry. Her influence was considerable until the death of Louis XV in 1774. She was then dismissed from court. The revolutionary tribunal tried her for having wasted the treasures of the state and worn mourning for the king, and she was executed.

BASEL, TREATIES OF. Two treaties, arranged by Napoleon with Prussia and Spain. The agreement with Prussia in April 1795 specified a line of demarcation drawn across Germany, within which all states were to be free from invasion. Napoleon's inducement for Prussian acceptance of the treaty was the withdrawal of French troops from the right bank of the Rhine. The treaty with Spain in July 1795 specified the return to Spain of the Spanish half of Hispaniola (*q.v.*). By pressing through the treaties, Napoleon had both Prussia and Spain withdraw from the European coalition. Other treaties were signed with Holland in April, Sweden in May, and certain other German states.

BASSANO, ITALY. Battle fought on September 8, 1796 between French and Austrian forces at Bassano del Grappa just northeast of Vicenza, Italy. The French won, taking over 3,500 prisoners, but General Würmser (q.v.) escaped. On September 9 Vicenza and Padua were occupied by Bonaparte.

BASSETERRE-ROADS, ST. CHRISTOPHER, WEST INDIES.
Comte de Grasse (q.v.), French admiral, was repulsed with loss in three desperate attacks on the British fleet, commanded by Sir Thomas Graves, January 25 and 26, 1782.

BASSEVILLE (BASSVILLE), NICOLAS, JEAN HUGON DE (1753-93).
Journalist and diplomat. Editor of the *Mercure nationale*, he was named (1792) as secretary to the legation at Naples. Later he received orders to go to Rome to protect the interests of the French, but was without official status. In Rome he announced himself as the protector of the extreme Jacobins in the city. He demanded the expulsion of the French émigrés and ordered that the fleurs-de-lys on the escutcheon of the French embassy be replaced by a picture of Liberty, painted by a French art student. He insulted the papal secretary of state and talked slightingly of church officials. His actions enraged a mob, who handled him so roughly that he died. Eventually the papacy paid compensation to his family.

BASTIA.
City on Corsica, the scene of major troubles in 1791, provoked by the civil constitution of the clergy. There was a major revolt resulting in the burning of the palace of the constitutional bishop and the local freemason's lodge. Order was reestablished by General Paoli. To punish Bastia, the Constituent Assembly (q.v.) moved the bishop's seat and the directory of the department to Corte. In 1793 Paoli marched against Bastia, which the Anglo-Paolist forces had besieged one year previously. The city fell to this force, and the defending soldiers were transported to Toulon (q.v.). Nelson, who commanded the *Agamemnon*, lost an eye during the siege. Bastia remained in English hands until 1796, when it was recaptured by Casalta.

BASTILLE.
Fortress commanding the eastern side of Paris built by Charles V in 1369 for the defense of Paris against the English. It was completed in 1383 and used as a state prison. Its most mysterious prisoner was "The Man in the Iron Mask" who died there in 1703. In 1789 it was no more than a state prison and ill-qualified to stand a siege. The garrison consisted of eighty-two pensioners (*invalides*) and thirty-two Swiss Guards (q.v.). It was attacked and captured on July 14, 1789 by workers from the Faubourg St. Antoine who feared that they might be caught between the king's hussars and the guns mounted on the Bastille's towers. There was also a need to capture the powder stored in the fortress. One hundred and seventy-one civilians were killed in the action. The dungeons were opened and the seven prisoners released. The governor, the Marquis de Launey, although given a safe passage to the town hall, was murdered by the crowd en route.

Godechot, Jacques L., *The Taking of the Bastille, July 14th, 1789*. 1970.

BASTILLE DAY. The Bastille (*q.v.*) fell on July 14, 1789. The event was celebrated by the erection of a stone column placed in the Place de la Bastille. Bastille Day is celebrated annually as a national holiday. In 1880 it was declared the foremost national holiday in France.

BATAVIAN REPUBLIC (1795-1806). The Batavian Republic consisted of Belgium and Holland, which were reorganized into a new state after their conquest by the French. In 1806 it was changed into a kingdom, under Louis Bonaparte, which lasted until 1810. The territory was part of France until 1814.

BATTLES.

April 28	1792	Quiévrain—French repulsed
September 20		Valmy—French defeat Prussians
November 6		Jemappes—French victorious
March 18	1793	Neerwinden—French beaten by Austrians
May 8		St. Amand—French defeated by English
May 23		Valenciennes—French defeated by English
July 26		Valenciennes—French defeated by English
August 18		Lincelles—Lake defeats French
September 7-8		Dunkirk—duke of York defeated
September 11		Quesnoy—reduced by Austrians
September 14		Pirmasens—Prussians defeat French
October 14-16		Wattignies—French defeat Coburg
December 19		Toulon—retaken by British
April 24	1794	Cambray—French defeated
April 30		Troisville, Landrecy—taken by Allies
May 4		Nimeguen—French victorious
May 18-22		Tourcoing—Moreau defeats Allies
May 22		Espierres—taken by Allies
June 1		Howe's naval victory
June 26		Charleroi or Fleurus—French defeat Allies
July 28		Misdon—Vendeans defeated
September 14		Bois-le-Duc—Duke of York defeated
September 17		Boxtel—Duke of York defeated
October 10		Maciejowice—Poles defeated
October 28		Nimeguen—French defeated
November 4		Praga—Warsaw taken by Suvarov
June 22	1795	Bridport's victory off Lorient
July 21		Quiberon—Emigrants defeated
September 20		Mannheim—taken by Pichegru
November 23-24		Loano—French defeat Austrians
April 12	1796	Montenotte—Bonaparte victorious
April 22		Mondovi—Bonaparte victorious
May 10		Lodi—Bonaparte victorious
June 4		Altenkirchen—Austrians defeated
July 5		Radstadt—Moreau defeats Austrians
August 3-5		Lonato and Castiglione—French defeat Austrians
August 10		Neresheim—Moreau defeats Archduke Charles
September 4		Roveredo—French defeat Austrians

September 8		Bassano—French defeat Austrians
September 16		Altenkirchen—Austrians victors
October 2		Biberach—French defeat Austrians
November 14-17		Arcola—Bonaparte victorious
November 21		Castelnuovo—Bonaparte victorious
January 14-15	1797	Rivoli—Bonaparte victorious
February 14		Cape St. Vincent—Spaniards defeated
March 16		Tagliamento—Bonaparte defeats Austrians
October 11		Camperdown—Duncan defeats Dutch
May 23	1798	Kilcullen—rebels successful
May 24		Naas—rebels defeated
May 26		Tara—rebels defeated
May 27		Oulart—rebels successful
June 4		Gorey or New Ross—rebels defeated
June 7		Antrim—rebels defeated
June 10		Arklow—rebels beaten
June 13		Ballynahinch—Nugent defeats rebels
June 21		Vinegar Hill—Lake defeats rebels
July 13-21		Pyramids—Bonaparte defeats Mamelukes
August 27		Castlebar—French auxiliaries victorious
August 1		Nile—Nelson defeats French fleet
September 8		Ballinamuck—French and rebels defeated
February 18	1799	El Arisch—French defeat Turks
March 7-10		Jaffa—stormed by Bonaparte
March 25		Stokach—Austrians defeat French
March 28-30		Verona—Austrians defeat French
April 5		Magnano—Kray defeats French
April 16		Mount Tabor—Bonaparte defeats Turks
April 27		Cassano—Suvarov defeats Moreau
April		Adda—Suvarov defeats French
May 4		Seringapatam—Tippoo killed
May 20		Acre—relieved by Sir Sydney Smith
June 5		Zurich—French defeated
June 17-19		Trebia—Suvarov defeats French
July 21		Alessandria—taken from French
July 25		Aboukir—Turks defeated by Bonaparte
August 15		Novi—Suvarov defeats French
September 9		Zuyper Sluys—French defeated
September 19 October 26		Bergen and Alkmaer—Allies defeated
September 24-25		Zurich—Massena defeats Russians
March 20	1800	Heliopolis—Kleber defeats Turks
May 3		Engen—Moreau defeats Austrians
May 5		Moeskirch—Moreau defeats Austrians
May 9		Biberach—Moreau defeats Austrians
June 9		Montebello—Austrians defeated
June 14		Marengo—Bonaparte defeats Austrians
June 19		Hochstadt—Moreau defeats Austrians
December 3		Hohenlinden—Moreau defeats Austrians
December 25-27		Mincio—French defeat Austrians

BEAUHARNAIS, ALEXANDRE, VISCOMTE DE (1760-94). Beauharnais served in the American Revolutionary War *(q.v.)* but returned to France to join the revolutionaries. He became secretary to the National Assembly, whose main objective was to draw up a constitution. Then in 1793 he commanded the army of the Rhine, where his failure to relieve the siege of Mainz angered the Committee of Public Safety *(q.v.)*. Despite his former work with the revolutionaries, suspicion fell upon him because of his noble birth, and in 1794 he was tried and guillotined. His wife was thrown into prison too and it was expected that she would be executed publicly at any time but in 1795, Marie-Joseph-Rose de la Pagerie de Beauharnais (her name at that time) was one of the thousands of prisoners released from the filthy dungeons.

Aged 32, penniless and the mother of two children, she was faced with many problems. She and Beauharnais had managed to give the children a good education up to the time of his death, but life was now very difficult for all three of them. However, it seems that she was still able to hold on to her status in society and her friends persuaded her, allegedly rather against her will, to marry a young general named Napoléon Bonaparte.

BEAUHARNAIS, JOSÉPHINE TASCHER DE LA PAGERIE, VICOMTESSE DE (1763-1814). Born in Martinique. Her first husband, Viscomte de Beauharnais *(q.v.)* was guillotined. She married Napoleon Bonaparte in 1796 and became empress in 1804. There were no children and Napoleon divorced her in 1809. Her children by de Beauharnais were Eugène (1781-1824), whom Napoleon made prince-viceroy of Italy, and Hortense (1783-1837), who married Louis Bonaparte and was the mother of Napoleon III.

BEAUMARCHAIS, PIERRE AUGUSTIN, COMTE DE (1732-99). Son of a Paris clockmaker, he received little formal education, being intended for his father's trade. In 1755 he obtained a minor post in the royal household, marrying the rich widow of his predecessor. When she, in turn, died, he lost her fortune. Later he was named as music master to the daughters of Louis XV. Beaumarchais received a considerable sum from a rich patron for a past favor and purchased a brevet of nobility and a more important office.

Throughout his life, Beaumarchais was involved in a series of adventures, financial enterprises, speculations and extensive litigation; he was jailed more than once. He was sent on a succession of secret missions to England and elsewhere by the governments of Louis XV and XVI. His many actions included organizing supplies for the insurgent American colonies and equipping the ships for their support. He defended the financial rights of dramatic authors against the actors' companies. During the Revolution, Beaumarchais, though an agent of the Committee of Public Safety *(q.v.)*, was in constant danger as a suspected émigré, but he survived. He is and was, in his time, best known as a dramatist, the author of *The Barber of Seville* (1775) and *The Marriage of Figaro* (1784). Characterized as an adventurer, with a great gift for making a noise, Beaumarchais was extremely versatile and wide-ranging. His importance as a dramatist stemmed from the audacity of his social satire, a revival of the comedy of intrigue. He was the first dramatist to use fully the principles of stage acting and craft conceived by Diderot (q.v.).

BED OF JUSTICE (LIT DE JUSTICE). A French court presided over by the king, whose seat was termed a "bed." It controlled the ordinances of the parliament. The last was held by Louis XVI at Versailles, November 19, 1787, to raise a loan. Once the king arrived personally in parliament, sitting on a pile of cushions, sovereignty of parliament was suspended and the king's ruling was final.

BELGIUM. The Belgian provinces were under Austrian rule from 1714 and were known as the Austrian Netherlands until 1790. Self-government was achieved in 1789 but in 1792 the French army began an occupation which lasted until 1814 apart from a short period in 1793-94 when the Austrians returned.

BELLEVUE, CHATEAU DE. Castle situated near Paris, between Sèvres and Meudon. It was constructed by the Pompadour and was inhabited by the king's aunts, Adélaide (q.v.) and Victoire, at the beginning of the Revolution. When they left France in 1791 the chateau was sequestrated. It was later turned into a barracks and, in spite of a Convention decree, sold and demolished.

BERNADOTTE, JEAN BAPTISTE JULES, PRINCE DE PONTE CORVO, KING OF SWEDEN (1763-1844). Born at Pau, he was an out-and-out republican from the beginning. In 1780, Bernadotte enlisted in the Regiment de Brassac, and by 1788 he was a sergeant-major in the Regiment Royal-Marine. From 1792 to 1796 he served successively in the armies of the Rhine, the North and Sambre-et-Meuse. He became *général de division* in October 1794. He won an action at Limborg in July 1796. In 1797 he was sent to join the army of Italy, where he commanded the Fourth Division, and helped Bonaparte cross the Tagliamento River.

In April 1798 Bernadotte was sent as ambassador to Vienna. During the War of the Second Coalition he commanded divisions in the army of Mainz. In 1799 he commanded the army of observation of the Lower Rhine, then the left wing of the army of the Danube. Disgusted with the conduct of the war, he traveled to Paris, throwing up his command, and was dismissed. From July to September 1799, Bernadotte was minister of war and, again, he was sacked. An ardent republican, with "Death to tyrants" tattooed on his arm, he refused to be involved in the coup d'état of 18 Brumaire. In January 1800 he was nominated as councillor of state. In 1804 he became governor of Hanover, and in May was made a marshal. In 1810 Bernadotte was elected Crown Prince of Sweden and his descendants rule to the present day.
Scott, F. D., *Bernadotte and the Fall of Napoleon*, 1935.

BERNARD, MOUNT ST. Mountain in the Alps where a monastery founded by Bernardine Menthon in 962 is situated. Velan, its highest peak, is about 8,000 feet high, covered with perpetual snow. Hannibal, it is said, conducted the Carthaginians by this pass into Italy (218 B.C.), and by the same route in May 1800 Bonaparte led his army of 30,000 men into Italy before the Battle of Marengo *(q.v.)*, June 14. This resulted in the breakup of the Second Coalition and the Treaty of Lunéville on February 9, 1801 *(qq.v.)*.

BERNE. Canton of Switzerland. It surrendered to the French under General Brune, April 12, 1798.

BERTIER DE SAUVIGNY, LOUIS JEAN (1742-89). Governor of Paris who was hated by the people. The excessive price of grain, and therefore bread, was attributed to him. During the early days of the Revolution, he was arrested at Compiègne and taken to Paris. On July 22, 1789 the mob called for his blood. He was seized and bayonetted to death. His head and pieces of his dismembered body were paraded about Paris.

BERTIN, LOUIS FRANÇOIS (1766-1841). Founder of *Journal des Débats* in 1799, edited afterwards by his sons Louis Marie Armand (1801-54) and Edouard (1797-1871).

BERTRAND DE MOLEVILLE, ANTOINE FRANÇOIS, MARQUIS DE (1747-1818). Minister under Louis XVI. In 1791 he was named minister of marine. He was hostile to the Revolution, and was repeatedly attacked and denounced during his time in the ministry. He was accused of being employed by France's enemies in the Saint-Domingue expedition. In spite of all evidence to support the accusations, Louis supported him, and this was a fact which contributed to the king's downfall. He resigned and was instructed by Louis to direct the secret police against the Jacobins *(q.v.)*. In doing so, he prepared a plan to stop the rapid development of the Revolution. He was denounced on June 20, 1792 and accused of preparing for another flight of the king, but he managed to escape to England, where he lived until 1814.

BIBLIOTHÈQUE DE L'ARSENAL. The second largest library of France on the site of the old arsenal of Paris. It was built in 1718 from designs by Boffin. In 1785-86 the comte d'Artois *(q.v.)* purchased the building and the library of Antoine-René d'Argenson, which he deposited in the Arsenal *(q.v.)*. It was confiscated during the Revolution. It now contains over a million books.

BIBLIOTHÈQUE DU ROI. *See* **Bibliothèque Nationale.**

BIBLIOTHÈQUE NATIONALE. Founded by Charles VIII, it received many fine additions during the reigns of Louis XIII and XIV. In 1725 it was allowed to purchase part of the Hôtel Mazarin, situated in the Rue Vivienne and Rue des Petits-Champs, in order to bring together the holdings of the king distributed through various buildings. By the reign of Louis XVI it held 150,000 volumes and in the Revolution changed its name from Bibliothèque du Roi to Bibliothèque Nationale.

BICÊTRE. Prison on the outskirts of Paris for young people and scene of the September Massacres *(q.v.)* in 1792.

BIENS NATIONAUX (NATIONAL PROPERTY). Property confiscated by the state from the clergy, the nobles and others during the Revolution.

BIGOT DE PRÉAMENEU, FELIX JULIEN JEAN, BARON (1747-1825). Advocate, legislator, councillor of state and minister. He was a member of the Legislative Assembly *(q.v.)* for Paris in September 1791 and a judge in the city. He voted, at first, with the Royalists, and was named as president of the Assembly.

BILLAUD-VARENNE, JACQUES NICOLAS (1756-1819). Son of an *avocat* (advocate) in the Paris Parlement, he originally trained for the church but did not take his vows. He went to Paris and bought a position as an *avocat* in the Parlement. In 1789 he published, in Amsterdam, his three-volumed *Despotisme des Ministres de la France*, and also adopted strong revolutionary principles.

From 1790 he became one of the most violent of the anti-Royalist orators. After the king's flight to Varennes, Billaud-Varenne published a pamphlet, *L'Acéphocratie*, in which he demanded the established right of a federal republic, and this demand was repeated at the Jacobin Club on July 1 and 15, where the speech was ordered, printed and sent to the branch societies throughout France. (*See* **Jacobins**.)

Elected one of the deputy commissioners of the section on August 10, 1792. He was accused, although the proof was lacking, of being an accomplice at the massacres in the Abbaye prison.

Billaud-Varenne was elected as deputy of Paris to the National Convention *(q.v.)*, and spoke in favor of the immediate abolition of the monarchy. At the king's trial he added new charges to the accusation, proposed to refuse defense counsel to the king, and voted for death "within twenty-four hours."

On June 9, 1793 he outlined at the Jacobin Club a program which the Convention gradually implemented: expulsion of all foreigners not naturalized, the establishment of a tax on the rich, the deprivation of the rights of all "anti-social" men, the creation of a revolutionary army, and the death penalty for all unsuccessful generals.

In August 1793 he was sent as a "representative on mission" to the departments of the Nord and the Pas-de-Calais; he was ruthless with all suspects.

After his return, Billaud-Varenne became a member of the Committee of Public Safety *(q.v.)*, which had decreed the arrest, en masse, of all suspects, and the establishment of a revolutionary army, and caused the extraordinary criminal tribunal to be named officially the "Revolutionary Tribunal" (October 29, *q.v.*). Billaud-Varenne attacked both Danton and Hébert *(qq.v.)*, and published *Les Éléments de Republicanisme*, in which he demanded a division of property, if not equally at least proportionally, among the citizens.

He attacked Robespierre *(q.v.)* on Thermidor 8, as a "moderate" and a Dantonist. Having denounced portions of the Thermidorean Revolution *(q.v.)*, he was attacked in the Convention in turn for his cruelty. A commission was appointed to examine his conduct and that of some former members of the Committee of Public Safety. He was arrested, to be sent to Cayenne in 1795. After 18 Brumaire, he refused the First Consul's *(q.v.)* pardon and died of dysentery in Haiti in 1819.

BIRON, ARMAND LOUIS DE GONTAUT, DUC DE LAUZUN, DUC DE (1749-93). He fought with Lafayette (*q.v.*) in America, later joining the revolutionaries in France, and defeated the Vendeans at Parthenay in 1793, but was later guillotined. (*See* **Vendéan Rebellion**)

BLACKS (NOIRS). Term of abuse, used against the opponents of the Revolution who sat at the far right in the Constituent Assembly (*q.v.*). They were usually clergy or aristocrats.

BLAKE, WILLIAM (1757-1827). English poet, painter, engraver and mystic. He was a radical and, until the Terror, supporter of the Revolution. His narrative poem dated 1791 was entitled "The French Revolution." Only one copy exists, and this is probably a proof. The poem was not published, probably because of the fear of prosecution for sedition.

BOISSY D'ANGLAS, FRANÇOIS ANTOINE, COMTE (1756-1828). Statesman. In 1789 he was elected by the Third Estate (*q.v.*) of the sénéchaussée (*see* **Baìllage**) of Annonay as deputy to the Estates-General, where he was one of those who induced the meeting to declare itself a national assembly on June 17, 1789. He was elected to the Convention (*q.v.*). Although he supported Robespierre during the Terror (*qq.v.*), he was one of those who helped in his downfall on 9 Thermidor. Boissy d'Anglas was elected a member of the Committee of Public Safety (*q.v.*). He presented the supporting decree of 3 Vêntose, Year III, which established freedom of worship. Boissy d'Anglas was the reporter of the committee which drew up the constitution of Year III, and his report presented reactionary measures against the reestablishment of "tyranny and anarchy." Boissy d'Anglas was suspected of becoming a Royalist, as a member of the 500. He presented a measure in favor of freedom of the press and attacked the Directory (*q.v.*). He left France and lived in England until the Consulate (*q.v.*). In 1801 he was made a member of the tribunate and in 1805 a senator.

BOLOGNA. Bologna, Italy was taken by the French in 1796 and by the Austrians in 1799. It was again in French hands after the Battle of Marengo (*q.v.*) in 1800 and finally restored to the pope in 1815.

BONALD, LOUIS DE, VICOMTE (1754-1840). Political philosopher. He emigrated in 1790 and was a conservative politician under the Restoration. He was a strong defender of the church and crown against the Revolution and held the Catholic religion and divine right as absolute truths.

BONAPARTE (BUONAPARTE) FAMILY. The name Bonaparte appeared in Florence and Genoa in the 13th century and in the 15th century a branch settled in Corsica. There were five sons and three daughters of the marriage of Carlo Bonaparte (1746-85) and Letizia Ramolino (1750-1836).

Joseph (1768-1844)	King of Naples
Napoleon (1769-1821)	Emperor of the French
Lucien (1775-1840)	Prince of Canino
Louis[1] (1778-1846)	King of Holland
Jerome (1784-1860)	King of Westphalia
Elisa (1777-1820)	Grand Duchess of Tuscany
Pauline[2] (1780-1825)	Princess Borghese
Caroline[3] (1782-1839)	Queen of Naples

[1]Married Hortense Beauharnais (daughter of Viscomte de Beauharnais [q.v.])
[2]Married first to Leclerc (q.v.)
[3]Married Murat (q.v.)

BONEY. Nickname for Napoleon Bonaparte.

BONNET ROUGE. The cap that became the emblem of the Revolution. It was worn during the Greco-Roman era by freed slaves. It appeared in the Paris streets in 1789. On June 20, 1792 Louis XVI was forced to wear an elaborately made red bonnet. On August 14, 1792 it was officially adopted as the headdress of members of the Commune of Paris (Commune de Paris, q.v.). It appeared on public papers, stamps etc. The first examples were grey, but red soon became the accepted color. After 9 Thermidor, it was gradually abandoned as a prominent symbol but still existed (and exists) as an emotive image, with similar power to that of the French cock.

BOUILLÉ, FRANÇOIS CLAUDE AMOUR, MARQUIS DE (1739-1800). General, he served in the Seven Years' War and as Governor of the Antilles waged war against the English during the American War of Independence (q.v.). He was op-posed to the Revolution and helped the king in his attempt to escape. After the king's arrest at Varennes he went to Russia and later served under Gustavus III of Sweden and the prince of Condé. Finally, he lived in England, where he wrote *Mémoires sur la Révolution* (1801).

BOULOU BALOU (FRANCE). Battle fought April 30, 1794 between France and Spain. The French under "Dugommier" (Jacques François Coquille) were the victors.

BOURBON, HOUSE OF. Name of the royal houses of France, Spain and Naples. The Bourbons were expelled from France in 1791 and restored in 1814. They were again expelled on the return of Bonaparte from Elba, and again restored in 1815. Charles X (q.v.) and his family were expelled in July 1830. Charles X had abdicated in favor of the Duke of Orleans and so the Orleans branch ascended the throne in the person of Louis Philippe (q.v.), "king of the French," August 9, 1830. Louis Philippe was deposed February 24, 1848 and his family was also expelled.

BOURDON DE L'OISE, FRANÇOIS LOUIS (1760?-97). Revolutionary who took part in the insurrection of 1792. He sat in the Convention *(q.v.)* and voted for the execution of Louis XVI, but in 1797 was sentenced to be transported to Cayenne, French Guiana *(q.v.)*, where he died soon after arriving there.

BOURGEOIS. Term having different meanings at various stages in history, but in the revolutionary period it described those French who supported the principles of constitutionality and the natural rights and dignity of man against the principle of the divine right of kings and the privileges of the aristocracy and clergy.

BOURG ST. PIERRE. Village in Switzerland through which Napoleon's army passed on its way to Italy in 1800. A bill for 45,334 Swiss francs (about $US20,000) was presented at the time for unreturned pots and pans, uprooted trees and local labor, but was never paid. French governments always maintained that all debts incurred by Napoleon had been settled by the Treaty of Vienna in 1815. However on May 19, 1984 the mayor, a direct descendant of the head muleteer who led Napoleon's baggage train over the Great St. Bernard Pass, accepted a bronze commemorative plaque and a handwritten note from President Mitterrand and the debt was cancelled by this French symbolic gesture.

BOURSIERS DE L'ÉGALITÉ (1792). The foundation scholars (boursiers) of the College Louis-le-Grand which had, in 1792, taken the name of the Institut de l'Egalité. There were more than 700, including the children of Camille Desmoulins, Brissot de Warville, Carrier, Buffon, Condorcet, Fabre d'Églantine, Jean-Bon Saint-André, Toussaint L'Ouverture *(qq.v.)*, and others.

BOXTEL, BRABANT. Battle on September 17, 1794. The British and allied army commanded by the duke of York was defeated by the French, who took 2,000 prisoners and eight pieces of cannon.

BREMEN. Hanseatic port, a free town of the German Confederation situated near the confluence of the Weser and the Wumme. The 1795 meetings of the émigrés *(q.v.)* occurred near here. The comte d'Artois *(q.v.)*, his son and others who had left France had considerable influence in the city. The émigré envoys to the Congress of Rastadt gained the guarantee of their territory.

BRESCIA. Town in Lombardy, taken and retaken numerous times. Finally taken by the French in 1796. It became part of the Cisalpine Republic in 1797 and the chief town in the Département de la Mella.

BRIENNE, ÉCOLE DE. Established in the town in the district of Bar-sur-Aube. Bonaparte started his military studies here (1779-1783). The school closed in 1790.

BRIENNE, LOMÉNIE, CARDINAL DE. *See* **Loménie de Brienne, Etienne Charles de.**

BRISSOT DE WARVILLE, JEAN-PIERRE (JACQUES-PIERRE) (1754-93). Lawyer and revolutionary born near Chartres. He abandoned the legal profession for that of authorship. His *Théorie des lois criminelles* (1780) was followed by his *Bibliothèque des lois criminelles* (1782-86), which established his reputation. He was imprisoned in the Bastille (*q.v.*) on the false charge of having written against the queen. He lived in London in 1787 and in 1788 visited North America as representative of the Amis des Noirs (*q.v.*). In 1789 he was elected representative for Paris in the National Assembly (*q.v.*) and also founded *La Patriote français*. As the Revolution proceeded he was recognized as the leading spirit of the Girondists or Brissotins (*qq.v.*). The Jacobin victory resulted in his fall and with 20 other Girondists he was executed.

Ellery, Eloise, *Brissot de Warville*, 1915 (reprinted 1970).

BRISSOTINS. Followers of Brissot (*q.v.*). The name was rarely used after the Brissotins joined the Girondists (*q.v.*).

BROGLIE, VICTOR FRANÇOIS, DUC DE BROGLIE (1718-1804). Marshal of France. He fought in the War of the Austrian Succession and in the Seven Years' War. He left France at the time of the Revolution and commanded the "army of the princes" in 1792. He entered Russian service when the Revolution ended.

BRUEYS D'AIGALLIERS, FRANÇOIS DE PAUCE DE (1753-98). Vice-admiral, he escorted Bona-parte's army to Egypt. On returning to France he was defeated and killed by superior British naval forces at Aboukir Bay on August 1, 1798. (*See* **Nile, Battle of the.**) His flagship was *L'Orient*, which blew up after his death.

BRUMAIRE. "Fog month" of the Revolutionary Calendar (*q.v.*) corresponding, according to the year, to October 22 or 23 to November 20 or 21.

BRUMAIRE, COUP D'ETAT OF. On 18 Brumaire (November 9, 1799) the Consulate (*q.v.*) replaced the Directory (*q.v.*). The Council of the Ancients and the Council of the Five Hundred (*see* **Councils**) were called to St. Cloud (*q.v.*) where it was put to these parliamentary bodies that the method of government was too cumbersome. There was some disagreement by a group of Jacobins (*q.v.*) and there were threats to kill Bonaparte. In the end a government was agreed by appointing three consuls, Bonaparte, Sieyès and Ducos (*qq.v.*).

BRUNSWICK, CHARLES WILLIAM FERDINAND, DUKE OF (1735-1806). General who fought in the Seven Years' War, commanded the Prussian and Austrian troops in France and at Valmy (*q.v.*). He retired from the army in 1793 and in 1806 became commander of the Prussian armies. He died of wounds soon after his defeat by Napoleon at Auerstädt.

BRUTUS. An historical figure of ancient Rome celebrated from the beginning of the Revolution. Founder of the Roman republic, Brutus had not hesitated to sacrifice his own sons to consolidate it, presiding over their punishment. "Brutus" became the first name of many children, and the Convention (*q.v.*) decreed that Brutus's bust should be conspicuous during all its meetings. A head of Brutus found in the ruins of Herculaneum was also placed in the Bibliothèque Nationale (*q.v.*).

BULLETIN DES LOIS. Because of the lack of control of departmental and municipal administration, it was decided that an official record of the laws enacted by the French government should be published. The first issue of *Le Bulletin des Lois* was published in May 1794.

BUREAU ACADÉMIQUE D'ÉCRITURE. The bureau was reorganized in Paris on January 23, 1779 by letters patent. It was made up of twenty-four members, twenty-four fellows and twenty-four associate writers and engravers. It taught its own students but was suppressed in 1791. It was replaced by the Société Académique d'Écriture.

BURKE, EDMUND (1729-97). British statesman, parliamentary orator and Whig political thinker. When the Revolution began Burke was hostile to it and was alarmed by its English supporters. His *Reflections on* *the Revolution in France* (1790) was provoked by a sermon given by the Protestant dissenter, Richard Price (1723-95), which welcomed revolutionary change. The book prompted many rebuttals, of which the best known is Tom Paine's *The Rights of Man* (1791). Two other notable replies are Mary Wollstonecraft's *A Vindication of the Rights of Men* (1790) and James Mackintosh's *Vindiciae Gallicae* (1791).

Freeman, Michael A. (ed.), *Burke and the Critique of Political Radicalism*, 1980.
Macpherson, Crawford B., *Burke*, 1980.

BUZOT, FRANÇOIS NICOLAS LÉONARD (1760-94). Lawyer and revolutionary. He was elected to the Estates-General as deputy in 1789 and became known for his advanced opinions. Buzot demanded the nationalization of all the possessions of the clergy and the right of the citizenry to bear arms. In 1792 he was a deputy to the Convention (*q.v.*) as a Girondist (*q.v.*). He demanded the formation of the National Guard (*q.v.*), drawn from the departments to protect the Convention, and this suggestion created much bitterness in Paris. Buzot had the decree of death for émigrés who did not return to France passed, and the same remedy for anyone who wished to reestablish the monarchy. On June 2, 1793 he was deposed, together with the other Girondists, and fled to Normandy, where he fomented an abortive federalist insurrection against the Convention. Outlawed, he later killed himself.

CABANIS, PIERRE JEAN GEORGES (1757-1808). Physician, philosopher and man of letters. He was elected to the Legislative Assembly (*q.v.*) as a deputy for the Seine in 1797. He was a friend and medical adviser to Mirabeau (*q.v.*), for whom he supplied material for speeches on public education. During the Terror (*q.v.*) he lived in retirement, and later taught in the medical school at Paris. He was a member of the Council of Five Hundred (*q.v.*) and later of the Senate (*q.v.*).

CABINET NOIR, LE. Bureau supported by the administrator general of posts which opened letters, made extracts and resealed the original without leaving any trace. Under Louis XIV, XV and XVI, the art of opening and resealing letters, covertly, became one of the unscrupulous measures perfected by the government. Under Louis XVI false letters were sent in order to compromise important officials.

CACHET, LETTRES DE (SEALED LETTERS). Letters or orders issued by the king under the royal seal (*cachet*). Best known for *cachets* used to imprison or punish without trial. In the 18th century they were often issued without names, which could be filled in later. *Lettres de cachet* were abolished by the Constituent Assembly (*q.v.*) in January 1790.

CADOUDAL, GEORGES (1771-1804). Using the name "Georges" he led the risings in the Vendéan Rebellion (*q.v.*) and was executed for conspiring to have Napoleon deposed and the monarchy restored.

CADRAN BLEU, LE. Restaurant situated on the Boulevard du Temple, frequented by playwrights of the many theaters in the area. Here the heads of the insurrection of August 10, 1792 used to meet to plan their strategy.

CAHIERS DE DOLÉANCES. List of grievances drawn up in towns, villages and by the guilds, which were presented by the deputies to the Estates-General in 1789. Demands were made for equality in legal matters, religious toleration, improvement in the condition of the parish clergy, an end to the sale of public offices and the abolition of seignorial judicial powers, such as the Gabelle (*q.v.*) and the Corvée (*q.v.*).

ÇA IRA (IT WILL COME TO PASS). The name and refrain of one of the earliest French revolutionary songs which was first heard when the Parisians marched on Versailles October 5-6, 1789.

As a rallying cry it was borrowed from Benjamin Franklin, who used to say, in reference to the American Revolution, *Ah! ah! ça ira, ça ira!* ("twill come to pass"). The refrain of the French revolutionary version by Ladré was:

Ah! ça ira, ça ira, ça ira,
Les aristocrates à la lanterne.

CALENDAR, REVOLUTIONARY.

The Gregorian calendar was introduced into France in 1582. The year began on January 1, and followed the festivals of the church. The new calendar's year began on September 22 (the autumn equinox) and consisted of 12 months, each of 30 days, totaling 360 days. Each month was, in turn, divided into three "decades" of periods of ten days, instead of the former seven-day weeks. This left five supplementary days, six in a leap-year, which were to be called "sans-cullotides" and were to be observed as national holidays. It was one of the more important actions for de-Christianizing France. The working party appointed by the Committee of Public Instruction included Fabre d'Églantine (*q.v.*) and it was charged with producing a "national" calendar. It aimed at universalization but for those living in the tropics it would have been foolish to operate under the illusion that their hottest month corresponded with the coldest months in France.

The days of the week were "Primidi," "Duodi," "Tridi," "Quartidi," "Quintidi," "Sextidi," "Septidi," "Octidi," "Nonidi" and "Décadi" (the day of rest). For saints' names, the names of grains, trees, roots, fruits and flowers were substituted.

On introduction, the calendar was antedated from September 22, 1792 (the day of the proclamation of the new republic) but its establishment was not decreed until November 24, 1793.

Autumn

Vendémiaire	"Vintage month"	September 22 to October 21
Brumaire	"Fog month"	October 22 to November 20
Frimaire	"Sleet month"	November 21 to December 20

Winter

Nivôse	"Snow month"	December 21 to January 19
Pluviôse	"Rain month"	January 20 to February 18
Ventôse	"Wind month"	February 19 to March 20

Spring

Germinal	"Sprouts' month"	March 21 to April 19
Floréal	"Flowers' month"	April 20 to May 19
Prairial	"Pasture month"	May 20 to June 18

Summer

Messidor	"Harvest month"	June 19 to July 18
Thermidor, or Fervidor	"Hot month"	July 19 to August 17
Fructidor	"Fruit month"	August 18 to September 16

Sans-cullotides, or Feasts dedicated to:

Les Vertus	The Virtues	September 17
Le Génie	Genius	September 18
Le Travail	Labor	September 19
L'Opinion	Opinion	September 20
Les Récompenses	Rewards	September 21

The Revolutionary Calendar was discontinued on January 1, 1806 having lasted for 12 years, 2 months and 27 days, and the Gregorian Calendar restored.

CALONNE, CHARLES-ALEXANDRE DE (1734-1802). Controller-general of finances. His attempts to refine the finances of France led to his dismissal in 1787 and indirectly to the beginning of the Revolution in 1789. He then lived in England, and remained a critic of the Assembly (*q.v.*). He returned to France in 1802.

Jully, P., *Calonne*, 1949.

CALUMNY, MOTIONS AND DECREES FOR REPRESSION OF. Accusations of calumny, raised against Royalist journalists and others, led to a motion in 1794 for its repression, but no one law was voted against it. Under the Directory (*q.v.*), the revolutionary newspapers redoubled their attacks on calumny, and a variety of methods of detection and punishment were suggested. Again, nothing positive was done. It was not until 1801 that the penal code laid down a law punishing a calumnist with six months' imprisonment, and a heavy fine.

CAMBACÉRÈS, JEAN-JACQUES RÉGIS DE (1753-1824). Legal expert who played an important part in the Convention (*q.v.*), then as second consul, and later in high official posts under the Empire.

CAMBON, PIERRE JOSEPH (1756-1820). Financial expert. A founder of the Montpellier Jacobin Club, he was elected a member of the municipality. He drew up the first petition to invite the Constituent Assembly to proclaim a republic on the flight of Louis XVI in 1791. As a member of the Committee of Finance he decreed the issue of *assignats* (*q.v.*) for war expenses in February 1793. He also worked to reduce the issue's depreciation through the Grand Livre in August 1793 and he instituted the *Great Book of Public Debt* (*q.v.*), by which all stock issued prior to the Revolution would be cancelled and a new, uniform stock reissued. Later, he was accused by Robespierre (*q.v.*) of being an aristocrat and antirevolutionary, and was attacked as a former Montagnard (*q.v.*) by the Royalists.

CAMPAN, JEANNE-LOUISE-HEN-RIETTE GENEST (1752-1822). Lady-in-waiting to Marie-Antoinette (1770-92). She wrote *Memoires sur la vie privée de Marie-Antoinette* (1823).

CAMP DE JALLÈS, CONSPIRACY OF THE. On the Plain of Jallès, at the foot of the Cevennes in the district of Largentière (Ardèche), a camp was formed in September 1790 of nobles who were opposed to the decrees of the Constituent Assembly (*q.v.*) and who wished to join with refractory priests to form a counter-revolutionary government. Under the pretext of holding a Fête de Fédération, the nobles and priests recruited 22,000 men, whose batallions carried a flag with a cross on it. The conspirators, established at the Château de Jallès, issued insurrectional decrees. On September 7, the National Assembly annulled these decrees and forbade all *camp fédératif*. The insurrectionists dispersed but renewed their attempts to create an insurrectionalist movement. They were finally disbanded in February 1791 by members of the National Guard (*q.v.*).

CAMPO-FORMIO, TREATY OF. Peace treaty concluded between France and Austria on October 17, 1797, ending Austrian involvement in the War of the First Coalition (*q.v.*). Austria gave up the Low Countries and the Ionian Islands to France, and Milan, Mantua, and Modena to the Cisalpine Republic. By a secret article the Austrian emperor gained Venice and the Venetian dominions.

CAMUS, ARMAND GASTON (1740-1804). Lawyer and revolu-tionary. In the debate on the power of the church he stated "The Church is within the state, not the state within the Church . . ." The Convention sent sent Camus and four colleagues, including the minister of war, to take Dumouriez (*q.v.*) prisoner in 1793 but Dumouriez handed them over to the Austrians. After an imprisonment of two and a half years, he was exchanged for the daughter of Louis XVI, and on his return to Paris was made member, and later president, of the Council of Five Hundred (*see* **Councils**), but he resigned in 1797.

CANON D'ALARME. Artillery placed in the different parts of Paris which, at any sign of danger, were sounded, in order to raise the citizen-ry and to call them together under arms. The most quickly understood cannon was that at the Pont-Neuf. It could be heard throughout the after-noon of the day on which the Prison Massacres occurred on September 2, 1792. After this occurrence, anyone who fired this piece faced the death penalty. On June 2, 1793 the *canon d'alarme* was fired again when Han-riot (*q.v.*), with his army of 80,000, went to the Convention (*q.v.*) at the time when the Girondins (*q.v.*) were about to be arrested and removed. The citizens of Paris dreaded the sound of this alarm.

CANTINIÈRE. Originally, a camp follower and then the woman who attended to the regimental canteen. Official recognition was obtained and the *cantinière* was put on the ration strength of her unit.

CAP OF LIBERTY. *See* **Bonnet Rouge.**

CAPET, LOUIS. *See* **Louis XVI.**

CAPETIAN. Family to which, for nearly nine centuries, the kings of France belonged. The origins of the name are in dispute, but the first of the family to whom the name applied was Hugh, elected king of the Franks in 987. The Capetian dynasty was France's third, preceded by the Merovingians and the Carolingians. From 987 to 1328 it comprised a direct line, from Capet to Charles IV, "Le Bel" (*d.* 1328). The Valois branch extended from Philippe VI to Henri III (1328-1589) and the Bourbon branch from Henri IV to Louis Philippe (1589-1848).

During the Revolution, Capet was the name given to Louis XVI and his family after their internment in the Temple because Hugh Capet was one of the chiefs of the Bourbon family. All of the judgment procedure against the king was made under the name of Hugh Capet, and he was condemned to death by the Convention (*q.v.*) under that name, without any other title or qualification.

Fawtier, Robert, *The Capetian Kings of France*, 1960.

CAPITAINERIES GARDE-CÔTES. All the territories along the coasts bordering the Channel, the Atlantic and the Mediterranean were divided into 110 *capitaineries*. At their head was a *capitain* or officer, who was in charge of watching at the defense and organization of the coast. In each of the parishes which went to make up the *capitainerie*, there was a coast-guard company. Each *capitainerie* had an effective strength of around 2,000. They were suppressed in 1791.

CAPORAL, LE PETIT. *See* **Corporal, The Little.**

CAPUCINES, CONVENT OF THE. Initially established on the Rue Saint-Honoré, facing the Capucins, and founded in 1604. Louis XV had it demolished, then rebuilt on the spot where the Rue Neuve-des-Petits-Champs ended. After 1790 and its suppression, presses were installed for the printing of *assignats (q.v.)*.

CAPUCINS DE LA CHAUSSÉE-D'ANTIN, DISTRICT OF. This district took its names from that of a convent, started in 1780 in the Chaussée-d'Antin quarter, where the Capucins of the Faubourg Saint-Jacques were established in September 1782. The convent was suppressed in 1790 and transformed into a hospice for those suffering from venereal diseases. In 1802 it became the Lycée Bonaparte and took the name of the Collège royal de Bourbon in 1814.

CARABOTS. Societies of sans-culottes which formed in numerous villages of Normandy. They carried a ribbon on their arms which had, at the extremity, a death's-head emblem and the words "L'exécution de la loi ou la morte." When the advocat Georges Bayeux was murdered in the streets of Caen in 1792, the cry of "Carabots" went up. The Girondin deputies visited Caen in 1793 to try and win support in their move to establish a government against that of the Convention (*q.v.*).

CARÊME CIVIQUE (CIVIC FAST). A Lenten fast by citizens in the countryside. To deliver surpluses of meat goods to those who had special needs and wants, they imposed on themselves the "carême civique."

CARÊME, LE. Order of the Paris Parlement on February 5, 1790 which stated that the display and sale of eggs in the markets and public places of the city, including the faubourgs, during the period of Lent of that year, should take place.

CARMAGNOLE. Originally the name of a workman's jacket from Carmagnola in Piedmont. It was first adopted by revolutionary marchers from Marseilles and introduced to Paris in 1792. It was also the name given to a popular song (authorship unknown), which was invariably used at the executions of 1792 and 1793, and a dance. The first verse of the song was:

Madame Veto avait promis
De faire égorger tout Paris,
Madame Veto avait promis
De faire égorger tout Paris,
Mais son coup a manqué,
Dansons la carmagnole,
Vive le son, vive le son,
Dansons la carmagnole,
Vive le son du canon.

It had 11 or 12 verses and they had constant revision. Speeches in favor of the execution of Louis XVI were called Barère des Carmagnoles.

The song was prohibited by Bonaparte when he became first consul.

"Madame Veto" was an epithet for Marie Antoinette, as she was supposed to have instigated the king's unfortunate use of the veto. Carmagnole was subsequently applied to other revolutionary songs such as "Ça Ira," the "Marseillaise," and the "Chant du Départ" (*qq.v.*).

CARMES, ÉGLISE DES. Situated in the Rue de Vaugirard, Paris, and the dependency of the convent of the Barefooted Friars, which was suppressed in 1790. It became a prison for refractory priests in 1791, and during the September 2, 1792 massacres (*q.v.*), Stanislas Maillard (*q.v.*), who had taken part in the storming of the Bastille, and a band of thugs entered the convent and 200 priests were murdered, either singly or shot together in groups in the garden and halls.

CARNAVALET, MUSÉE. Built as the Hôtel de Carnavalet in 1544, it is situated on the Rue Culture-Sainte-Catherine and a corner of the Rue Neuve. Madame de Sévigné (1677-96) lived there for some years. The office in charge of libraries was situated here after the Revolution. Since 1866 it has held books, documents and manuscripts concerning the Revolution.

CARNOT, LAZARE NICOLAS MARGUERITE (1753-1823). General and minister of war (1793-97). "Organizer of victory" in the Revolution, he instituted the *levée en masse* (*q.v.*). In 1791 he became a member of the Legislative Assembly (*q.v.*), and later, in the Convention (*q.v.*), voted for the death of Louis XVI. He was elected to the Committee of Public Safety (*q.v.*) and entrusted with raising the 14 armies (*q.v.*). In 1797 he was sentenced to exile as a suspected Royalist. He returned to Paris at the 18th Brumaire (*q.v.*) and in 1800 was

appointed minister of war. He opposed Napoleon's plans for the empire but served again as minister of the interior during the Hundred Days. He was exiled again during the Second Restoration.
Palmer, R. R., *Twelve who Ruled*, 1958.

CARRIER, JEAN BAPTISTE (1756-94). Radical politician. He helped to form the revolutionary tribunal in the Convention (*q.v.*), voted for the death of Louis XVI, sought the arrest of the duc d'Orleans and assisted in the overthrow of the Girondists (*q.v.*). At Nantes in 1793 he massacred, in four months, 16,000 Vendéan and other prisoners, chiefly by drowning them in the Loire. (*See* **Noyades.**) He helped to bring about the fall of Robespierre (*q.v.*) on July 27, 1794 but, immediately afterwards, Carrier was tried for mass murder and was guillotined.

CARTES DE SURETÉ. Identity cards of two kinds. The first was for people domiciled in Paris for at least 14 years, the second for those who, as outsiders (*externes*), needed authorization to stay in the city. Any citizen who could not produce his card when asked was arrested as a suspect. The delivery of the cards involved a great many formal procedures. In 1794 and 1795, the *certificat du payement des impositions* was necessary to receive the cards. Later, they became a right of entry into the primary assemblies (*q.v.*). In 1797 they became obligatory if one wished to leave the canton of Paris.

CASERNE DE LA NOUVELLE FRANCE. Paris barracks at 76 Rue du Faubourg Poissonière that was a center of revolutionary activity with-

in the army. Both Hoche and Lefebvre (*qq.v.*) were billeted there.

CASSATION, COURT OF. Highest court of appeal in France, instituted on December 22, 1790. On April 19, 1791 it was organized as a supreme court to maintain uniformity of jurisprudence. It had the right of revising all judgments that had been passed that violated the law or promoted a false application of the law. It was placed at the top of the judicial organization and was composed of forty-five members elected by the forty-five departments.

CASTLEBAR. *See* **Killala.**

CATEL, CHARLES-SIMON (1773-1830). Composer. During the Revolution he became associated with the band of the Garde Nationale for which he wrote military music. His "Hymn of Victory" was to celebrate the Battle of Fleurus (*q.v.*), June 26, 1794, and the work was performed on June 29.

CATHERINE II (1729-96). Known as the Great, she was empress of Russia from 1762 to 1796. Although she welcomed the Enlightenment (*q.v.*) and was a friend of writers such as Voltaire and Diderot (*qq.v.*), she had no wish to give up her own privileges. Towards the end of her life she was increasingly perturbed by the successes of the revolutionary armies and the increase of radical views, and particularly by the death of Louis XVI.
Grey, Ian, *Catherine the Great*, 1961.

CATHOLIC CULT, ABOLITION OF. *See* **Abolition of the Catholic Cult.**

CAZALÈS, JACQUES ANTOINE MARIE DE (1752-1805). Orator and leader of the monarchists in the early stages of the Revolution. From 1791 to 1803 he was an émigré in Coblenz and in England. He fought with the émigré army and returned to France in 1802.

CENS. The annual manorial tax made to a seigneur was the essential mark of "commoner" land. The land holding for which *cens* was paid was a *censive,* and the person responsible for paying it was a *censitaire.*

CENSORS, ROYAL (CENSEURS ROYAUX). Officials charged with examining books, which could not be published without the agreement of the king. They numbered seventy-nine and were placed in ten classes for each series of human knowledge. Architecture had only one censor; newspapers were under the scrutiny of many more special censors. Censors received their directions from the chancellor and were placed under the direction of the lieutenant of police. They were abolished with the 1791 constitution, which declared freedom of thought and opinions to be part of humanity's natural rights. This guaranteed that all citizens had the liberty to speak, write and publish their opinions without prior scrutiny. In 1795 the Directory (*q.v.*) renewed these principles, but the day after the coup d'état of 18 Fructidor, the newspapers were subjected to police inspection and the right to prohibit publication.

CENTIÈME DENIER. One-percent annual tax on the income from an office to insure its inheritability, paid during the ancien régime.

CERTIFICAT DE CIVISME. Certificate sent to Paris by the general council of the commune which affirmed that the individual named was in accord with all of the obligations and responsibilities demanded of citizens of the republic. Only those who occupied themselves with public affairs had to be provided with one. It was not dropped during the Terror (*q.v.*) although a large number of people demanded it, but was abolished by the law of 18 Fructidor, Year III.

CERTIFICAT DE VIE. By a decree of the Convention (17 Fructidor, Year II), birth certificates of non-French persons whose country was at war with the republic, had to be signed by two agents of neutral countries in order to be recognized by the national treasury.

CERTIFICAT D'INDIGENCE. In 1795 this certificate was required of widows and children of citizens killed during the course of serving in the Revolution to help them obtain pensions or other entitlements.

CERTIFICAT DE RÉSIDENCE. Certificate issued during the years 1795-96 and, subsequently, to attest that the person who possessed it had always resided within the commune. Its object was to show that the bearer had never emigrated. The production of this certificate was demanded for the payment of pensions and salaries.

CHAMFORT, NICOLAS-SÉBASTIEN ROCH (1741-94). Writer and playwright. Sponsored by high society because of his writings and wit, he became disillusioned and became a revolutionary and a friend of Mirabeau (*q.v.*), writing for the *Mercure de France*. He also became secretary of the Jacobin Club. Shocked by the Terror (*q.v.*), he attempted suicide and later died.

CHAMPART. Manorial tax consisting of a portion of the produce of the land. Also called *agrier* and *terrage*.

CHAMP DE MARS. Large open space and chief military parade ground of Paris (1770-89) on the left bank of the Seine, where the Eiffel Tower stands today. During the Revolution it was used for staging the great festivals such as the anniversary of the capture of the Bastille (*q.v.*) on July 14 and the Festival of the Supreme Being in 1794.

CHAMPS ÉLYSÉES. Originally the Champs de Culture, Marie de Medici opened up, alongside the Seine, three great garden lanes of four rows of trees, which were closed off by iron gates at both ends. This promenade was named the Cours la Reine and was a rendezvous for the court. In 1670 the avenues were opened and the area took the name *Champs Élysées*. In 1697 the area was separated from the Tuileries by muddy fields, which made the promenade practically impassable and inaccessible, so this area was deserted and periodically taken over by tramps and vagabonds.

On July 13-14, 1789 foreign regiments that had been camped in the Champs moved to Versailles. On October 5, 1789 the group of women led by Stanislas Maillard (*q.v.*) met here to demand bread of the king. Fêtes were held here in 1790 and 1791 by the federalists who had come from their departments.

CHANCELIER DE FRANCE (CHANCELLOR OF FRANCE). This office disappeared with the monarchy. It was the highest and most important of the great offices of the kingdom. The chancellor was chief of all the tribunals, presiding officer of the Privy Council. He held the highest position of rank and prerogatives and he presided over the council of peers and dukes. The only permanent minister, he could be exiled but not dismissed. He carried the Great Seal. The office was changed in a variety of ways during the Revolution and its title became Ministre de la Justice.

CHANT DU DÉPART, LE. Revolutionary song written by Marie Joseph Blaise Chénier (*q.v.*) in 1793 with music by Étienne Nicolas Méhul. It was written to commemorate the fall of the Bastille and subsequently became the official song at national festivals. The refrain runs:

La République nous appelle,
Sachons vaincre ou sachons périr:
Un Français doit vivre pour elle,
Pour elle un Français doit mourir.

CHAPELIER, ISAAC RENÉ GUY, LE (1754-94). Politician and lawyer. He was elected as deputy to the Estates-General (*q.v.*) for Rennes and was one of the founders of the

Jacobin Club. Having considerable influence in the Constituent Assembly *(q.v.)* he was elected president on August 3, 1789. Le Chapelier, a leading member of the committee which drew up the new constitution, presented a paper on the liberty of theaters and one on literary copyright. He opposed Robespierre *(q.v.)* when the latter proposed that members of the Assembly should not be eligible for election to provide the new Assembly. After Varennes *(q.v.)*, Le Chapelier became more moderate and brought forward a motion to restrict the freedom of the clubs. Having visited England in 1790, he was denounced for conspiring with a foreign nation and executed.

CHAPELIER'S LAW. *See* **Law, Chapelier's.**

CHAPPE, CLAUDE (1763-1805). Priest and engineer. During the Revolution he devoted himself to the invention of the semaphore visual telegraph, which in 1794 enabled news of battles to be reported at what was then tremendous speed. His brother, Ignace Chappe (1760-1829), was a member of the Legislative Assembly (q.v.), which gave its backing to several experiments.

CHARLES X (1757-1836). King of France (1824-30). Younger brother of Louis XVI and Louis XVIII, successor of Louis XVIII known as the comte d'Artois *(q.v.)*. He left France in 1789 but returned to lead the Vendéan revolt in 1795. (*See* **Vendéan Rebellion.**) He returned at the Restoration having lived in England for most of the intervening years. His attempts to revive absolutism led to the Revolution of 1830.

Beach, Vincent, *Charles X of France: His Life and Times*, 1971.

CHARTREUSE, LA GRANDE. Chief of the monasteries of the Carthusian order, situated near Grenoble. In 1792 the monks were expelled and their library destroyed. They returned to the monastery after the restoration of 1815.

CHATEAUBRIAND, FRANÇOIS AUGUSTE, VICOMTE DE (1768-1848). Author. Chateaubriand traveled in America (1791-92) but returned on hearing of the arrest of Louis XVI, fought with the émigré army, and was wounded at Thionville, escaping to England in 1793. He returned to France only in 1800. He was appointed to the embassy at Rome by Bonaparte but he resigned from the post in disgust at the execution of the duc d'Enghien *(q.v.)*. He was anti-Bonaparte, pro-Catholic, and became one of Louis XVIII's ministers at Ghent.

CHATELET DE PARIS. Headquarters of the ancient provostship and viscounty of Paris. In 1789 the marquis de Boulainvilliers carried the title of provost of the city, the conservator of the royal privileges of the university, and was head of the Grand Tribunal. On August 24, 1790 its jurisdiction was abolished, making way for the new judicial reorganization.

CHATELET, LE GRAND. Fortress built on the Right Bank of the Seine. Under Louis XVI the dungeons of the Grand Chatelet were not used, and prisoners were placed in less appalling circumstances. The Constituent Assembly *(q.v.)* ordered its demolition in 1790 but this was not achieved until 1802.

CHATELET, LE PETIT. Prison situated on the Left Bank of the Seine, at the head of the Petit Pont and on the Quay Gloriette. Like the Grand Chatelet *(q.v.)*, it was first constructed of wood but was rebuilt in stone in 1368. The provost of Paris lived here. The prison was closed, following a report by Necker *(q.v.)*, in 1780 (demolished in 1782) and the Hôtel de la Force was converted into a prison with better conditions for prisoners.

CHAUFFEURS. Brigands who operated in the departments of the west after the routing of the *chouans (q.v.)*. They struck at farms, murdering, torturing and stealing. They operated in Normandy until 1800. They also existed in the eastern departments and in the Midi from 1795 until about 1803.

CHAUMETTE, PIERRE GASPARD (1763-94). Revolutionary leader. An extreme sansculottist, he was appointed procurator of the Paris Commune (Commune de Paris, *q.v.*) and did much to improve social conditions. He was a promoter of the anti-Christian cult. Although he did not advocate rebellion by the sansculottes *(q.v.)* he was arrested and guillotined in 1794.

CHAUVELIN, FRANÇOIS BERNARD, MARQUIS DE (1766-1832). Diplomatist and administrator, he was master of the king's wardrobe in 1789 but joined the Revolution. He served in the army of Flanders, and was ambassador to Britain in 1792, his aim, to encourage England to remain neutral in the war which was to break out between the French and the king of Bohemia and Hungary. On the execution of Louis XVI he was told to leave England. He was imprisoned as a suspect during the Terror, *(q.v.)*, and was released after 9 Thermidor *(q.v.)*.

CHÉNIER, ANDRÉ (1762-94). Poet. After service in the army he traveled to Switzerland and Italy. He worked at the French embassy in London from 1787-90. He was active in the early days of the Revolution, but protested against the excesses of the monarchists and of the Terror *(q.v.)*. He was arrested and after being imprisoned for four months, he was executed two days before 9 Thermidor *(q.v.)*.
Scarfe, F. H., *André Chénier: His Life and Work,* 1965.

CHÉNIER, MARIE-JOSEPH-BLAISE (1764-1811). Politician, poet and dramatist, brother of André Chénier *(q.v.)*. He was a member of the Convention and the Council of Five Hundred *(qq.v.)* and served on the Committee of General Security and the Committee of Public Safety *(qq.v.)*. The patriotic hymn *Chant du départ (q.v.)* was written by him.

CHERASCO, PEACE OF. Armistice signed on April 28, 1796 by Bonaparte and the king of Sardinia after the Battle of Mondovi. The terms of this armistice stated that the Sardinians should deliver up to the French the three fortified places of

Conti, Tortone and Alexandrie, permit the passage of couriers to France in order to be able to continue operations against the Austrians, and to consent to retire from the coalition. This armistice was converted into a peace treaty on May 15, 1796.

CHOLET, BATTLE OF. Town in the department of Maine-et-Loire. It was taken and retaken during the wars of the Vendée, its commerce totally ruined. In March 1793 it was the general quarters for the Vendéan Rebellion (*q.v.*) and the center of its operations. On October 17 a battle was fought with the republicans. It lasted for two days and the republicans were the victors. On March 18, 1794 the Vendéan army entered the town again, the republicans having retreated, first destroying all of the defenses, burning all the provisions and sacking all the buildings and houses.

CHOUANNERIE, LA. In Brittany and Normandy in 1792, an insurrection started which should not be confused with that of the Vendée. (*See* **Vendéan Rebellion.**) The supporters of the insurrection were vagabonds, malcontents, religious fanatics, military deserters, opportunists. They operated from the Misdon, Fougère and Pertre forests, striking at farmers, villages, and the authorities. The first bands had, as their chiefs, the four Cottereau brothers, of whom the most celebrated was Jean, named "Jean Chouan."

In 1793 the Chouannerie was just organized as the Vendéan army marched on Laval. Jean Chouan's corps joined with this army, forming a distinct group under the command of the prince de Talmont. They were called the "Petit Vendée" and took part with the Vendéans in most of their battles, and continued their own fighting from the woods after the major fighting was over.

An act of truce or pacification was eventually signed with the republic, after considerable pressure by General Hoche (*q.v.*). Considerable concessions were made by the government: the sequestrations raised against their properties were lifted; they were guaranteed the free exercise of the Catholic faith; the republic engaged to pay out of the treasury to the value of a million and a half the notes signed by the leaders of the Chouans (*q.v.*); the Chouans could dispense with the laws relative to military requisitions; and indemnities were given to the victims of the war. Attempts were made to keep the fight going, but the Chouannerie ceased to exist after the government's concessions, although there was still sporadic violence during the following years.

CHOUANS. Name given to the Bretons during the Vendéan Rebellion (*q.v.*) in 1792. It is a dialect word for "screech owl," the sound used by their leader, Jean Cottereau, as their signal.

CHRISTOPHER, ST. (ST. KITTS). Island in the West Indies discovered in 1493 by Columbus. Settled by the English and French in 1623 or 1626. Ceded to England by the peace of Utrecht, 1713. Taken by the French in 1782, but restored the following year.

CI-DEVANTS. Name (literally "the former ones") given during the Revolution to those who, as a result of the abolition of titles, were known but by their family names. Marie Antoinette, for example, was tried as "Widow Capet."

CISALPINE REPUBLIC. Republic formed on June 29, 1797 by Bonaparte, comprising the provinces he had conquered in 1796-97; Lombardy, the old Venetian territories west of the River Adige and south as far as Modena, Reggio nell'Emilia, Ferrara and Bologna. It received a new constitution in September 1798. In 1802 it became the Italian Republic and merged into the Kingdom of Italy in 1805.

CISPADANE REPUBLIC. Republic which Bonaparte formed in Italy in 1796 comprising the province of Emilia. It became part of the Cisalpine Republic (q.v.) in June 1797.

CITIZEN. *Citoyen* and *citoyenne* became the only titles in France from October 10, 1792 until the Empire.

CIVIC MILITIA. *See* **National Guard.**

CIVIC OATHS. Public oaths taken during the Revolution by officials and citizens. The first of many was taken by the Third Estate (q.v.) deputies on June 17, 1789, in the Jeu de Paume at Versailles. On August 9, 1789 Mounier (q.v.) proposed that troops should be required to swear the oath of obedience before the civil magistracy and this was passed by the Constituent Assembly (q.v.). On December 29, 1789 the order went out for all priests to swear fidelity, before the primary assemblies, to the constitution. In January 1790 it was decreed that the national militia should take the oath of fidelity to the nation, the law and the king, and to uphold the constitution.

CLERGY, CIVIL CONSTITUTION OF THE. Law passed in July 1790 which allowed changes in the dioceses and for the election of bishops and priests by the laity. This repudiated the Concordat of 1516. The clergy were required to take an oath of loyalty to the constitution. Many refused and were deemed to have resigned. The measures were condemned by the pope. The breach within the French church was not healed until the Concordat of 1801 (q.v.).

CLOOTS, JEAN-BAPTISTE DU VAL DE GRACE, BARON DE (1755-94). Politician and revolutionary. Self-styled "Anarcharsis Cloots" who joined the Encyclopédistes. He advocated a universal family of nations and a cult of reason. He obtained French citizenship in 1792 and he was a member of the Convention (q.v.). He was executed with the Hébertists (q.v.) on March 23, 1794.

CLUB BRETON. *See* **Jacobins.**

CLUBS, FRENCH. They were essentially political, and greatly concerned in the Revolution. The Club Breton was later known as Club des Jacobins (q.v.), and the Club des Cordeliers (q.v.) comprised among its members Danton and Camille Desmoulins (qq.v.). From these two came the mountain party which overthrew the Girondists *(q.v.)* in 1793, and fell in its turn in 1794. The clubs disappeared with the Directory *(q.v.)* in 1799. They were revived in 1848.

COCKADES (COCARDES). Military insignia, made of different colored papers. They had been used frequently as a symbol since the beginning of the 18th century. On July 11, 1789 Camille Desmoulins *(q.v.)* took a green leaf from a tree in the garden of the Palais Royal and put it in his hatband while speaking to a large crowd; the people followed his example. Soon the revolutionary cockade's colors became identical to those of the tricolor. A series of ordinances elevated and protected the cockade, and the Convention ordered the arrest of those citizens who did not wear it.

COLLIER, L'AFFAIRE DU. *See* **Diamond Necklace Affair.**

COLLOT D'HERBOIS, JEAN MARIE (1751-96). Revolutionary, formerly a provincial actor and theater manager. In 1793 he became president of the Convention *(q.v.)* and a member of the Committee of Public Safety *(q.v.)*. He wrote *Almanach du père Gérard* in 1791 as revolutionary propaganda. He joined the successful plot against Robespierre *(q.v.)* in 1794 but was later expelled from the Convention, and deported to Cayenne, French Guiana *(q.v.)* in 1795, where he died.

COMITÉ CENTRAL RÉVOLUTIONNAIRE. Established by the Paris Commune (Commune de Paris, *q.v.*) in early May 1793. It greatly aided the invasion of the Convention

(q.v.) on June 1 and 2, and helped to force through the Girondin law.

COMITÉ DE SALUT PUBLIC. *See* **Committee of Public Safety.**

COMITÉ DIPLOMATIQUE. At the time of diplomatic correspondences between the Austrian emperor and the Legislative Assembly in March 1792, before the declaration of war, the Assembly renewed its comité diplomatique, composed of 18 members. The committee studied the changes which were occurring in European diplomacy, and to put France in a position where its voice could be heard, diplomatically.

COMITÉ INSURRECTEUR. Committee which prepared the work for the attack on the Tuileries of August 10, 1792. It was composed of the principal federalists of the departments and the members of the Paris faubourgs. The committee's membership was composed of five members, who gave the signal for the attack.

COMITÉ MILITAIRE. Created on October 1, 1789, it was composed of 12 members who, together with the minister of war, were to try to work out an organizational plan for the army, to submit to the Constituent Assembly *(q.v.)*.

COMITÉS RÉVOLUTIONNAIRES. Name given to clubs and popular societies, founded and organized throughout France in 1790, known at the time as *Comités de Surveillance*. In September 1793 the committees were charged by the Convention *(q.v.)* to arrest suspects, without the intervention of the authorities, and to pursue conspirators and foreigners. In August 1794 the *comités révolutionnaires* were suppressed, except in the chief towns of the departments and in communes with more than 8,000 people where national agents were in charge of surveillance.

In June 1795 the Convention ordered that the *comités révolutionnaires* return to their original title, that of *comités de surveillance.*

The committees had a great influence on the course of the Revolution and were composed of, in the main, sincere republicans and patriots. In fighting strongly against counterrevolutionaries and Royalists they did, however, commit excesses.

COMMITTEE OF GENERAL SECURITY (COMITÉ DE SURÉTÉ GÉNÉRALE). Established by the National Convention on October 2, 1792. It controlled the police and prisons, and was responsible for arrests.

COMMITTEE OF PUBLIC SAFETY (COMITÉ DE SALUT PUBLIC). Emergency executive body formed on April 6, 1793 by a decree of the National Convention *(q.v.).* It had 9 and later 12 members which included Danton, Robespierre, Carnot, Saint-Just *(qq.v.).* It was largely responsible for the Terror *(q.v.)* but also organized the revolutionary armies *(q.v.).* It was abolished in 1795 on the establishment of the Directory *(q.v.).*

COMMITTEES (COMITÉS). In 1790 and 1791 the work of the Constituent Assembly *(q.v.)* was under-

taken by various committees, clearly defined by their respective titles. The first, established in 1789, was for surveying the deputies to the Estates-General *(q.v.);* the second was charged with the drawing-up of the Declaration of the Rights of Man and of the Citizen *(q.v.);* the third, the most important (along with finances), was charged with drawing up the constitution. Between 1791 and 1792 the Legislative Assembly had six committees, but later this number rose to twenty-three.

In September 1794 the Convention reorganized the system into sixteen committees: Public Safety (twelve members); General Security (twelve members); Finances (forty-eight members); Legislation (sixteen members); Public Instruction (sixteen members); Agriculture and the Arts (sixteen members); Commerce and Provisions (twelve members); Public Works (twelve members); Mines and Quarries (twelve members); Transport, Post and Messengers (twelve members); Military Committee (sixteen members); Marine and the Colonies (twelve members); Public Relief (twelve members); Division (twelve members); Decrees and Archives (sixteen members); Petitions, Correspondence and Despatches (twelve members); Inspectors of the National Palace (sixteen members). A quarter of the committees were replaced each month but those leaving were eligible to sit again.

COMMUNE DE PARIS (COMMUNE OF PARIS). Administration of the city of Paris from 1789 to 9 Thermidor. On August 10, 1792 an insurrectionalist council, with Pétion de Villeneuve *(q.v.)* as mayor and Louis-Pierre Manuel as procurer general syndic, was formed. This council forced the Legislative Assembly *(q.v.)* to take the decision that the royal family should be transferred to the Temple. When the Convention took over from the Legislative Assembly, the commune declared itself for the Mountain *(q.v.)*, and struggled with the Girondins *(q.v.)* and the ministers. The commune reclaimed the establishment of the revolutionary tribunal and were involved in the accusations against Dumouriez *(q.v.)*; the arrests of the Girondins; encouraged and applauded the Terror *(q.v.)* and its excesses; moved against Catholicism with the Cult of Reason. Robespierre *(q.v.)* turned on the commune leaders savagely, when it appeared that his power was being weakened and his influence lessened. With the fall of Robespierre 73 commune members were executed. The influence of the commune was terminated, and with the division of Paris into 12 arrondissements *(q.v.)* in 1795, the municipality was no longer involved in administrative affairs.

COMMUNES, CHAMBRE DES. Name which was taken by the chamber of deputies to the Third Estate *(q.v.)*, when they arrived at the Estates-General at Versailles in 1789. The communes claimed the right to sit with the two other orders, the nobility and the clergy.

COMPAGNIE DE JÉSUS OU DU SOLEIL. Secret association formed after the fall of Robespierre *(q.v.)* by the royalists. Under the pretext of gaining revenge for the victims of the Terror *(q.v.)*, they promoted assassinations in Lyon, Marseille, the Jura and throughout the entire Midi. The gilded youth (jeunesse dorée) were responsible for these assassinations.

Their violence plunged areas of France into turmoil. The company's members considered it to be a sign of strength to carry the symbol of a splash of blood on their hands. They flourished for a period of six years, and were not finally wiped out until under the Consulate *(q.v.)*.

COMPTE RENDU AU ROI. Report to the king by the controller-general of finance, especially the report of 1791 by Jacques Necker *(q.v.)*. Necker's principal undertaking was to finance participation in the American War of Independence *(q.v.)* through additional taxation. In trying to raise the necessary loans, the *Compte rendu au Roi* was published in 1781; its figures were a complete fabrication. This account claimed a surplus of ten million livres when there was, in fact, a deficit of 46 million. There was opposition from Comte J.-F. Phélypeux de Maurepas, the Prime Minister, and the queen, and as a result Necker was forced to resign on May 19, 1781.

CONCIERGERIE, LA. Paris prison which forms part of the Palais de Justice. Inmates included Hébert, Brinvilliers, Damiens, Marie-Antoinette, Corday, Danton and Robespierre *(qq.v.)*.

CONCORDAT OF 1801. Concluded between Napoleon and Pope Pius VII, it was promulgated on Christmas Day 1802. This reestablished the Catholic religion in France as the form of worship recognized and endowed by the state. In principle, it was drawn up on the lines of the Concordat of 1516, assuring to the head of the French state in his dealings with the papacy the same prerogatives as had formerly been enjoyed by the king. The chief of these was that he appointed the bishops, who afterwards had to ask the pope for canonical institution.

The territorial distribution of dioceses was preserved practically as it had been left by the Civil Constitution of the Clergy (q.v.). The state guaranteed the payment of salaries to bishops and curés, and the pope agreed to renounce all claims referring to the appropriation of the goods of the clergy made by the Constituent Assembly (q.v.).

Later a decree restored to the *fabriques* (or vestries), such of the former possessions as had not been alienated, and the churches that had not been alienated were restored for the purposes of worship. The law of 18 Germinal, Year X, ratified the Concordat, and reasserted, under the names of "articles organiques du culte catholique," all the main principles centered in the old doctrine of the liberties of the Gallican church. Religious orders and organizations were not restored.

CONDÉ. The name of Condé, from the town of Condé-sur-l'Escaut, was borne by a branch of the House of Bourbon. Its first member was the Huguenot leader Louis de Bourbon, the fifth son of Charles de Bourbon, duc de Vendôme. Louis Joseph, prince de Condé (1736-1818), son of Louis Henry, duc de Bourbon, was governor of Burgundy. At the Revolution he became commander of the Royalist army of Condé, and fought with the Austrians until the Treaty of Campo-Formio (1797, q.v.). He then served the emperor of Russia in Poland, and in 1800 went over to the English and fought in Bavaria. On the restoration of Louis XVIII, Condé returned to France, having lived in England for seven years. Louis Henry Joseph, duc de Bourbon (1756-1830), son of the above, was the last prince of Condé. At the Revolution he fought with the émigré army at Liège. Between the return of Bonaparte from Elba and Waterloo, he fought and headed an unsuccessful rising in the Vendée.

CONDORCET, MARIE-JEAN-AN-TOINE-NICOLAS CARITAT, MARQUIS DE (1743-94). Mathematician, philosopher and politician. He was a member of the Convention (q.v.) and secretary of the Académie des Sciences (q.v.), a member of the Académie française (q.v.). A friend of d'Alembert, Turgot and Voltaire (qq.v.), he was anti-monarchist and anti-clerical. He incurred the opposition of Robespierre (q.v.) and during the Terror (q.v.) he took poison to avoid the guillotine.

CONGÉABLE. Legal term, "held under tenancy at will."

CONSCRIPTION. Military conscription was proposed at the Constituent Assembly (q.v.) on September 12, 1789 but was not carried. On September 5, 1798 the Council of Ancients adopted the principle for males aged 20 to 25 years, from whom recruits were selected.

CONSEIL D'ÉTAT DU ROI. Senior of the five councils (q.v.). It concerned itself with external relations and policy, and its decisions were executed by the other councils. It met, under the ancien régime, twice a week.

CONSEIL DES DÉPÊCHES. Council which dealt mainly with internal affairs, composed of the king, the keeper of the seals and two councillors of state.

CONSEIL ROYAL DES FINANCES. One of the five councils of the king, created in 1661 and concerned with duties and taxation, loans, and the state of funds.

CONSERVATOIRE. The singing school at Paris, founded in 1784 and closed at the beginning of the Revolution in 1789. It reopened in 1793 as the Institut National de Musique. After being reorganized it became the Conservatoire de Musique in 1795.

CONSPIRATION DES PRISONS. Event occurring after the trial and convictions of Danton and Camille Desmoulins (qq.v.), who were kept in the Luxembourg prison. Desmoulin's wife, Lucile, attempted to gain entry into the prison to get in touch with the accused. The attempt failed. Lucile was executed on April 13, 1794 after the Dantonists, along with Jacques René Hébert's wife, Chaumette, Gobel, the bishop of Paris, General Beysser, the gatekeepers of the prison, and 19 others. A plot did not exist, and most of the accused were totally innocent of any crime.

CONSPIRACY OF THE EQUALS. See **Babeuf Plot.**

CONSTITUENT ASSEMBLY. See **Assembly, National.**

CONSULATE. Government of France between November 1799 and 1804, established when Bonaparte overthrew the Directory (q.v.). It had three legislative chambers with an executive headed by three consuls. In fact Bonaparte dominated the Consulate throughout its existence. It lasted until he established the Empire and declared himself emperor in 1804.

CONTRIBUTIONS PUBLIQUES. In the early days of the Revolution the name was gradually substituted for that of "impôt" (tax, duty), and entered the language of politics and finance. The Constituent Assembly (q.v.) decreed that taxes should be paid by all citizens proportionate to their property and resources, and that the impôt was to be voted annually.

CONTROLEUR GÉNÉRAL DES FINANCES. Under the ancien régime the controleur général was a great officer of state, charged with controlling and registering all the acts which related to finances, assigning the payment of all the ordinances, and directing the collecting and application of the state revenues. He was the right (droit) member of the Conseil des finances et du commerce, the only person who could grasp the nature of all the affairs considered. He depended upon the surintendant des finances for his briefings but, after the disgrace of Fouquet, the controleur général filled the position of the surintendant. In the single year of 1787, Bouvard de Fourqueux, Lomenie de Brienne, de Villedeuil, Lambert and Necker (qq.v.), succeeded each other as *controleur général*. During the Revolution this post became the *ministère des finances*.

CONVENTION, NATIONAL. The National Convention succeeded the Legislative Assembly *(q.v.)* on September 21, 1792, and proclaimed the Republic on September 22. It governed France until October 1795 and was the most long-lasting of the three revolutionary assemblies. It was succeeded by the Directory *(q.v.)*.

COQ GAULOIS, LE. The cock, as a symbol and as a national emblem, appeared on flags during the Revolution. Its origin is uncertain, but it had the characteristics of a fighting bird; it symbolized the protector of territories and was aggressive and fought until death.

CORDAY D'ARMONT, MARIE CHARLOTTE (CORDAY, CHARLOTTE) (1768-93). Politician and assassin. Corday welcomed the Revolution but she was horrified by the actions of the Jacobins *(q.v.)*. This intensified after discussions with Girondists *(q.v.)* who had fled to Caen. She decided to assassinate one of the leaders of the Jacobins and went with that aim to Paris. On the evening of July 13, 1793 she gained an audience with Jean Paul Marat *(q.v.)* who was in his bath, and she stabbed him in the heart. She came before the revolutionary tribunal, but showed no repentance. In the Conciergerie *(q.v.)* she was painted by Hauer, and on July 17 she was guillotined.
Corday, M., *Charlotte Corday*, 1931.

CORDELIERS' CLUB. French revolutionary club of the left founded in 1790 by Danton, Marat, and Camille Desmoulins *(qq.v.)*, which met in the old convent of the friars of the order of St. Francis of Assisi, instituted about 1223. They are clothed in coarse grey cloth, having a girdle of cord. Hence the name, first given to them by St. Louis of France, about 1227. The club was also called the "Society of the Friends of the Rights of Man and of the Citizen" and nicknamed the "Pandemonium." Its members were the first to demand the abolition of the monarchy, but the club declined after the execution of its leaders in 1794.

CORPORAL, THE LITTLE. Name given to Bonaparte by his troops.

CORPS LEGISLATIF, LE. Term used briefly by the revolutionary assembly but generally applied to the lower house of the legislature. However, by the Constitution of Year VIII the Corps Legislatif was the Assembly of Deputies, instituted to exercise legislative power with the Tribunal. It replaced the Council of Five Hundred *(q.v.)* and its powers were considerably reduced. It could no longer propose laws as this task lay solely within the province of the executive. It was composed of 300 members (all over thirty years of age) and voted secretly, without public discussion, having heard the speakers representing the Tribunal and the government. Each decree of the Corps was promulgated six days after the vote, the issue having been judged constitutional by the Senate. Meetings of the Corps were public but only 200 people were allowed access. The Corps sat for four months out of every twelve. Each department was represented by at least one deputy. The Corps disappeared with the Restoration.

CORRESPONDING SOCIETY OF LONDON. Society formed in 1792 to counter the severity of the British government's response to the Revolution. Several members of the society were tried for treason and acquitted October 1794. The society's meetings at Copenhagen Fields and elsewhere, in 1795 and 1796, were declared treasonable. In April 1798 some members were tried for corresponding with the Directory (*q.v.*).

CORSICAN, THE. Name given to Bonaparte, born in Corsica, which became a French possession in 1768.

CORVÉE. Peasant's obligation, introduced in the 1730's, to do unpaid labor on the roads. The government alleged that the work occurred at the time of the year when agricultural labor was not in great demand and it was preferable to raising a tax. The obligations were reduced in 1787 and in 1790, and totally abolished by the Convention on July 17, 1792.

COUNCIL OF FIVE HUNDRED. Established by the constitution of August 22, 1795. In April 1795 a constitutional committee came to the conclusion that the constitution of 1793 was impracticable, and proceeded to frame a new one. The draft was submitted to the Convention in June. The constitution established a parliamentary system of two houses:

a Council of Five Hundred, and a Council of Ancients (250 in number). Members of the Five Hundred were to be at least thirty years of age, while the Ancients had to be at least forty. The system of indirect election was maintained but universal suffrage was abandoned. A moderate qualification was required for electors in the First Degree, a higher one for electors in the Second Degree. When the 750 people necessary had been elected, they were to choose the Ancients out of their own body. A legislature was to last for three years, and one-third of the members were to be renewed every year. The Ancients had a suspensory veto, but no initiative in legislation. The executive was to consist of five directors, chosen by the Ancients and drawn out of a list elected by the Five Hundred. One director was to retire every year. The Council of Five Hundred was unceremoniously dissolved by Bonaparte on November 10, 1799.

COUNCILS. The Council of Ancients, consisting of 250 members, together with the Council of Five Hundred, were established on November 1, 1795. The executive was a Directory (*q.v.*) of five. However, on November 9, 1799 Bonaparte dispersed the Council of Five Hundred, declaring himself, Roger Ducos and Sieyès (*q.v.*), provisional consuls.

COUPERIN, GERVAIS-FRANÇOIS (1759-1826). Composer, son of Armand-Louis Couperin (1725-89). He was organist of St. Gervais in 1789. The Revolution disrupted his work but he managed to save the organ from being destroyed and took up his post in 1795. His compositions include variations on the revolutionary song, "Ah, ça ira" (1790). (*See* **Ça ira.**)

COUR DES AIDES. Under the ancien régime a court of appeal in tax cases, particularly the collection of *aides (q.v.)*. Its abolition was called for by the various communes and it was abolished by the laws of September 7 and 11, 1790.

COUTHON, GEORGES (1755-94). Lawyer and revolutionary. He was a member of the Legislative Assembly, the Convention and eventually president of the Committee of Public Safety *(qq.v.)*. At Lyons he crushed the rebellion with fanatical severity. He was guillotined with Robespierre *(q.v.)* and Saint-Just. They were known as "Le Triumvirat de la Terreur."

CROAKERS (TOADS) **OF THE MARSHLAND** (LES CRAPAUDS DE LA MARAIS). Name given to moderates in the National Convention (1792-95, *q.v.*).

CURÉ. Parish priest.

CUSTINE, ADAM PHILIPPE, COMTE DE (1740-93). General. He served in the Seven Years' War, and against England during the American War of Independence *(q.v.)*. In 1789 he was elected to the Estates-General but he rejoined the army as a lieutenant-general in 1791 and was known to his soldiers as "General Moustache." He became general-in-chief of the Army of the Vosges. From September to October 1792, Custine took Spires, Worms, Mainz and Frankfurt. During the winter, a Prussian army forced him to evacuate Frankfurt, recross the Rhine and fall back on Landau. Accused of treason, he was defended by Robespierre *(q.v.)*. He was sent back to the Army of the North, but did not take the offensive against the Austrians, who were besieging Condé *(q.v.)*. In Paris, Custine was found guilty of having conspired with the enemies of the Republic by the revolutionary tribunal, and was guillotined.

CUSTOMS SYSTEM, UNIFICATION OF. Under the ancien régime, the customs system was divided into three parts but in 1790 the Constituent Assembly *(q.v.)* unified the tariff throughout the country, and a central administration was organized in 1791.

DANDY KING, THE. Nickname of Joachim Murat (1767-1815, *q.v.*), from his fondness for personal adornment.

DANTON, GEORGES JACQUES (1759-94). Politician, orator and lawyer. One of the great figures of the Revolution, Mirabeau (*q.v.*) was one of the first to recognize his genius. With Marat and Camille Desmoulins (*qq.v.*), Danton had instituted the Cordeliers' Club (*q.v.*) and he became its leader. Danton first appeared in a revolutionary capacity as president of the popular club, or assembly, in his district—the Club of the Cordeliers, so called because its meetings were held in the old convent of the Cordeliers. From the first, the Cordeliers were the "popular" part of the Revolution, carried to its extreme. They were the earliest to suspect the court of being totally hostile to both elementary reforms and freedoms, and those who most strongly urged root-and-branch measures. At the beginning of 1791, Danton was elected as the administrator of the Paris department, but it was not until 1792 that he came into prominence as a great revolutionary chief. He was a member of the Legislative Assembly (*q.v.*) and was a leader of those who stormed the Tuileries (*q.v.*) in 1792. He voted for the death of the king in 1793 and was an original member of the Committee of Public Safety (*q.v.*). In the Convention (*q.v.*) his aim was to topple the Girondins (*q.v.*), which he achieved in 1793.

Danton joined the Mountain (*q.v.*), sitting with Marat (whose extreme views he never accepted), and with Robespierre (*[q.v.]* whom he did not esteem, but whose moderate aims, in many respects, were his own). Camille Desmoulins and Phélippeaux were Danton's chief supporters and friends.

Attacked by the Girondins for his part in the September Massacres (*q.v.*), Danton considered that, while these murders were unfortunate, they were all part and parcel of building a total, cohesive control of Paris and its environs. The Germans were poised on the northeast frontier, and the reactionaries were stirring in the interior of the country. "Paris is the natural and constitutional center of free France. When Paris shall perish, there will no longer be a republic," he said.

The fierce upheavals between the Girondins and Jacobins at a time of active and acute national crisis may have encouraged Danton to instigate the insurrections of May 31 and June 2, which ended in the purge of the Convention and the proscription of the Girondins. While Danton accepted that popular violence was an inevitable part of the process leading toward international unity and a concentration of national effort, unlike the Girondins, he was most unwilling to countenance the repeated use of violence and terror.

In June 1793 the Mountain had complete control in the Convention, but the actual power was in the hands of the Committees of Public Safety and General Security (q.v.). Danton was not a member of the revived Committee of Public Safety and abstained from joining that group, which he had done his utmost to make supreme in the state.

Danton attempted to control the extremists in both Paris and the provinces, such as Carrier, Collot d'Herbois, Hébert and Chaumette (qq.v). Anticipating the rise of the Hébertists, the authorities struck first, executing the majority membership in March 1794; this was the first victory of the revolutionary government over the extreme insurrectionary party.

Now regarded as being excessively moderate by the membership of the committees, Danton's enemies moved to have him struck off. Robespierre defended Danton twice, but after Billaud-Varenne ([q.v.] the most prominent Committee member after Robespierre) persuaded the latter to join him against Danton, the Convention and the Committee assented. Danton, Desmoulins and others of the party were arrested on March 30. Fearing Danton's oratorical abilities to enlist popular support before the Revolutionary Tribunal (q.v.), the Committee agreed to Saint-Just's (q.v.) proposal that sentence should be passed immediately, as Danton had shown no respect for justice. His trial was a farce and he was guillo-tined on April 5, 1794. Three months later Robespierre was himself executed.

Hampson, Norman, Danton, 1978.

DAUNOU, PIERRE CLAUDE FRANÇOIS (1761-1840). Priest and historian, he was a member of the Convention (q.v.). He was against the execution of Louis XVI but was arrested when the Girondists fell. Imprisoned in 1793-94 he returned to public life and served in the Directory (q.v.). He was responsible for organizing important legislative innovations.

DAUPHIN. Title borne by the eldest son of the king of France from 1349 to the revolution of 1830.

DAVID, JACQUES LOUIS (1748-1825). Painter. David was an enthusiastic revolutionary and in 1792 became a representative for Paris in the Convention (q.v.). He voted for the death of Louis XVI and was a member of the Committee of Public Safety (q.v.). He was twice imprisoned, and narrowly escaped execution. Released from prison in 1795 he produced The Rape of the Sabines in 1799.

The France of David's early years was going through a political and artistic revolution. The earlier rococo style was fading, to be replaced by a return to the more classical tendencies of French art, particularly those portrayed by Poussin in the 17th century; also, the beauty and correctness of antique Greek and Roman art were coming into fashion.

David's progress toward the style that was to make him the most influential French painter of his time commenced with his *Antiochus and Stratonice* (1774); this work gained him the Prix de Rome, enabling him to spend four years in Italy, at the French government's expense. His five years in Rome (1775-80) were spent in studying ancient monuments and sculptures, as well as works of the Renaissance and the baroque, and convinced him of the need to adopt a more vigorously classical style.

Returning to France, David drew together all of the elements associated with Neoclassicism in his *Oath of the Horatii* (1785), which was called by one contemporary critic "the most beautiful painting of the century." Echoing, perfectly, the "noble simplicity and calm grandeur," this work has often been cited as heralding the Revolution. Throughout this period David's work shows his involvement in every activity, whether organizing festivals celebrating revolutionary events, or composing a drawing such as the *Oath of the Tennis Court* (1791), a work that shows a large number of clearly-identifiable figures involved in an important contemporary event. His *Death of Marat* (1793) shows much more than a man known and admired by David: it is an icon, glorifying the revolutionary who had been assassinated for his beliefs.

David specified Bonaparte as "his hero," and the latter used David's fame and skill to spread his image throughout Europe. The first Napoleonic commission, *Bonaparte Crossing the Saint Bernard Pass* (1800), was succeeded by a number of works on which, as "Premier Peintre" to the emperor, David concentrated on the contemporary reality, but his first love was classical painting, revolutionary in character. In 1804 he was appointed court painter by Napoleon. After the Bourbon restoration he lived in Switzerland and died in Brussels in 1825.

Dowd, David Lloyd, *Pageant-Master of the Republic: J. L. David and the French Revolution,* 1948.

DAY OF THE SECTIONS. Rising of the Parisian Royalists on October 5, 1795 (14 Vendemiaire) which was crushed by government troops under the command of Bonaparte. It was initiated by constitutional Royalists who, having approved the passage of the 1795 constitution, were convinced that their case would benefit from the free election of new representatives; the Convention *(q.v.)* wished to avoid this possibility. On August 22, 1795 the Convention passed the principle that no less than two-thirds of the first legislative body should be elected from its own ranks. The Convention itself provided that legislative body to be renewed annually by one-third. By this decree it meant that three years would pass before a completely new parliament would come into being.

Both armies faced each other from morning to afternoon of October 5. There was sporadic fighting, but with Bonaparte's "whiff of grapeshot," the leaders of the insurrection scattered during the night. There were about 300 killed and wounded on either side.

For the first time since the Revolution a rising in Paris had been broken by military force. Bonaparte was considered the genius behind the victory. The result was that the sovereignty of sections and the Royalist cause were ruined. Paris was firmly under military control. The National Guard *(q.v.)* was disarmed and incorporated into the Army of the Interior.

DÉCADE. One "decade" was ten days and there were three *décades* in a month. *See* **Calendar, Revolutionary.**

DÉCLARATION DES DROITS DE L'HOMME ET DU CITOYEN, LA. Guiding principles of the Revolution, modeled on the American Declaration of Independence. *See* **Rights of Man, Declaration of the.**

DEFENSEUR DE LA CONSTITUTION, LE. Newsletter founded by Robespierre *(q.v.)* in 1792 to expound and defend his theories of the Revolution. It ran until 1793.

DEFICIT, MADAME. Name given to Marie Antoinette, who had taken an active part in the registering of the edicts on the territorial subsidy and the stamp duty in 1787.

DÉPARTEMENT (DEPARTMENT). A decree of February 1790 by the Constituent Assembly *(q.v.)*, divided France into 83 *départements* for administrative purposes. Work started in November 1789 with the aim of preserving unity and the removal of provincial rivalries.

DEPORTATION. Law which exiled a condemned person from France, almost unknown before the Revolution. The first law was that of June 1791. The deported person could not exercise any civil right himself. Criminal tribunals were allowed to pronounce a sentence of temporary punishment or a life of punishment through deportation. Deportation covered refractory priests and, gradually, men seen as dangerous because of their political opinions. Later it was extended for sedition. Some members of the Convention *(q.v.)* were sent to French Guiana *(q.v.)*. The law applied equally to those who had broken the agrarian law. After 18 Fructidor, two members of the Directory (Carnot *(q.v.)* and Barthélemy), deputies of the two councils, Royalists, generals and journalists, were sent to Guiana. The major settlements abroad were Madagascar, Sinnamari and Cayenne.

DESAIX DE VEYGOUX, LOUIS CHARLES ANTOINE (1768-1800). General. He refused to emigrate during the early years of the Revolution. In 1794 he was a general of division, and he held important commands in 1795. He commanded Jourdan's *(q.v.)* right wing and assisted Moreau *(q.v.)* in the invasion of Bavaria. He was provisionally appointed as commander of the "Army of England" by Bonaparte. Veygoux went to Egypt and it was his division which bore the brunt of the attack at the Battle of the Pyramids *(q.v.)*. He enhanced his reputation by defeating Murad Bey in Upper Egypt. Veygoux was one of the small party who accompanied Bonaparte when he turned over his command to Kléber *(q.v.)* to return to France. He assisted in Italy and was killed at Marengo (June 1800, *q.v.*).

DESORGUES, JOSEPH-THÉODORE (1763-1808). Composer of revolutionary songs, best known for "Hymne à l'Être Suprême."

DESMOULINS, CAMILLE (1760-94). Revolutionary and journalist. Following the fall of the Bastille *(q.v.)*, in which his oratory had been a contributory factor, he began the witty *Revolutions de France et de Brabant,* which appeared weekly until July 1792. Desmoulins was a founder-member of the Cordeliers' Club *(q.v.)* and was elected by Paris to the National Convention *(q.v.).* He voted for the death of the king. In the struggle between the Girondists and the Mountain *(qq.v.)* he took an active part. In December 1793 he published the *Vieux Cordelier,* which expressed his, and Danton's, view that the Terror *(q.v.)* should be moderated. On March 30, 1794 Desmoulins was arrested with Danton *(q.v.)* and on April 5 he was guillotined.

DESTUTT, (TRACY), ANTOINE LOUIS CLAUDE, COMTE DE (1754-1836). Philosopher. He was elected as a delegate of the nobility to the Estates-General. In the spring of 1792 he was a *maréchal de camp,* but retired because of the increasing influence of the extremists. He settled at Auteuil where, with Condorcet and Cabanis *(qq.v.),* he devoted himself to scientific study. He was imprisoned for a year during the Terror *(q.v.),* during which time he studied Condillac, Locke and others, abandoning the natural sciences for philosophy.

DEVIENNE, FRANÇOIS (1759-1803). Composer, flautist and bassoonist. A member of the band of the Garde Nationale *(q.v.)* he was important in revolutionary music. He became teacher of the flute at the Institut National de Musique, which was known as the Conservatoire in 1795.

DIAMOND NECKLACE AFFAIR. A diamond necklace was offered to Queen Marie Antoinette by Boehmer, the court jeweler, in 1785 but she did not take up the offer. Comtesse de la Motte forged the queen's signature, persuaded Cardinal de Rohan, the queen's almoner, to undertake the negotiations with the jeweler, and thus de la Motte obtained the necklace. She was tried in 1786 and sentenced to be branded on the shoulders and imprisoned for life. She escaped to London, where she died by falling from a window-sill, in an attempt to escape arrest for debt. De Rohan was tried and acquitted on May 31, 1786 but was stripped of all offices and exiled. The general public suspected the queen of being a party to the fraud and the affair did much to discredit the monarchy on the eve of the Revolution.

DICTATORS. During the Revolution, Marat and Robespierre *(qq.v.)* were accused of aspiring to become dictators and the Thermidorian Revolution *(q.v.)* turned out to be a dictatorship. Bonaparte's actions in 1799, against the rights and privileges of the Council of Five Hundred *(q.v.),* created an enormous reaction with cries of "À bas le Cromwell! À bas le dictateur!".

DIDEROT, DENIS (1713-84). Encyclopedist; member of a group known as the *philosophes* who brought about the Enlightenment *(q.v.).* His *Encyclopédie* was an important factor in bringing about this new thinking. He was coeditor with the mathematician d'Alembert *(q.v.).* Work on the *Encyclopédie* covered the years 1751-72 and was originally based on Chambers's *Cyclopaedia.* Diderot wrote many articles on philosophical and mechanical subjects but he gathered a galaxy of scholars, including Buffon (*q.v.*), Montesquieu, Rousseau, Turgot and Voltaire (*qq.v.*), to contribute additional ones. When the *Encyclopédie* was complete he was short of money. Catherine the Great of Russia (*q.v.*) purchased his library and made him its librarian with a lifetime salary.

Crocker, Lester G., *Diderot, the Embattled Philosopher*, 1966.

Wilson, A. M., *Diderot: The Testing Years, 1713-1759*, 1957.

DIRECTOIRE. *See* **Directory.**

DIRECTORY, THE. The Constitution of August 22, 1795 that followed the fall of Robespierre vested the executive authority in five directors. The "Five Majesties" were Barras (*q.v.*), Reubell, Sieyès (*q.v.*), Letourneur, and La Revellière. Sieyès retired at the outset and was replaced by Carnot (*q.v.*). The directors were assisted by a Council of Five Hundred (*q.v.*) and a council of 250 known as the Council of Ancients. (*See* **Councils.**) Its rule was ended with Bonaparte's coup d'état of November 9, 1799 when the Consulate (*q.v.*) was established.

Lefebvre, Georges, *The Directory*, 1965.
Lyons, Martin, *France under the Directory*, 1975.

DISTRICTS OF PARIS. Paris was divided into 60 districts for the election of the deputies to the Estates-General. After the fall of the Bastille (*q.v.*) the electors of Paris continued to meet and declared themselves to be permanently established. Each of the districts had its own battalion of the National Guard, its own flag and artillery. The Cordeliers and the Petits-Augustins' districts were the most celebrated. The law of May 21, 1790 replaced these 60 districts with 48 sections.

DISTRICTS OF DEPARTMENTS. Subdivisions of the departments, which existed from 1790 to 1800. The 544 districts which the Constituent Assembly (*q.v.*) established were themselves divided into cantons, and the cantons into communes. They were administered by their district council and their directory, which was composed of four members named by the General Council.

DIXIÈME, DÎME. Tithe, or tenth part of the harvest, which the church demanded from farmers and peasants. No payment was made for this. On August 8, 1789 the Constituent Assembly (*q.v.*) decided that the *dîme* should be suppressed, without repurchase. The clergy agreed after several days of discussion and argument. The liquidation of the *dîmes* took three years.

DON GRATUIT. "Free gift"—a subsidy that the clergy, and also the pays d'état (*q.v.*), paid annually to the king, taken in lieu of taxes. It was voted by the representatives of the Three Orders. That of the clergy was reasonably raised, but it was never in anything like true proportion to the enormous incomes that the church itself raised. The *don gratuit* pressed most heavily on the parish priests, while the bishops and archbishops gained a relative advantage from this donation. It disappeared along with the *taille* (*q.v.*) and the other taxes of the ancien régime.

DROWNINGS (NOYADES DE NANTES). Drownings of Royalists in the Loire at Nantes, by order of Jean Baptiste Carrier (1756-94), lawyer and member of the Convention (*q.v.*). He was an influential member of the Cordeliers and Jacobins Clubs. In March 1793 Carrier helped to establish the revolutionary tribunal. In July 1793 he was sent on a mission to Normandy and later, in August, he was sent to Brittany and ordered to secure Nantes against the insurgents of the Vendée. (*See* **Vendéan Rebellion**.) He arrived in Nantes on October 7, established a tribunal and formed gangs of thugs (the Compagnie Marat) to ruthlessly and quickly kill prisoners and suspects held in the jails. Trials were abandoned and the victims were sent to the guillotine or shot en masse.

A large number of prisoners, mainly priests, were put on barges fitted with trap doors and sunk in the Loire.

Carrier was recalled by the Committee of Public Safety (*q.v.*) on February 8, 1794. His superiors were appalled by the ruthless and indiscriminate manner in which he had acted to put down the rebellion. He took part in the Thermidorean attack on Robespierre (*q.v.*) but was himself brought before the revolutionary tribunal and guillotined on December 16, 1794. (See also **Thermidor Revolution**.)

DUCOS, PIERRE ROGER (1754-1816). Born at Dax, he was an advocate when elected deputy to the Convention (*q.v.*) by the department of Landes. He voted for the death of the king, without appeal or delay, but played no significant role in the Convention. A member of the Council of Five Hundred (*q.v.*), he presided over it on 18 Fructidor, Year V. At the end of his term he became a justice of the peace, but after the parliamentary coup d'état of 30 Prairial, Year VIII, was named a member of the Executive Directory by Barras (*q.v.*).

Ducos was accepted by the coup d'état of Bonaparte, on 18 Brumaire, and was one of the three provincial consuls. He became vice-president of the Senate. In 1814 he abandoned Napoleon, and voted for his deposition. Seeking to gain favor of the restoration government, he was exiled in 1816 by virtue of the law against regicides. It was said that in spite of his absolute lack of talent he attained the highest of positions, an exceptional fact in the history of the French Revolution.

DUMAS, GUILLAUME MATHIEU, COMTE DE (1753-1837). General; with Lafayette (*q.v.*) he commanded the escort that conducted Louis XVI from Paris to Varennes. In 1792 Dumas was president of the Assembly. He left and returned to France several times, and was proscribed as a Royalist/monarchist.

DUMOURIEZ, CHARLES FRANÇOIS (1739-1823). General during the Seven Years' War. Commander-in-chief of the revolutionary armies, he defeated the Prussians at Valmy and the Austrians at Jemappes. At Neerwinden on March 18, 1793 he sustained a severe defeat from the Austrians. He was a constitutional monarchist at heart and eventually he was denounced as a traitor and summoned to Paris. To save himself he went over to the Austrians. He finally settled in England.

DUNKIRK. Port on the Channel, chief town of the department of the same name. Jean Bart, the pirate or corsair, attacked English shipping from here during the 17th century and the same activity occurred during the periods covering the American Revolutionary War and the French Revolution.

Dunkirk was under siege by the British army, commanded by Frederick Augustus, Duke of York and Albany (1763-1827), in 1793. Carnot (*q.v.*) placed all his best troops in a concentrated manner and attacked the British army before Dunkirk. Severe fighting on September 6 and 8, 1793 occurred at Hondschoten. The British had to fall back, and rejoined the Austrian army at Tournay.

DUPONT DE NEMOURS, PIERRE SAMUEL (1739-1817). Politician, economist and statesman. He belonged to the physiocrats (*q.v.*) and popularized their doctrines through his writings. A friend of Turgot (*q.v.*), he supported him during his brief holding of power. Dupont de Nemours was a deputy to the Estates-General in 1789 and, after having been proscribed for a period, a member of the Council of Ancients. (*See* **Councils**.) As a constitutional monarchist, he was hostile towards the Directory (*q.v.*). In 1799 he voluntarily emigrated to the United States. Jefferson (*q.v.*) thought highly of him. In 1802 Dupont de Nemours conveyed, unofficially, to Bonaparte a threat against the French occupation of Louisiana (*q.v.*). Earlier, Jefferson had asked him to prepare a scheme of national education, which was published in 1800. Dupont de Nemours retired to France in 1802, leaving again for Delaware after the return of the emperor in 1815.

DUPORT, ADRIEN (1759-98). Politician. He was an influential advocate in the Parlement, against Calonne and Lomènie de Brienne (*q.v.*). In 1789 he was the member for Paris in the Estates-General representing the nobility. Duport was remarkably eloquent, a learned jurist who contributed in the Constituent Assembly (*q.v.*) during the organization of the judiciary. With Barnave and Alexandre de Lameth, Duport formed a group known as the Triumvirate. He became unpopular after. As a member of the commission charged to question the king, he distanced himself from any extreme position. Thus, he left the Jacobins (*q.v.*) and joined the Feuillants (*q.v.*). After the Constituent Assembly, he became president of the Paris criminal tribunal. He was arrested during the August 10, 1792 insurrection and fled (thanks to Danton's help). He returned after the 9 Thermidor, Year II coup, and was in exile again after the coup of 18 Fructidor, Year V. (*See* **Thermidor Revolution** and **Directory**.)

DUPUIS, CHARLES FRANÇOIS (1742-1809). Scientific writer, mathematician and politician. Member of the Convention (*q.v.*) sitting for the department of Seine-et-Oise, he was considered a moderate. He became secretary to the Assembly (*q.v.*) and eventually a member of the Council of Five Hundred (*q.v.*). After Bonaparte's coup d'état of 18 Brumaire (*q.v.*), he was elected by Seine-et-Oise as a member of the legislative body and became president, but he later resigned from politics.

DYING SAYINGS. Danton (*[q.v.]* to the executioner): "Be sure you show the mob my head. It will be a long time ere they see its like."

Louis XVI (on the scaffold): "Frenchmen, I die guiltless of the crimes imputed to me. Pray God my blood fall not on France!"

Marie Antoinette: "Farewell, my children, forever. I am going to your father!"

Murat (King of Naples, to the men detailed to shoot him): "Soldiers, save my face; aim at my heart. Farewell."

Madame Roland (last words before her execution): "O liberty, What crimes we committed in your name!"

EAST, ARMY OF THE. Army that went as an expeditionary force to Egypt with Bonaparte in May 1798. It continued under that title, gaining some considerable victories and a number of significant defeats until August 22, 1799 when Bonaparte returned to France.

EAUX ET FORÊTS, MAÎTRISE DES. Administration under the ancien régime responsible for enforcing laws and settling disputes concerning rivers, lakes and wooded lands.

ÉCHARPE TRICOLORE. Band of material with three longitudinal lines, red, white and blue, which, during the Revolution, was worn by magistrates and administrators, either as a sash or as a shoulder-belt. It was worn during public ceremonies and fêtes, and during the exercise of the wearer's duties.

ÉCHECS (CHESS). Chess was very popular in France under Louis XVI and during the Revolution. In 1793 Guyton de Morveau (*q.v.*) proposed that the principal figure on the chessboard, the king, should be changed, along with the others who symbolized the ancien régime. The intention was to republicanize the game and its terms. Chess became known as "le

jeu de la petite guerre." The king was replaced by the "standard bearer" the piece formerly the queen was known as the "adjutant," knights became "cavaliers," bishops became "light cavalry," castles became "cannon," and so forth. It was a military game, totally republican in spirit. The changes were not a great success. Under the Directory (*q.v.*) the Royalists continued to play chess in the old way, publicly.

ÉCHEVINS. Town councillors of the highest rank who were appointed by the king through the intendant (*q.v.*), or by the local lord. With the mayor, they formed the executive committee of the municipality, usually translated as "aldermen." In some southern cities, they were called consuls.

ÉCOLE AÉROSTATIQUE DE MEUDON. Founded by Guyton de Morveau in 1793 and authorized by the Committee of Public Safety (*q.v.*), on the condition that sulphuric acid was not used in the blowing up of balloons to be used in military (field) operations.

ÉCOLE DE DROIT (SCHOOL OF LAW). In 1789 the universities were closed but the École de Droit's function as a teaching institution continued. Two écoles de droit were established during the Revolution, the first adopting the title of Académie de Législation, the second, Université de Jurisprudence.

ÉCOLE DE MARS. Following a report of the Committee of Public Safety *(q.v.)* the Convention *(q.v.)* decreed on June 1, 1794 that each district was to send six young citizens *(élèves de Mars)* aged from six to seventeen-and-a-half to receive a revolutionary education. Half the children were selected from the sans-culottes *(q.v.)* in the country. The other half, to be chosen from like children in the towns. Children of revolutionary volunteers were to be given preference.

The School was located at the Plaine des Sablons in Paris, facing the Bois de Boulogne. It was a military school, the curriculum was influenced by revolutionary doctrines. The school was short-lived.

ÉCOLE DES GÉOGRAPHES. In October 1795 the Convention *(q.v.)* instituted a school made up of 20 pupils to be instructed in geographical and topographical operations, and in the appropriate calculations for map-design. The pupils were required to submit to an entrance examination, having first spent time at an *école polytechnique.* Having entered the geography school they were given a yearly stipend. Eventually a corps of fifty surveyors was developed. They were sent out for service in the army or in public administration, where they were known as *ingénieurs topographes.*

ÉCOLE MILITAIRE. Founded under Louis XV in 1750 to serve in the instruction of 500 gentlemen-orphans, the preference for selection of whom was that their fathers had died in service and that they possessed four generations of nobility. On September 9, 1793 a decree ordered the sale of all the property and goods of the Paris school and the colleges in the country, except for Auxerre, which was kept open. The Paris school then served as a grain depot and quarters for cavalry.

ÉCOLES NAVALE. Created by the Constituent Assembly *(q.v.)* in 1791, these naval colleges were established in maritime towns under the control of the municipalities and elected professors. The Directory *(q.v.)* gave them the name of *écoles de navigation,* forming two new establishments for the merchant marine, at Arles and at Morlaix.

ÉCOLE POLYTECHNIQUE. Military academy at Paris, established in 1794 by the Convention *(q.v.).* Initially a civilian day school, it was transformed by Bonaparte into a military college for boarders.

ÉCOLES DE SANTÉ (SCHOOLS OF HEALTH). In 1795 the Convention *(q.v.)* established three schools of health, in Paris, Montpellier and Strasbourg, and the old *écoles de chirurgie* (schools of surgery) in the three cities were closed and refounded within the new schools. Teaching professors were chosen by the Committee of Public Instruction.

ÉCOLES D'HYDROGRAPHIE ET DE MATHÉMATIQUES. The schools were established on April 19, 1791 by the Constituent Assembly (*q.v.*). To gain admission it was necessary to pass an examination designed to select young men aged 15 to 16 who were destined for the marine. On admittance they would serve for three years on warships under the title of *aspirant*. The *aspirants* were paid during their three years' study.

ÉCOLES SPÉCIALES. One of the last acts of the Convention (*q.v.*) was to create special, or specialized, schools within the Republic for specific studies: astronomy; geometry and mechanics; natural history; medicine; veterinary science; rural economy; antiquities; political science; painting, sculpture and architecture; music. It was also decreed that there should be schools for the deaf and dumb and the blind.

ÉCU (CROWN). Unit of money under the ancien régime. One écu equaled about three francs.

EDEN, WILLIAM, LORD AUCKLAND (1744-1814). Statesman and diplomat. He was lord of the Committee of Council on Trade and Plantations. Britain's major concern was for the benefit of English trade by a commercial treaty with France, a difficult, intricate affair. French thinkers, influenced by thoughts of free trade promulgated by the physiocrats (*q.v.*), were in favor of it but French statesmen were uncertain. Dupont de Nemours (*q.v.*), the French negotiator, quickly agreed to the terms of the treaty, but the French ministry made matters difficult. In September 1786 the treaty was signed, followed, in January 1787, by a commercial convention. In August 1787 an agreement settling the disputes of the French and the English East India companies was signed, followed by a treaty (November 1787) settling the French and the English differences regarding Holland. During the years 1791-93 Eden remained at The Hague as ambassador extraordinary.

EDICT OF VERSAILLES. At the beginning of Louis XVI's reign there were strong efforts by Turgot (*q.v.*) to grant civil rights to Protestants. Their marriages were not legal, their wills were without force and their children bastards. In 1785 work began on reforms.

On November 19, 1787 the edict was published "concerning those who do not belong to the Catholic religion." While the Catholic-Apostolic-Roman religion would continue to possess the exclusive right to public worship, "we . . . allow those of our subjects who profess a different religion . . . to enjoy all the possessions and rights that may now or in the future belong to them as property or inheritance, and to carry on their business, crafts, trades and professions without being disturbed or disquieted on account of their religion."

However, dissidents were still excluded from the judicature, from municipal appointments that were offices and to which were attached judicial functions, and from all posts which allowed them to teach publicly. They were incapable of "forming in our kingdom a corporation, community or special society and could not, therefore, deliberate together or formulate joint demands." Pastors were not to assume status officially, wear a special form of dress in public or issue any marriage certificates. Dissidents had to respect the Catholic religion and its ceremonies, abide by police regulations on Sundays and feast days, and contribute to the cost of repairing Catholic churches.

Protestants could contract marriages that had, in civil law, the same consequence as Catholic marriages, provided that they had the banns published by the *curés* or offices of justice and notices of them affixed to church doors. They could be married by the *curé* or the judge, provided that the banns had been published; they could assure the authority that parental consents had been given; and could provide four witnesses. They would then be declared united under the law. Marriages previously entered could be regularized within a year.

Births of non-Catholic children were recorded either by a certificate of baptism or a declaration made by the father and two witnesses, or four witnesses, before a judge.

Declarations of death were to be made to a *curé* or judge by the two closest relatives or neighbors of the deceased and registered. A cemetery was to be designated for non-Catholics, by town, city and village administrators. Bodies of the deceased were not to be shown outside the house, nor were funerals to be followed by singing or recited prayers.

Lutherans in Alsace and those subjects previously granted religious tolerance kept their privileges.

The French General Assembly of the Clergy saw the need for non-Catholics to be given civil status but they favored obligatory Catholic baptism.

ÉGALITÉ. Philippe, duc d'Orléans (1747-93) assumed this name when he renounced his title and voted for the death of Louis XVI. It is taken from the revolutionary motto "Liberty, *Equality*, and Fraternity." When his son, Louis Philippe (r. 1830-48, *q.v.*), defected to the Austrians with Dumouriez (*q.v.*), Philippe fell under suspicion, was arrested and later guillotined.
Schoder, E. S., *Prince of the Blood*, 1938.

EHRENBREITSTEIN (HONOR'S BROADSTONE). Often besieged Prussian fortress on the right bank of the Rhine. General Beurnonville, the French minister of war, and the four commissioners to the armies (*q.v.*) were handed over to the Austrians here on June 24, 1793 by Dumouriez (*q.v.*). The fortress surrendered to French General Jourdain on January 24, 1799 after a four-month siege.

EL ARISCH, EGYPT. Captured by the French under Reynier in February 1799, a convention was signed here between the grand vizier and Kléber (*q.v.*) for the evacuation of Egypt by the French on January 28, 1800.

ELBA. Island situated in the Mediterranean between Corsica and the Italian coast. It was ceded to France in 1802 and was Napoleon's place of exile (1814-15), at which time it was an independent principality. Elba became part of Tuscany in 1815.

ELIZABETH, MADAME (1764-94). French princess and sister of Louis

XVI. Sharing the fate of her brother, she was guillotined.

ÉMIGRÉS (EMIGRANTS). Opponents of the 1789 Revolution, particularly Royalists and the privileged classes, who were forced to flee France. Many were members of the nobility and some actively worked to promote a coalition of European sovereigns against the Revolution. The revolutionaries themselves enacted various punitive decrees against the émigrés. Bonaparte, as first consul, declared a general amnesty and when the Empire fell, they were rewarded with favors by Louis XVIII (*q.v.*).

Greer, D. M., *The Incidence of the Emigration during the French Revolution*, 1951.

Weiner, Margery, *The French Exiles, 1789-1815*, 1960.

ENCYCLOPÉDIE, L'. Denis Diderot (*q.v.*) the founder of the *Encyclopédie*, defined it as a reasoned inventory of the sciences, arts, letters, the manual professions and all of the creations of human genius and intelligence. This work had a profound influence on events leading up to the Revolution. Its publication started in 1751 and ran over a period of 21 years, forming 28 folio volumes of text and 15 volumes of engraved plates. Diderot had, as the principal collaborators, D'Alembert (*q.v.*), who wrote the Preface, Turgot (*q.v.*), Condillac, Helvétius, Mably, Marmontel, Raynal (*q.v.*), Grimm, Buffon, Rousseau (*q.v.*), and many others. In 1759 the Parlement ordered the burning of all the volumes of the work published to that date, along with Voltaire's *Dictionnaire philosophique*. Those who wrote for the great work, the Encyclo-

pédistes, used to meet together in the salons of Madame Geoffrin, facing the Convent of the Capucins (*q.v.*).

Darnton, Robert C., *The Business of Enlightenment: A Publishing History of the Encyclopédie, 1775-1800*, 1979.

Lough, John, *The Encyclopédie*, 1971.

ENGHIEN, LOUIS ANTOINE DE BOURBON CONDÉ, DUC D' (1772-1804). Eldest son of the prince of Condé (*q.v.*). Enghien fought in the émigré army from 1792 to 1801. After the Peace of Luneville, he settled near Baden and was kidnapped in 1804 by Napoleon's agent, tried and shot. He was accused of an assassination plot against Napoleon. Although his father survived him, he was the last of the House of Condé.

ENLIGHTENMENT. A period in the late 17th and the 18th century that was also known as the "Age of Reason," when critical reason was used to replace prejudices, accepted and unexamined authority, and general oppression by the church and state. Its basic tenet was that through reason people could find knowledge and happiness.

To some extent the Enlightenment was an almost inevitable growth of human enquiry and thought, fueled and encouraged by such factors as increasing sophistication in the fields of science, economics and the social sciences, philosophy, classical studies and so forth, which rapidly developed in breadth and sophistication. In doing so, it encouraged a fairly "democratic" spirit (society's good and gain would come from an increase in the number of people who contributed to it, by education and exposure to the new theories), which was raised against a rigid and old-fashioned system of government, religion and social order. Ideas vs. orthodoxy (or the *status quo*) was perhaps the most "revolutionary" principle of all, and as is commonly known, the revolutionary period was perhaps one of the most dynamic and exciting periods for a multiplicity of ideas. The *Encyclopédie* of Denis Diderot *(qq.v.)* was the embodiment of this surge of scientific and intellectual development.

ENRAGÉS (ANGRY ONES/MADMEN). Extremist political group recruited mainly from the sans-culottes in 1793 led by the abbé Jacques Roux. Their main demand was for economic control of the price of food.

EQUALS, THE. Group of egalitarian communists led by François Noel Babeuf *(q.v.)*, known as "Gracchus" (1760-97), which called for the abolition of the 1795 constitution and the return of the constitution of 1793. They were totally against the existing social order, called for its destruction and the confiscation of all private property, believing that this would allow the restoration of democratic freedom and equality. It was a popular dictatorship, with the leaders carrying the sovereignty of the people until the opposition had been eliminated. On May 10, 1796 the group was betrayed and tried by the Directory *(q.v.)*. In the spring of 1796 its leaders and major participants were deported or executed.

ESPIONS (SPIES). The Convention *(q.v.)* issued a decree that ordered the death penalty against all foreigners or French citizens who had been convicted of spying in fortified places and in the armies *(q.v.)*. They were judged by military commissions. In April 1794 numerous agents of foreign powers were arrested and in the armies, spies paid for by England, mostly émigrés, were discovered.

ESPRIT, SAINTE (HOLY SPIRIT). Order of knighthood founded by Henry III of France in 1578 and abolished in 1791.

ESTATES-GENERAL. Ancient assembly of France that was first summoned in 1301. Before the Revolution it had not met since 1614 under Louis XIII. The estates consisted of three orders, the clergy, nobility, and commons or Third Estate. They were convened by Louis XVI and met at Versailles on May 5, 1789; the aim was to solve the financial problems of France. A dispute arose as to whether the three orders should sit separately or as one assembly. The Third Estate insisted on one assembly and on June 17 assumed the title of the "National Assembly," and on November 5 distinctions between the three estates were finally abandoned.

Estate	Numbers	Seats
First Estate (clergy)	100,000	300
Second Estate (nobility)	400,000	300
Third Estate (rest of the population)	22,500,000	300

ÉTRANGER, CONSPIRATION DE L'. On November 26, 1793 Danton *(q.v.)* demanded a speedy report, to be published and presented to the Convention (*q.v.*), on foreign conspiracies. These conspiracies, many of which originated from England, had been occurring since 1792. Money had been sent to Paris and the departments for the purpose of calming unrest. Pitt (*q.v.*) was considered to be the chief instigator of the troubles by pouring in vast sums to undermine national morale. The Convention denounced the English government and, on behalf of its citizens, ordered the immediate arrest of all foreigners who had not been domiciled in France since the fall of the Bastille (*q.v.*).

ÊTRE SUPRÊME, L'. *See* **Supreme Being, Cult of.**

EXPOSITION PUBLIQUE, PEINE DE L'. A degrading punishment that consisted of fastening, by an iron collar to a stake erected on a scaffold in a public place, anyone who had been condemned to the galleys. A decree of the Legislative Assembly (*q.v.*) of August 31, 1792 suppressed the punishment of the iron collar for pregnant women. In this case, only the judgment was fixed to the stake in the public place.

FABRE D'ÉGLANTINE, PHILIPPE FRANÇOIS NAZAIRE (1750-94). French dramatist, poet and revolutionist. After winning the Prix de L'Églantine he took the name Églantine. He wrote *Le Philinte de Molière, ou la Suite du Misanthrope* (1790), a sequel to Molière's *Le Misanthrope*. A member of the National Convention *(q.v.)* and a leading revolutionary journalist, he devised some of the new names of months for the Revolutionary Calendar *(q.v.)*, but, having fallen foul of Robespierre *(q.v.)*, was eventually guillotined, together with his friends Danton and Desmoulins *(qq.v.)*.

FARMERS-GENERAL (FERMIERS GÉNÉRAUX). Before 1789 a system of indirect tax collection in which persons, often royal favorites, obtained the right to collect taxes in return for payment of a fixed sum. Taxes were leased on a six-year contract, often to the highest bidder. They retained any surplus for themselves and consequently grew rich. The system was grossly abused during the ancien régime and led to much dissatisfaction and discontent prior to the Revolution.

FAUBOURGS. Originally the sub urbs of Paris lying outside the city. By 1789 they had been enclosed within the city boundaries. The most famous were the working-class faubourgs of St. Antoine and St. Marcel and the richest, St. Honoré.

FEAR, GREAT. *See* **Great Fear.**

FEDERALISM. System used by the Girondins *(q.v.)*, to make the 83 departments into so many states, equal amongst themselves and confederated along the lines of the United States of America.

FEDERATION, FÊTE DE LA. The National Assembly approved on June 5, 1790 a suggestion, put forward by the Paris Commune (Commune de Paris, *[q.v.]*), that on July 14 there should be a fête in the Champ de Mars *(q.v.)*, made up of the delegates of all the towns in the kingdom, in order to celebrate the anniversary of the fall of the Bastille *(q.v.)* and administer the oath to the constitution. It was attended by 60,000 delegates from the 83 departments. The Bishop of Autun (Talleyrand, *[q.v.]*) celebrated mass in the Champ de Mars.

FÉDÉRÉS. Term applies to delegates from the towns who assisted in the fête at the Champ de Mars (*see* above) but more particularly to the young revolutionaries from Marseilles, led by Barbaroux (*q.v.*), who marched to Paris in 1792 to aid the Revolution.

FERMIERS GÉNÉRAUX. *See* **Farmers-General.**

FERRARA, CAPTURE OF. Town in Italy taken by the French in June 1796. On September 4, after the French departure, the pope sent a vice-legate to take back possession. In November, Ferrara formed a confederation with Reggio, Modena and Bologna. Under an invitation from Bonaparte, who was then general-in-chief, the central administration decreed the abolition of the inquisition, the exclusion of religious foreigners and the suppression of all distinction of title or rank on an hereditary basis. After the peace treaty with the pope was signed in February 1797, the legations of Ferrara, Bologna and of all the Romagna were ceded to France. Ferrara became part of the Cisalpine Republic (*q.v.*) and, in 1802, was designated as the chief center of the Departement du Bas-Po in the Italian Republic.

FERSEN, HANS AXEL, COMTE DE (1755-1810). Swedish statesman sometime in the service of France and a favorite at court. He idolized Marie Antoinette and it was he, disguised as a coachman, who drove the royal fugitives part of the way to Varennes (*q.v.*) in 1791.

FERVIDOR. *See* **Thermidor.**

FÊTE(S) DE LA RAISON (FESTIVAL(S) OF REASON). The first was celebrated in Notre Dame on November 10, 1793 with the aim of eliminating Christianity. An actress played the part of Goddess of Reason. Subsequently many churches were closed and converted to Temples of Reason.

FÊTE DE LA SOUVERAINETÉ DU PEUPLE (FEAST OF THE SOVEREIGNTY OF THE PEOPLE). A law of February 1, 1798 established the celebration of this fête on 30 Ventose of each year. In Paris, it occurred in each of the 12 municipalities.

FÊTE DE L'ÊTRE SUPREME. (FEAST OF THE SUPREME BEING). On May 7, 1794 the National Convention (*q.v.*) instituted the Cult of the Supreme Being (*q.v.*). Robespierre (*q.v.*) had rejected the "Cult of Reason" and wished to create a unified, aesthetically-satisfying form of worship likely to unite patriots. In April 1794 Georges Auguste Couthon (1755-94, *q.v.*) submitted a project for the Festival of the Supreme Being to the Convention. Jacques Louis David (1748-1825, *q.v.*) was put in charge of the organization of the festival, to take place in the Jardin des Tuileries on June 8, 1794.

The new god, sanctioned by Robespierre (*q.v.*), was a mirror-image of Rousseau's "vicaire savoyard," and the fount of revolutionary justice, patriotic obligations and civic morale. Atheism, in Robespierre's eyes, was aristocratic, while the worship of the Supreme Being was social and republican. Only those who truly believed in providence could be encouraged to greater bravery in combating tyranny and greater love of their country. It was a civic religion. The decree ordered that the Supreme Being was to be celebrated annually at the festivals of July 14, 1789, August 10, 1792, January 21, 1793 and May 31, 1793.

On June 8, Robespierre played the senior role, setting fire to a large effigy of Theism, while people sang the "Hymne a l'Être Suprême," words written specially for the occasion by André Chénier (1762-94, *q.v.*), the music by François Joseph Gossec (1734-1829, *q.v.*). In addition to the figure of Atheism, representations of Discord and Egoism were also burned; in the middle of these fires the figure of Wisdom suddenly appeared. The crowd then marched to the Champ de Mars (*q.v.*) to plant the Tree of Liberty. Here a vast mountain stood, crowned by a single huge tree, with the members of the National Convention placed under its branches. Robespierre dominated the Fête, a point that was not missed by his critics and those terrified of the recent purges of the Hébertists (*q.v.*) and Dantonists. (*See* **Danton.**) Some saw the festival as a plot to restore Catholicism, while others believed it to be Robespierre's intention to set himself up as the "pontiff" of a new religion. Catholics saw no difference at all between this festival and the Feast of Reason (*q.v.*). The festival itself marked the end of Thermidorean coalition. (*See* **Thermidor Revolution.**)

FÊTE DES VICTOIRES. National festival held on October 21, 1794 to celebrate the victories of the revolutionary armies and the departure of foreign invaders from French soil.

FEUILLANT, CLUB OF. Founded by moderate Jacobins in 1791. Among its members were Siéyès, Barère, Lafayette, Lameth and Barnave. The proper title of the club was the Société des Amis de la Constitution and the popular name was derived from its premises in the Rue St. Honoré, formerly a convent of the Feuillants. A chief aim of the club was to obtain for France a constitutional monarchy.

FIEFFÉ. A nobleman was said to be enfieffed if he held feudal title to land. This was a requirement for admission to the Second Estate in some provinces.

FIEFS. Expanses of land where the rights are held by the seigneur, to whom the rents are due and to whom fealty and homage must be rendered. In 1789 France was no more than an assembly of fiefs, placed under the tenure of the king. In February 1790 all honorific distinctions, superiority and power resulting from the feudal system, fealty, homage and all other purely personal service, were abolished. In 1793, the Convention (*q.v.*) decreed that all the fiefs which were paid to the crown would be taken over by the Republic.

FIGUERAS. Fortified town in Catalonia, Spain, which served as a rallying place for the émigrés (*q.v.*). It was taken by the French in a battle, November 17-19, 1794.

FIRST COALITION, WAR OF THE. *See* **War of the First Coalition.**

FIRST CONSUL. The most powerful and senior of the three consuls after the coup d'état of November 9, 1799. Three consuls were chosen, Sieyès (*q.v.*), Bonaparte and Roger Ducos (*q.v.*), by the application of the constitution of 1799, which gave the Senate (*q.v.*) conservator the right to choose the consuls. Bonaparte and Cambacérès were chosen for a period of ten years, while Lebrun rated only five. As first consul, Bonaparte had the greatest power. He nominated all the civil and military employees, and chose the members of the Council of State. His annual income, at half-a-million francs, was over three times that of each of his fellow consuls. As head of the government, he was installed in the Palais des Tuileries. In May 1802 his functions as first consul were extended by another ten years and on August 2 he was named consul for life. Following this, on May 18, 1804, he was proclaimed emperor of the French, Napoleon I.

FIRST GRENADIER OF THE REPUBLIC. Title given by Napoleon to La Tour d'Auvergne (1743-1800), a man of extraordinary courage and self-effacement. He refused all promotion beyond that of captain, as well as this title.

FLANDERS. Provinces of the Netherlands that, at the time of the Revolution, were part of France, Belgium and Holland. French Flanders had been constituted by Louis XIV, who had seized one part of this province, Hainaut, Cambresis and Artois, whose possession was confirmed by the treaties of the Pyrenees, Aix-la-Chapelle, Nimwegen and Utrecht.

Belgian Flanders, after having cut itself off from Emperor Joseph II, participated in the revolt in the Netherlands. In 1792 it demanded to be allowed to unite with France, and this occurred in 1794, resulting in the departements of Lys, with the major town being Brussels, and l'Escaut. Gand, as the center of Belgian Flanders, was part of France until 1814.

FLESSELLES, JACQUES DE (1721-89). Provost of merchants at Paris, Flesselles applied a rigorous set of rules dictated by the court, but yet tried to promote more moderate measures within the city. Caught in the middle of extreme and moderate forces, he was doomed. He was shot in the head and decapitated, his remains stuck on a pike by a mob.

FLEUR-DE-LIS. Said to have been brought from heaven by an angel to Clovis, it was the national emblem until 1789, when the tricolor (*q.v.*) was adopted.

FLEURUS, BATTLE OF. Small town in Belgium in the Hainaut near Charleroi, on the right bank of the Sambre River. It was the scene of a battle on June 26, 1794 between the French, commanded by Jourdan, general-in-chief of the Armée de Sambre-et-Meuse, and the armies of the Coalition, under the orders of the prince of Cobor, the archduke Charles, de Beaulieu and the prince of Orange. Although outnumbered, the French forced the Coalition to retreat. It was a major battle, which probably saved France from being invaded. On this occasion a balloon was used by Jourdan and others to study the course of the battle. This was its first military usage and contributed to Jourdan's success.

FLORÉAL. Flowers' month, April 20 to May 19. *See* **Calendar, Revolutionary.**

FLORENCE. Situated on the Arno River, capital of the Grand Duchy of Tuscany at the time of the Revolution. Relations between the grand duke and the French minister in Florence had always been difficult. On March 24, 1799 Ferdinand III, the grand duke, left Florence on the approach of the French, who had invaded Tuscany. Ferdinand settled in Vienna, advising his subjects to remain calm. Equally, the pope quit the city to seek refuge in Parma. During the last days of 1799, General Macdonald entered Florence with his army, but six months later he evacuated the city, which was ceded to France in 1801 by the Treaty of Lunéville. Ferdinand III returned to power in 1814.

FONTENAY-LE-COMTE, BATTLE OF. Ancient capital of Bas-Poite, the chief center of the department of La Vendée in 1790. During the first troubles in the west, the Royalists attempted to take the city on May 16, 1793, but were repulsed. On May 25 the Royalists were reinforced, and the republicans were defeated.

FORCE, PRISON DE LA. Paris prison situated on the Rue Paveé-au-Marais and the Rue-de-Sicile. It had belonged to the duc de la Force and was transformed into a prison in 1780. It held those condemned for not being able to pay the monthly due for the nursing of their children, police prisoners, women, tramps and those jailed for debt. It was in the courtyard of this prison that the princesse de Lamballe was murdered during the massacres *(q.v.)* of September 1792.

FOUCHÉ, JOSEPH (1759-1820). Statesman, a member of the Convention *(q.v.)* from 1792. He was a supporter of Robespierre *(q.v.)* and was one of those responsible for the mass-shootings of anti-Jacobin rebels at Lyons in 1793. Later he became an opponent of Robespierre because of the Cult of the Supreme Being *(q.v.)*, which he despised. Under the Directory *(q.v.)* he became minister of police, even with his record of blood-thirstiness, and retained the post with breaks until 1815. He was created duke of Otranto in 1806. After the Bourbon restoration he regained office and served, for a time, as ambassador to Dresden.

FOULON, JOSEPH FRANÇOIS (1717-89). Minister of the King's Household, appointed after the dismissal of Necker *(q.v.)* in 1789. He was very unpopular and detested by the Farmers-General *(q.v.)* because of his severity. He was loathed by the Parisians for his ostentation and indifference to their misery. After the fall of the Bastille *(q.v.)*, he was returned to Paris, carried off to the Hôtel de Ville with a bundle of hay on his back, and hanged from a lamp-post.

FOUQUIER-TINVILLE, ANTOINE QUENTIN (1747-95). Revolutionary politician. He was public prosecutor to the Revolutionary Tribunal *(q.v.)* from 1793 until July 1794, and superintended all the political executions during the Reign of Terror *(q.v.)*, sending, among others, Robespierre, Danton and Hébert *(qq. v)* to their deaths. He was guillotined in 1795.

FOURIERISM. Charles Fourier (1772-1837) proposed the establishment of cooperative agricultural communities (phalanxes), which were to be federated under a central government. The wealth created of each phalanx was to be subject to common ownership. The system was attempted in both France and the United States.

FOX, CHARLES JAMES (1749-1806). British statesman and orator. In 1787 Fox unsuccessfully opposed the commercial treaty with France. He believed that France, or at least the Bourbons (q.v.), were the natural enemies of England. Fox welcomed the Revolution, and saw the 1789 Estates-General as the downfall of a despotism hostile to England. He maintained that, essentially, the Revolution was just, and should not be condemned for either its errors or its crimes. Thus, he opposed Pitt's (q.v.) foreign policy, which he saw as a crusade against freedom in the name of despotism. Between 1790 and 1800, Fox was alone in Parliament, denounced as an enemy of his country.

In 1797 Fox left Parliament, reappearing to take part in the vote of censure on ministers for declining Bonaparte's peace overtures. This resulted in the fall of Pitt's first ministry, the formation of the Addington (q.v.) cabinet, the Peace of Amiens (q.v.), and the establishment of Bonaparte as first consul (q.v.).

FRANC FIEF. Under the feudal system this term designated the fiefs that originally could be held only by people who were franchised or noble. This became significant when possessors of such fiefs had to sell their rights, permitting commoners to buy and hold their properties. This was considered to be most humiliating.

FRANCIS II (1768-1835). The last Holy Roman Emperor (1792-1806). An absolutist who hated constitutionalism, he declared himself the first Austrian emperor as Francis I in 1804. His first campaign against Napoleon Bonaparte ended with the Peace of Campo Formio (q.v.) in 1797, when Austria exchanged the Netherlands and Lombardy for Venice, Dalmatia and Istria; the second ended with the Treaty of Lunéville in 1801 after defeats at Marengo (June 14, 1800, q.v.) and Hohenlinden (December 3, 1800). Then followed the campaign of 1805 when the French victories at Ulm (October 20, 1805) and Austerlitz (December 2, 1805) and the capture of Vienna compelled Austria to purchase the peace at Pressburg in 1805 by the cession of Venetia, Tyrol and Vorarlberg. With the establishment of the Confederation of the Rhine in 1806, Francis renounced the title of German-Roman emperor. The Treaty of Vienna in 1815 saw the return to Austria of Lombardy, Venetia and Galicia, thanks largely to Prince Metternich.

Bibl, Victor, *Kaiser Franz*, 1938.

FRANKFURT ON MAIN. German city, one of the four "Free Cities" of the German Confederation. Leopold II was crowned here on October 4, 1790. The city served as a refuge for the émigrés (q.v.). Custine (q.v.) seized it on October 22, 1792, but on December 7 the inhabitants massacred the French and the Prussians regained the city. In July 1796 the Armée de Sambre-et-Meuse retook the city, and in 1799 and 1800 the city again suffered from the war.

FRANKLIN, BENJAMIN (1706-90). American statesman and scientist. During the American Revolutionary War (*q.v.*) Franklin arrived in Paris (December 1776) and enjoyed immense popularity and success. Seen by the French as the embodiment of enlightened simplicity, he successfully negotiated the Franco-American alliance (1778).

On Franklin's death, the Constituent Assembly (*q.v.*) went into mourning for three days. Funeral ceremonies and memorial services were held throughout France.

Crane, Verner W., *Benjamin Franklin and a Rising People*, 1954.

van Doren, Carl, *Benjamin Franklin*, 1948.

FREIBURG. Town of the canton of the same name in Switzerland, 17 miles from Bern. Its magistrates were hostile toward the Revolution from the very beginning, and it became a haven for émigrés and priests. It was taken on March 10, 1798 by General (later Marshal) Guillaume Brune, after the defeat of the Bernois.

FRÉJUS, VAR, FRANCE. Town founded by Julius Caesar. On his return from Egypt, Bonaparte landed at the port of Saint-Raphael on October 9, 1799. Fifteen years later he left from Fréjus to go into exile at Elba (*q.v.*).

FRENCH COMPANY OF THE INDIES. From 1604 to 1769, five companies obtained the privilege to exploit the commerce of the Indies, but none of these enterprises was successful. In 1769 the state took over the last company, which had functioned since 1604 and possessed the privilege exclusively to provide France with all the merchandise of the Indies, setting its own prices. The royal government abolished this privilege, which was reestablished in 1785, nevertheless leaving the freedom of commerce between France's islands and those of Bourbon. Lorient was the only entry port.

On April 3, 1790, the Constituent Assembly (*q.v.*) canceled the company's dividend and in September 1792 the Legislative Assembly (*q.v.*) decreed heavy reimbursements. Later, pensions were given to sailors who had served on the company's vessels to induce them to leave the service. In July 1793 the Convention (*q.v.*) ordered the company's holdings, including merchandise at Lorient, to be frozen, the company having been accused of providing sums to encourage the counterrevolution. Its holdings and assets were ordered to be sold. Fabre d'Églantine (*q.v.*) was accused of falsifying the decree relative to the company's debt, and he and a number of others implicated in this cover up were executed.

FRENCH GUIANA. A French colony from 1677. During the Revolution it served as a place of exile for Royalists and counterrevolutionaries. Its administrators demanded that Cayenne, the main settlement, no longer be a place assigned for deportations and that slavery be abolished. The Assembly chose to ignore the former demand, and the victims of 18 Fructidor were sent to Cayenne. (*See* **Directory.**) Slavery was abolished by the Convention (*q.v.*) in 1794 and reintroduced by Napoleon in 1802. The colony was held by the French until 1809, when it was taken by the English and Portuguese and became a French possession again in 1817. It has been an overseas department of France since 1946.

FRÉRON, LOUIS MARIE STANISLAS (1754-1802). Journalist and revolutionist, the son of Elie-Catherine Fréron, editor of *L'Année Litteraire*. He managed the publication after his father's death in 1776 and in 1789 founded *L'Orateur du Peuple.* In 1793 Fréron and Barras (*q.v.*) were sent by the Convention (*q.v.*) to suppress counterrevolution in Toulon and Marseilles. He was savage with his reprisals, but soon after joined the Thermidoreans. Fréron became their leader, and the head of the Jeunesse Dorée (*q.v.*). His paper became the official organ of the reaction. Fréron was elected to the Council of Five Hundred (*q.v.*), but not allowed to take his seat. He failed as a suitor for the hand of Pauline Bonaparte, one of Napoleon's sisters, and in 1799 went as a Commissioner to Saint Domingue, where he died.

FRIMAIRE. Sleet month, November 21 to December 20. *See* **Calendar, Revolutionary.**

FRUCTIDOR. Fruit month, August 18 to September 16. *See* **Calendar, Revolutionary.**

FRUCTIDOR. Coup d'état of 18 Fructidor, year 5 (September 4, 1797). *See* **Directory.**

FRUCTIDOR CONSTITUTION. Promulgated in France on the 5th Fructidor, year 3 (August 22, 1795). *See* **Directory.**

G

GABELLE. Tax on salt, first imposed by Philip the Fair in 1286 and abolished on May 19, 1790. The word was originally applied to any indirect tax but later was restricted to salt and was a royal monopoly. All the salt made in France was sold at a price fixed by the government. Some areas had to pay twice as much as others and everyone above the age of 8 had to purchase a minimum quantity weekly. The tax produced 38 million francs under Louis XVI.

GALÉRIANS. Those condemned to penal servitude, who formerly had served their sentences on galleys. In 1793 the galérians who had been condemned for desertion were set free and a further decree from the Convention permitted them to wear the red cap. In the same year the galérians distinguished themselves at the siege of Toulon by the allies, saving the Arsenal and preventing a number of defensive positions from being destroyed.

GALLICANISM. French doctrine which emphasized the king's authority, or that of the French bishops, over the French church in ecclesiastical matters. The Papal Bull *Unigenitus* of 1715 was regarded by many clergy and parliamentarians as being a combined attack by Louis XIV and the pope on Gallican liberties. It provided forty years of civil wars and political controversies in France. The destruction of the monarchy and the church of the ancien régime did not put an end to the Gallican movement in the broadest sense. Bonaparte's Organic Articles (1802) established the complete control of the French church by the state and introduced a new form of Gallicanism, which remained after the Restoration (1815) and represented the overriding authority of the French bishops over the lower clergy.

GARAT, DOMINIQUE-JOSEPH (?1750-1832). Editor of the *Journal de Paris*. He was a member of the Estates-General *(q.v.)* in 1789 and minister of justice under the convention *(q.v.)*. He was a member of the Senate *(q.v.)* under Napoleon.

GARDE CONSULAIRE (GARDE DES CONSULS). Formed after 18 Brumaire *(q.v.)* of a section of the Directory guard which had been favorably disposed toward the coup d'état. Only those who could prove that they had been involved in at least four campaigns and actions of bravery were admitted to this force. It was composed of 360 men at the beginning, increasing to 2,000 and then 7,000 by the beginning of the

Empire. It formed the nucleus of the Imperial Guard.

GARDE DÉPARTEMENTALE. Guard composed of the citizens of the 83 departments, at the disposal of the Convention *(q.v.)*. On October 8, 1792 Buzot's *(q.v.)* report proposed that each department should send as many as four infantrymen and two cavalrymen to be deputies to the Convention. The National Guard were to be in barracks and to be paid the same amount as received by the National Guard at Paris. They were elected by the general councils of the departments, after having produced a civil certificate for their communal general council and that of their district. Their commandant was to be named by the National Convention. The entire issue became a violent controversial center for the arguments between the Girondins and the Montagnards. *(See* **Mountain, The.***)* Many departments, concerned by the ultrarevolutionary influence of the Paris-based communes, organized their volunteers for the protection of the Convention. After the victory of the Montagnards over the Girondins, these forces were suppressed on August 12, 1793. They were not taken seriously as a national force and were seen as being a rallying-point for antirevolutionary forces.

GARDE DU CORPS LÉGISLATIF. Guard serving the Council of Ancients and later by the Council of Five Hundred *(q.v.)*, it originally consisted of 1,000 men provided by the departments. The Council of Five Hundred organized 1,200 of the guard's members into grenadiers. It served as a considerable force, backing

Bonaparte on his attempt to move into the main room of the Orangerie de Saint-Cloud, instead of protecting the Five Hundred, who were meeting there on 19 Brumaire.

GARDE DU DIRECTOIRE. Guard consisting of 360 men, with 240 foot-soldiers and 120 cavalry. On 18 Brumaire *(q.v.)* this force did not defend the Palais du Luxembourg, where the Directors were in session, when Bonaparte sent General Moreau *(q.v.)* to take over the building. Later many joined the Garde Consulaire *(q.v.)*.

GARDE INVALIDE. Veteran invalid company which came into service for the king at Versailles. On July 28 and 29, 1789 the French and Swiss guards quit the garrison for Paris. The bourgeois militia came forward to take over the vacant posts, but the *invalides* also presented themselves as guards. The conflict was resolved when it was agreed that the *invalides* should take duty in the inner courts, the militia posting themselves at the gates. The king then reversed this positioning. Later, the *invalides* were sent to fortified places and garrisons in the provinces.

GARDE MUNICIPALE DE PARIS. In 1789 the guard was composed of 950 infantry and 528 cavalry recruited from line troops. It consisted of three companies of the Gardes de l'Hôtel de Ville and one company of the Guet de Paris, specially charged with prison-service and attached to the Châtelet. *(See* **Châtelet de Paris.***)* They enjoyed a certain number of nontaxable privileges, but were replaced in 1792 by the Gendarmerie.

GARDE NATIONALE. Citizen militia instituted by the Commune of Paris (*q.v.*) July 13, 1789. At first it numbered 48,000 men, but was increased to 300,000 when it was organized throughout the whole country. Lafayette (*q.v.*) was its first commander. It was reorganized by the Directory and by Napoleon, and again under the Bourbons and was dissolved in 1827.

GARDES FRANÇAISES. Infantry established by Catherine de' Medici to guard the king. It was composed of 4,880 men formed into 6 battalions of 6 companies, one of which was a grenadier company. Four companies were, each day, on service to the king. The guards wore a blue uniform and carried white caps with braid. In July 1789 some of the guards instructed the citizenry in the use of arms in the Place Louis XV, and on July 14, a number joined those storming the Bastille (*q.v.*). The king was forced to authorize Lafayette (*q.v.*) to incorporate the Gardes Françaises into the bourgeois militia of Paris, where they formed grenadier companies, and were assured of subsistence and support. On July 31, four companies left Versailles, with the consent of the king, carrying their flags; no officers came with them. They were soon licensed by Louis after their incorporation into the National Guard. By a decree of October 12, 1792 they became part of the active army and were among the first units to see service on the frontiers.

GENDARMERIE NATIONALE. On December 21, 1790 the Constituent Assembly decided that the old constabulary should be replaced by the National Gendarmerie, composed of men both on foot and on horseback. This force was comprised of 28 divisions and distributed in groups of five men throughout all France. There were 1,560 brigades of men on horseback and foot throughout the localities. A small troop of 33 *gendarmes nationaux* on horseback was attached to the armies in 1792, charged with enforcing the judgments passed by the courts-martial and the correctional tribunals, and ensuring that good order was maintained in the camps. Members kept their civilian rank during their period of war service, and were allowed to return to their original posts after the end of the hostilities.

GENERAL FARMERS (FERMIERS GÉNÉRAUX). Company of financiers who, under the ancien régime, numbered between 40 and 60, who, every six years, came to an agreement with the crown in which they were obliged to pay the king an advance and an annual fee. In return, the company was granted the right to collect the indirect taxes and the income from the royal domain and to manage the royal monopolies, which included those of salt and tobacco.

GÉNÉRALITÉS. Thirty-four areas into which France was divided for tax and other administrative purposes.

GENÈVE, RÉPUBLIQUE DE. Founded in the middle of the 16th century under the dictates and directions of John Calvin. In 1789 it experienced the backlash of the Revolution and later an excess of revolutionary fervor. The Directory (q.v.) prepared for the union of Geneva with France, which had been demanded by its inhabitants. French troops entered the republic on April 15, 1798, and on May 17, after its union with France, it became the Département du Léman, with its chief center being Geneva.

GÉNIE, LE (GENIUS). One of the sans-culottides (q.v.) September 18.

GENS DE COULEUR. Free citizens of the French colony of Saint-Domingue who had some Negro blood. Also known as *affranchis*, they numbered about 28,000. In the social structure they ranked below the "grand" and "petit" blancs ("whites", q.v.) and just above the 500,000 slaves who possessed no rights at all. The *couleurs* suffered social and legal humiliations from the *blancs*, but were championed by the Société des Amis des Noirs (q.v.).

In April 1792 (*affranchis* had been granted some political rights in 1789) the National Assembly decreed the enfranchisement of *gens de couleur* and in February 1794 the French Convention decreed the emancipation of the slaves. Revolutionary principles quickly spread in Saint-Domingue and the first mulatto risings occurred in the spring and autumn of 1790. In August 1791 a slave revolt broke out. The arrival of the Jacobin commissioners in September 1792 aggravated the divisions between competing groups. The *gens de couleur* were supported by the commissioners at the cost of the *blancs*. Support was then transferred to the blacks, who were newly emancipated. Later the British landed to help the whites, at their request.

The struggle between the blacks, the British force of occupation and the mulattoes continued until the British were defeated in 1798 by Pierre Dominique Toussaint l'Ouverture (1746-1806, q.v.), the leader of the blacks, who then turned on the mulattoes. In 1801 Spanish Santo Domingo was occupied and the constitution published. Toussaint declared himself governor-general for life. In 1802 Napoleon sent General Leclerc (q.v.) to reestablish slavery and French authority. Toussaint was captured and died a prisoner in France in 1803. The blacks and mulattoes rose again against the restored slave trade and fought a successful war of independence.

GEOFFRIN, MARIE THÉRÈSE (1699-1777). Patroness of literature. She provided funds for the publication of the *Encyclopédie* (q.v.).

GEORGE III. (1738-1820). King of Great Britain and Ireland, Elector (later, King) of Hanover. In the American Revolution, the personal responsibility for the loss of the colonies lay not with any assertion of his royal prerogative. The Americans were, in fact, ready to admit his personal supremacy. What provoked their hostility was George's alignment with Parliament, which had strongly asserted its supremacy in American affairs. By 1779, Parliament had grown tired of the war but the king argued that, although it was totally indefensible on economic grounds, it must be pursued on the lines of ideology and basic principle. In 1778 after France had joined the Americans in their fight, George argued that French finances would collapse under the strain before those of Great Britain. In summary, the king's determination prolonged this war by a period of two years. After the outbreak of the extended war with revolutionary France, all but the most radical Whigs joined the government. To the upper and middle classes, this war seemed to be an absolute battle for national survival, a feeling precipitated by the early successes of the French on the continent.

GERMINAL. Sprouts' month, March 21 to April 19. *See* **Calendar, Revolutionary.**

GERMINAL INSURRECTION. Riots that occurred in the faubourgs of Paris, suppressed on April 1, 1795.

GERTRUIDENBERG, FORTRESS OF. Fortress in Holland taken by the French on March 5, 1793 after a siege of seven days. The taking was made extremely difficult by the enemy and the enormous water-filled moats. The French were later forced to give way to considerable pressure by a Dutch force, and were allowed to leave the fortress with full honors on April 5, being escorted to the border by a Dutch force.

GIACOBINI. Liberal nobles of Lombardy, interested in French revolutionary affairs.

GIRONDINS (GIRONDISTS). An important middle-class republican party during the Revolution, principally composed of deputies from the Gironde region of southwest France. Their leaders were Brissot *(q.v.)*, Roland *(q.v.)*, Pétion *(q.v.)* and Vergniaud *(q.v.)*. They sat in the Legislative Assembly of 1791 and in the Convention of 1792 *(qq.v.)* Having rushed into war with Britain, Holland and Spain, they were attacked by the Jacobins *(q.v.)* after its early reverses. They were overthrown on June 2, 1793 and their leaders were guillotined on October 31, 1793.
Sydenham, Michael John, *The Girondins*, 1960.

GLORIOUS FIRST OF JUNE. On June 1, 1794 the British Channel fleet, under Lord Howe, gained a decisive victory over the French under Admiral Villaret Joyeuse. Off Ushant, six French ships were captured and one sunk, but the convoy of corn ships that they were escorting, got through to Brest.

GODWIN, WILLIAM (1756-1836). English social philosopher; a rational anarchist who influenced Coleridge and Shelley and who anticipated the arguments of John Stuart Mill and Proudhon. The Revolution profoundly influenced the course of Godwin's career. He did not support all aspects of it because of the revolutionary tendency to forsake reason, but he thought it generally beneficial. Godwin served on a small committee that secured the publication of Paine's *Rights of Man*, in response to Burke's *Reflections*. Godwin, however, felt that a thorough analysis of society and government was required, rather than a refutation of Burke. His *An Enquiry concerning the Principles of Political Justice, and its Influence on General Virtue and Happiness* (1793) was a futuristic study. *Caleb Williams, or Things as they are* (1794) is Godwin's doctrinaire novel.

Godwin supported radical and corresponding societies, but did not support the physical destruction of government because he thought that one tyranny would be replaced by another. He believed in progressive enlightenment, which would free man from the social and political deficiencies of society.

GOSSEC, FRANÇOIS-JOSEPH (1734-1829). Composer of much official music for outdoor performances during the Revolution. This music included "Hymne à l-Être Suprême" and "Le Triomphe de la République."

GOUGES, OLYMPE DE (MARIE-OLYMPE GOUZE) (1748-93). Feminist and revolutionary. In 1790 she founded the Club des Tricoteuses, and wrote the feminist polemic *Déclaration des droits de la femme et de la citoyenne* in 1791. She also wrote several successful comedies and oriental tales which included *Le Prince philosophe* (1792). She was an opponent of Robespierre *(q.v.)* and was arrested after protesting the death of Louis XVI. She was guillotined in 1793.

GOURNAY, SEIGNEUR DE. *See* Raigecourt.

GRANDE ARMÉE (GRAND ARMY). Reorganized army of Napoleon from 1805 to 1812 that incorporated all the separate armies of France.

GRANDE CHAMBRE. Name given to the principle chamber of each *parlement (q.v.)*. Here the king held his "lits de justice" and all of the magistrates met together. Appeals against abuses, civil requests and other major causes were carried out in this place. In Paris, the Grand Chamber of the Parlement was known as the "chambre dorée" because of its gilded ceiling. During the Revolution it served as the room of the revolutionary tribunal, and was later the great chamber of the Cour de Cassation *(q.v.)*.

GRANDE PEUR, LA (GREAT FEAR). Panic that spread throughout France, with the exception of Alsace, Lorraine, Brittany and Lower Languedoc, from July 20 to August 6, 1789. It originated in a rumor that brigands in the pay of aristocrats were going to attack in order to restore the status quo. The peasants took up arms and barricaded their homes and property. Though no attack was forthcoming, once armed, the peasants made many attempts to destroy châteaux, and considerable destruction of manorial records resulted.
Lefebvre, Georges, *The Great Fear of 1789*, 1973.

GRANDS AND PETITS BLANCS. The French colony of Saint-Domingue was controlled by whites, who numbered about 35,000, divided into the *grands blancs*, who were generally aristocratic planters and higher civil servants, and the *petits blancs*—the remainder. The whites were also divided, yet again, into Creoles (natives) and Europeans (foreign-born). Each class despised the other and those below them—the *gens de couleur* (*q.v.*) and the slaves.

A minority of the *grands blancs* insisted on sending delegates to the Estates-General to press for self-government for the island, with them in control. Fearing a revolt on the island, royal authority to convoke a colonial assembly responsible only to the Crown was granted, but it was too late. In April 1792 Jacobin commissioners were sent from France. The slaves were emancipated in February 1794. Following extended warfare on the island, and with the independence of Haiti in 1804, virtually no whites remained.

GRAND LIVRE DE LA DETTE PUBLIQUE (GREAT BOOK OF PUBLIC DEBT). Register opened in August 1793 in which Joseph Cambon (*q.v.*) wrote the certificates of all the income due by the public treasury. The principle was to liquidate all the debts acquired prior to the Revolution by the monarchy, the provincial estates, religious houses, corporations and the old orders that had been suppressed, and, since the beginning of the Revolution, by the nation, departments, districts and communes.

GRAVE, PIERRE MARIE, MARQUIS DE (1755-1823). General and minister of war. He fought in the Spanish War, 1783. He became first equerry of the duc de Chartres (afterward, Louis Philippe [*q.v.*]). Regarded as being aggressive and retrograde, he was accused of being responsible for the defeats suffered by the Armée du Nord. He was accused but escaped to England, returning to France only in 1804.

GRASSE, FRANÇOIS JOSEPH PAUL, MARQUIS DE GRASSE-TILLY, COMTE DE (1722-88). French admiral. Born at Bar, Department of Alpes Maritimes. In 1734 he entered the service of the Order of Malta. In 1740 he entered French service, being promoted to chief of squadron in 1779.

De Grasse took part in the naval operations of the American Revolutionary War (*q.v.*) and distinguished himself at the battles of Dominica and Saint Lucia (1780), and of Tobago (1781). At St. Kitts he was defeated by Admiral Hood. In April 1782 de Grasse was defeated and taken prisoner by Admiral Rodney. Retired to France, he published a *Mémoire Justificatif*, and was acquitted by a court martial in 1784.

GREAT ST. BERNARD. The Great St. Bernard, an alpine pass at 8,111 feet (2,469 meters), leads from Martigny in the Rhône Valley in Switzerland to Aosta in Italy. In May 1801 Bonaparte led an army over the pass into Italy. After the coup d'état of 18 Brumaire (*q.v.*) Bonaparte had become de facto ruler of France. To maintain his hold on the country it was vital to gain at least a temporary peace, thus supporting his reputation as the peacemaker of Campo Formio (*q.v.*). The rapid, brilliant Second Italian Campaign helped to achieve this end. Placing himself unofficially at the head of the Army of the Reserve, he led the army over the Alps, taking the Austrian army in the rear. He met the enemy in the Po Valley near Alessandria, defeating them in the hard-fought Battle of Marengo (*q.v.*).

GRÉGOIRE, HENRI (1750-1831). Prelate and revolutionary. Curé of

Embermènil in Lorraine, he was sent to the Estates-General of 1789 (q.v.) as a deputy of the clergy. He worked for a union with the Third Estate and for the abolition of Negro slavery. He took the oath of allegiance and was elected constitutional bishop of Loire-et-Cher. In 1792 he proposed the abolition of the monarchy and that Louis XVI be brought to trial. At the Fête de la Raison (q.v.) he refused to renounce Christianity. He opposed the coup d'état of 18 Brumaire (q.v.) and the proclamation of the Empire, and in 1814 proposed the deposition of Napoleon. The Concordat forced him to resign his bishopric. He died unreconciled with the church.

GRENELLE. Commune near Paris, on the left bank of the Seine, the scene of an explosion on August 31, 1794, when the local gunpowder mill blew up. The Convention (q.v.) took it upon itself to ensure that the families of the workmen killed or hurt in the explosion were looked after.

GRENIER À SEL. Storehouse from which salt was issued for controlled sale by the *grenetier*, in connection with the levying of the *gabelle* (q.v.).

GRENVILLE, WILLIAM WYNDHAM, BARON GRENVILLE OF WOTTON-UNDER-BERNEWOOD (1759-1834). British politician. In 1791 he was appointed to the Foreign Office by William Pitt (q.v.) as the man best fit to carry out policy with France. Over the years he and his chief were frequently at variance on important questions of foreign policy. In 1801 he resigned with Pitt because King George III (q.v.) would

not consent to the introduction of any form of Catholic emancipation.

GRÉVE, PLACE DE. Sandy stretch on the edges of the River Seine in Paris. Originally the location for fêtes and other public festivities held by the Parisians. It was also the place where, until 1830, public executions were held. Now called Place Hôtel de Ville.

GRIBEAUVAL, JOHN BAPTISTE DE (1715–89). General. In 1764, after distinguished service in the Austrian army during the Seven Years' War, he became Inspector of Artillery. He promoted numerous reforms within the French artillery that were to be especially important during the Revolutionary and Napoleonic periods.

GUADELOUPE. Department of France situated in the West Indies, the island was discovered by Columbus in 1493. Conquered by the French in 1635, it was successively occupied by the French and the English alternately. By 1789 it was in French hands and had become a prosperous center with a population of 109,246, divided into 13,958 whites, 5,149 persons of mixed race and 90,139 slaves. A civil war began in 1793, resulting in serious troubles in the interior. In 1794 the English tried to retake the island but were repulsed by French forces led by Chrétien and Victor Hugues, the commissioners sent by the Convention (q.v.). Guadeloupe was retaken in 1810 and again during the Hundred Days, returning to France on July 25, 1816.

GUADET, MARGUERITE ÉLIE (1758-94). Lawyer. Guadet was made administrator of the Gironde in 1790, and in 1791 president of the criminal tribunal. Elected to the Legislative Assembly (q.v.), he became a Girondist (q.v.) and supported the 1791 constitution. He forced Louis XVI to accept the Girondist ministry of March 15, 1792. Guadet moved for the removal of all non-juring priests, the disbanding of the Royal Guard, and for the formation of a camp of fédérés (q.v.) in Paris; he remained, however, a Royalist. On August 10, as the presiding officer in the Assembly, Guadet opposed the Paris Commune. (See **Commune de Paris.**) On his motion of August 30 the Assembly voted for its dissolution, which was reversed the following day. In March 1793 Guadet met Danton (q.v.), who wanted a reconciliation between the Girondins and the Montagnards during the Vendean Rebellion (q.v.), but Guadet refused to cooperate with those whom he held responsible for the September Massacres (q.v.). He was guillotined in 1794.

GUARD, NATIONAL. See **Garde Nationale.**

GUIDES. Corps in the French army especially charged with the protection of the person of the general.

GUILLOTIN, JOSEPH IGNACE (1738-1814). Physician, regent of the College of Medicine in Paris. Under the name of *Pétition des six Corps* he wrote a brochure in 1788 in which he demanded more equal representation of the Third Estate (q.v.).

He was Paris deputy in the Estates-General and occupied himself with issues of medicine.

On December 1, 1789 there were two proposals regarding capital punishment. The second, by Guillotin, was that it should be decapitation by a machine, as decapitation was no longer the privilege of the nobility, and that it should be swift and painless. On October 6, 1791 decapitation was placed in penal code and the means for this method referred to a committee, under the direction of Dr. Antoine Louis, secretary to the Academy of Surgeons. A German named Schmidt was hired to build a machine for each department. The first one was placed in the Place de Grève for the execution of a highwayman named Pelletier on April 25, 1792.

Guillotin was imprisoned during the Terror (q.v.). After his release he founded the Academie de Medicine.

GUILLOTINE. An instrument for causing immediate and painless death, named after a physician, Guillotin (q.v.), who proposed its use. At a meeting of the Legislative Assembly in 1789 he expressed an opinion that capital punishment should be the same for all classes. Dr. Guillotin proposed that it should be carried out mechanically. The Assembly adopted this proposal and a German mechanic named Schmidt built a machine to the specifications of Dr. Antoine Louis (1723-92), then secretary of the French College of Surgeons. It was first used on April 25, 1792, and for a while referred to as "Louisette" after Dr. Louis.

A similar instrument consisting of a falling blade, weighted, running between two upright posts, had been used previously in Scotland, England

and parts of the continent. In Scotland the "Maiden" was used in 1581 for decapitating the Regent Morton. In 1661 it executed the marquis of Argyll and in 1685 to dispose of the earl of Argyll, the marquis' son. In Germany it was in general use during the Middle Ages, called, variously, "Diele," "Hobel" or "Dolabra." In Italy during the 13th century it was used for the execution of criminals of noble birth. In France in 1632 it was used to execute Marshal Montmorency at Toulouse, and functioned in the south of France.

It was first referred to as a "guillotine" in the *Journal des Revolutions de Paris* on April 28, 1792.

GUILLOTINE SÈCHE, LA. Punishment by deportation, used instead of executions. It was frequently employed under the Directory (*q.v.*).

GUYTON DE MORVEAU, LOUIS BERNARD, BARON (1737-1818). Born in Dijon, at the age of 24 he became advocate-general in the *parlement* there, an office he held until 1782. Studying chemistry in his off-hours, he published his thoughts on phlogiston, crystallization and so forth in 1772. In 1774 he published courses of lectures on *materia medica*, mineralogy and chemistry. His essay on chemical nomenclature, which he published in the *Journal de Physique* for May 1782, was ultimately developed, with the aid of Lavoisier (*q.v.*), Berthollet and Fourcroy, into the *Methode d'une Nomenclature Chimique* (1787), a work which was adopted throughout Europe. A Lavoisierian, he was an ardent anti-phlogiston, publishing his findings in the first volume of the *Encyclopédie Methodique* (1786) as "Chymie, Pharmacie et Metallurgie." The *Encyclodédie's* articles on chemistry were written by him, as well as some of the entries in the second volume (1792). Having conducted some aeronautical experiments in Dijon ten years earlier, in 1794 he was appointed to superintend the construction of balloons for military purposes.

In 1791 Guyton de Morveau was a member of the National Assembly (*q.v.*), and in the following year of the National Convention (*q.v.*), to which he was reelected in 1795. In 1798 he acted as a provincial director of the École Polytechnique having been influential in its foundation. From 1800-14 he was master of the mint, and was made a baron of the French Empire in 1811.

H

HA, FORT DU. Fort situated near Bordeaux, built by Louis XIV. Its great tower was turned into a military prison and part of the remaining structure into a civil prison by the Constituent Assembly *(q.v.)* in May 1791.

HAGUE, TREATY OF THE. Treaty signed between France and the new Batavian Republic *(q.v.)* on May 16, 1795. The first anti-French coalition fell apart with the withdrawal of Austria (1794) and Prussia (1795), the latter's defection exposed Britain's ally, the Batavian Republic, to French attack and forced the Dutch to come to terms with France.

HAGUENAU, BATTLE OF. Fortified town near Strasbourg on the Moder River in the department of Bas-Rhin. After the taking of the lines of Wissemburg, the duke of Brunswick and General Würmser resolved to chase the French, who had retreated behind the lines of the Moder. The battle began on October 17, 1793 with the center of the French army established at Haguenau. After a sustained defense the French were obliged to fall back under the walls of Strasbourg. On December 17, 1794 the Armée du Rhin took the high ground around Haguenau and six days later the Austrians were forced to evacuate the town.

HALLES, LES. Wholesale food market.

HAMBURG. Town on the right bank of the Elbe River. One of the three German "Hanseatic towns." Initial reaction to the Revolution was favorable, until the execution of Louis XVI, when the French envoy was expelled. Hamburg became the center for a colony of some 40,000 émigrés. They had their own theater, newspapers and reviews, and a café where they met. In 1798 French Consul General Legot requested the support of French residents in Hamburg against the English. At the Congress of Rastadt, Hamburg insisted in adopting a policy of total neutrality. After various exchanges between Hamburg and France, the Directory *(q.v.)* ordered a total embargo on all the Hamburg ships which were found in the ports of the Republic.

HANOVER, ELECTORATE OF. Since the German Confederation (1815-66), it was governed by the king of England, who added to his titles that of king of Hanover, after the accession of George Louis, elector of

Hanover, to the English throne in 1714. The electorate took a firm stand against the French émigrés (q.v.) who had come to Hanover, ordering them to leave. In 1793 the Hanoverians were compromised with English subjects through the decree of arrest directed against English people present in France. Accordingly the comte d'Artois (q.v.) and the émigrés were expelled from Hanover. In 1801 Hanover was occupied by the Prussians, and in 1803 it was seized by the French, who exchanged it with the Prussians for Anspach, Cleves and Neûchatel.

HANRIOT, FRANÇOIS (1761-94). Revolutionary and an orator for the sans-culottes (q.v.). In May 1793 Hanriot was provisionally appointed as commandant-general of the Paris armed forces by the council general of the commune. He was a commune delegate to the Convention (q.v.), and demanded the dissolution of the Committee of Twelve and the proscription of the Girondists on May 31, 1793. (See **Commune de Paris.**) Hanriot was in command of the insurrectionary forces of the commune during the riot of June 2. On July 1, he was elected by the commune as permanent commandant of the Paris armed forces, which gave him enormous power until 9 Thermidor (q.v.). Hanriot's arrest was decreed, he had the generale and the tocsin (q.v.) sounded, and he tried to rescue Robespierre (q.v.). Arrested, he was guillotined with Robespierre and supporters on 10 Thermidor.

HÉBERTISTS. Followers and supporters of Jacques René Hébert (1755-94, q.v.). After the fall of the Girondins (q.v.), the Montagnards (Mountain, The [q.v.]) split into two factions: the Indulgents (Danton, Camille Desmoulins, Fabre d'Églantine [qq.v.]), who were reasonably moderate; and the Hébertistes (Jean Baptiste de Cloots [q.v.], Jean B. J. Gobel and Pierre Gaspard Chaumette [q.v.]), commune-based, violent and irrational. Robespierre (q.v.) and the Committee of Public Safety (q.v.) stood above both groups.

The Hébertistes gained their support from the Paris mob, who could be called out in short order through Hébert's newspaper Le Père Duchesne. Extremists, they alienated themselves from the center of power by their violent actions. Robespierre attacked Hébert's atheistical views and, through him, the rise of a "Commune insurrectionnelle de Paris." By summarily destroying Hébert and his supporters, Robespierre was in a strong position to turn on, and remove, Danton and the Indulgents.

HÉBERT, JACQUES RENÉ (NICKNAME: PÈRE DUCHESNE) (1755-94). Revolutionary. At the outbreak of the Revolution he became a prominent Jacobin (q.v.) and editor of Le Père Duchesne, a newspaper established to ruin a constitutional newspaper of the same title. As a member of the revolutionary council he played a conspicuous part in the September Massacres (q.v.). As a commissaire-investigator appointed to examine Marie Antoinette, he accused her of incestuous practices with the dauphin, but the revolutionary tribunal did not use his evidence. He helped to organize the Worship of Reason, in opposition to the theistic cult of Robespierre (q.v.). His alienation from the center was hastened by this move, and the fact that he had not consulted the Convention (q.v.) before taking the important decision to press for the suppression of Christianity. He and his associates were responsible for converting Notre Dame into the Temple of Reason. Hébert also attempted to incite a popular movement against Robespierre and attacked the chiefs of the Mountain (q.v.). Both Danton (q.v.) and Robespierre saw clearly that he wished to substitute the power of the commune for that of the Convention.

He was condemned and guillotined with 18 of his colleagues on March 24, 1794 for planning the massacre of the Convention.

HELIOPOLIS, BATTLE OF. Situated in Lower Egypt near Cairo, Heliopolis was the site of a battle on March 20, 1800 between the French army, led by General Kléber, and the Egyptians and Mamelukes. Kléber was the victor.

HERAULT DE SECHELLES, MARIE JEAN (1759-94). Politician and lawyer. On December 8, 1789 he was appointed judge of the Court of the First Arrondissement in the department of Paris. He was a deputy for Paris to the Legislative Assembly (q.v.), a growing leftist and a member of the diplomatic committee that presented the report demanding that the nation should be declared to be in danger. He cooperated with Danton (q.v.) during the August 10, 1792 revolt, and was appointed president of the Legislative Assembly and a deputy to the National Convention (q.v.). It was he who, on the rejection of the proposed constitution drawn up by Condorcet (q.v.), was charged with preparing a new one, which became the 1793 constitution. Herault was a member of the Committee of Public Safety (q.v.), charged with diplomacy, but he was suspected by his fellow committee members, especially Robespierre (q.v.), and expelled from the committee in December 1793. Herault was accused of treason and condemned with Danton.

HISPANIOLA. Caribbean island settled by the Spanish in the early 16th century. Later the seat of the republics of Haiti and Santo Domingo (now the Dominican Republic). By the Treaty of Ryswick (1697) Spain gave France the western half of Hispaniola. The eastern half became Santo Domingo, which was ceded to France in 1795. The island was the scene of Pierre Dominique Toussaint l'Ouverture's (q.v.) revolt. Napoleon sent his brother-in-law General Charles Victor Emmanuel Leclerc (1772-1802 [q.v.]) to put the island under French control again. Toussaint was treacherously seized and sent to France where he died in prison. Expeditions directed against the blacks by the French were repulsed by Jean Jacques Dessalines (1758-1806) and independent Haiti was declared on January 1, 1804.

HISTOIRE DES GIRONDINS. Historical work that glorified the Girondins (q.v.) and was written with revolutionary fervor by Alphonse Marie Louis de Lamartine (1790-1869), published in 1847. It was extremely popular at the time of publication. There are descriptions of the September Massacres (q.v.), Louis XVI's trial and the fall of the Girondins, and sketches of leading revolutionaries such as Charlotte Corday and Robespierre (qq.v.).

HOCHE, LOUIS-LAZARE (1768-97). General of the revolutionary armies. He defended Dunkirk against the duke of York, drove the Austrians out of Alsace in 1793 and commanded the Army of the West (1795-96), which finally pacified the Vendée. (*See* **Vendéan Rebellion**) He then led an abortive expedition intended to seize and hold Ireland against the English. He died suddenly while in command of the Army of Germany, possibly by poisoning.

HOLBACH, PAUL HEINRICH DIETRICH, BARON D' (1723-89). German-born French philosopher. He was one of the Encyclopedists, he explained the natural principles of morality in his *Systéme de la Nature* (1770) and believed that self-interest is the dominating motive of man.

HONDSCHOOTE, BATTLE OF. A large English army of 18,000, commanded by the duke of York, was defeated by a French army, led by Houchard, in a battle fought September 6-8, 1793 in the Netherlands. Hondschoote is in the district of Dunkirk.

HOOD, ALEXANDER, FIRST VISCOUNT BRIDPORT (1727-1814). British sailor and brother of Samuel Hood. (*See* below.) During the Revolution he served under Howe in the English Channel and the Strait of Gibraltar and was at "the glorious first of June" off Ushant in 1794.

HOOD, SAMUEL, FIRST VISCOUNT HOOD (1724-1816). British sailor and brother of Alexander Hood. (*See* above.) He served in the Seven Years' War and later in the West Indies, during the American Revolution, where he was successful in an action off St. Kitts and Nevis in 1792, when the islands were attacked by the French admiral Comte de Grasse. He was commander in chief in the Mediterranean and captured Toulon in 1793 and Corsica in 1794.

HÔPITAUX MILITAIRES (MILITARY HOSPITALS). Under the ancien régime, military hospitals were administered by a commissioner of wars in the major towns and cities of the kingdom. They had been instituted in 1769 by Choiseul, with a medical service supported by the government. This was a fortunate reform, as previously the service had been run by entrepreneurs, who had made excessive profits at the cost of the well-being of the sick. In 1769, Choiseul organized a system of special inspectors. In 1792 the Legislative Assembly (*q.v.*) decreed the establishment of fixed and ambulatory hospitals behind the troops. Before and during the Revolution there were three military hospitals in Paris: the Hôpital Militaire, founded in 1765 by the duc de Biron and containing 264 beds in 1792; the Hôpital de Montaigu, which in 1793 became both a military hospital and a prison, adopting the name of the old Collège de Montaigu; and the Hôpital Val-de-Grâce.

HOSPITALIÈRES, COUVENT DES. Founded in 1624 for poor and sick women, it was situated in the Rue Saint-Antoine. It was suppressed in 1792 and was converted into a cotton spinning mill. The Hospitalières de la Rue Mouffetard possessed 40 beds;

that of the Place Royale held 23 beds; and that of the Roquette, 25 beds. These three maisons were suppressed by the Convention decree of January 17, 1795. The infirm who were in these places, who paid, were given the chance to go into a Hospice de Bienfaisance Nationale, under the same conditions, and those who were indigent were placed in the Hospices Nationaux, according to their specific conditions. The Hospitalières de Saint-Mandé, who possessed many beds in that commune, were suppressed by the same decree, and the same resettlement principles followed.

HOSPITALITÉ, FÊTE DE L'. Instituted by the Convention in honor of foreign patriots who were refugees in France, it was celebrated in the Champ de Mars in April. There they sang a hymn of circumstances, composed in 1793 by Doin, secretary of the public prosecutor's office of the commune.

HOSTAGES, LAW OF (LOI DES OTAGES). Measures which were taken on July 12, 1799 against the parents of émigrés who were suspected of violent acts occurring in the departments. Any individuals responsible or thought to be responsible for unlawful acts, or being in any way connected with groups or individuals acting against the established order, were to be considered as hostages, and declared personally responsible. Magistrates were given the right to detain suspects in prison for as long a time as they considered fit. If there was an assassination in the neighborhood, magistrates were empowered to choose one of the

detained and to have him deported. This law was abolished by Bonaparte after 18 Brumaire (q.v.).

HÔTEL CARNAVALET. See **Carnavalet, Musée.**

HÔTEL DES INVALIDES. Hospice for old soldiers, the wounded or disabled. It was founded by Louis XIV in 1670 at the western extremity of the Faubourg Saint-Germain and that of the Gros-Caillou, and was opened in 1674. On July 14, 1789 the Paris populace, hearing of a considerable number of weapons deposited in the dome, broke into the Hôtel where nearly 26,000 firearms, pikes, sabres and some cannons were discovered. From here the mob moved on to the Bastille (q.v.). In 1800 General Lalanne hung 96 flags, captured in Egypt, in the Hôtel. A simultaneous celebration was held to commemorate Washington. In September of 1800 the remains of Marshal Turenne (1611-1675) were transferred to the Invalides, from their resting place in the Musée des Petits-Augustins; they had previously been removed to here after the destruction of the tombs of Saint-Denis. The two churches and the great dome were started in 1675 and finished in 1705. In the nave of the first church were placed nearly 960 flags by the end of the Revolution and the Empire. The other church, placed under the great dome, held the tombs of Napoleon and of Turenne and other great men of war (Napoleon's in the center, the others in the six side chapels). On August 10, 1793 the members of the National Convention (q.v.) met on the great Esplanade des Invalides, which ran from the front of the Invalides almost to the Seine, to celebrate the constitution and the first year of the republic. Under the Convention, a statue of Hercules (the emblem of Robespierre, *q.v.*) was placed in the middle of the Esplanade. It was later removed, to be replaced temporarily by the great Lion of Saint Mark, removed from Venice by the Armée d'Italie.

HÔTEL DE VILLE DE PARIS. Headquarters of the city government. The first stone was laid by François I, following the plans of the Italian Boccardo. The major work, started under Henri II, was not finished until 1628. The façade looked over the Place de Grève and was marked by 13 windows, surmounted by a bell tower in which was placed the city clock in 1781, built by André Lepaute. To the north, the ancient chapel of Saint-Ésprit and part of the hospice of the same name were found backing the Hôtel. The south side provided another building for the bureaux, brought into the principal portion of the Hôtel by the old Arcade Saint-Jean. Near the end of the Directory, the different services of the city of Paris required more space, and other annexes were built on the sites of the churches of Saint-Jean and Saint-Ésprit.

Louis was returned here with his family by the citizens of Paris. The Assembly of the Third Estate (*q.v.*) of the city of Paris was installed here on July 13 and 14, 1793. Three days after the fall of the Bastille (*q.v.*) the king was received here by Bailli, the mayor of Paris. Martial law was signified by the red flags draped from the Hôtel's windows on July 17, 1791. During the Revolution it was a rallying-point and meeting place for a variety of groups and organizations. Robespierre (*q.v.*) was confined in the theater at the Hôtel after his downfall, before being taken to his execution.

HÔTEL DIEU. Hospital situated in the Place du Parvis Notre Dame. It contained 1,700 beds, of which there were 800 where the sick slept three and four to a bed. Annually, 27,000 patients passed through the Hôtel. By a decree of November 15, 1793 the Convention (*q.v.*) reunited the Hôtel Dieu with the archbishop's palace, and authorized the municipality to give each sick person a single bed. The Hôtel was enlarged in 1804.

HOUPPES ROUGES, LES. Catholic fanatics of Nîmes who, in 1790, armed themselves against the Protestants and revolutionaries. On June 13, 1790 the Montagnards (*q.v.*) of Cévennes stormed the Couvent des Capucins at Nîmes, where they massacred all of those defenders wearing the *houppe rouge* (red top-knot).

HOWE, RICHARD, EARL (1726-99). British admiral. He commanded the channel fleet at the Battle of the First of June (Ushant) in 1794.

HUIT MILLE, PÉTITION DES (PETITION OF 8,000). Petition by the État-Major of the National Guard (*q.v.*) carrying 8,000 signatures, it was directed against a decree of the minister of war that had ordered the formation of a camp of federal soldiers to defend Paris. It was denounced on June 9, 1792 in the Legislative Assembly (*q.v.*) by a deputation from the Bataillon des Petits-Augustins. It was suggested that, like the army, the National Guard had no right of petition. Those apologists for the petition said that the signatories had signed as citizens, not as soldiers. After considerable debate, it was decreed that the original petition would be burnt and that those citizens who possessed printed copies of it should destroy them. Those National Guard who had signed it were to be excluded from both revolutionary and civil committees.

I

IDEOLOGUES. A group of thinkers and writers active during the Directory *(q.v.)* who were disciples of Abbé de Condillac *(q.v.).*

ILDEFONSO, ST., SPAIN. A treaty between France and Spain, August, 19, 1796, and another, October 1, 1800, by which France regained Louisiana, were signed at St. Ildefonso.

IMPARTIAUX, CLUB DES. Founded by an aristocratic group, this club met at the Grands-Augustins in several rooms that had for some time served as a meeting place for the higher clergy and for the Chevaliers du Saint-Ésprit. It held centrist views and, under the leadership of Malouet *(q.v.)*, vainly tried to influence opinion in Paris. After sustained attacks against the Jacobins *(q.v.)*, the club disappeared. The "Impartiaux" were, in addition, moderate members of the Constituent Assembly *(q.v.)*, called the "Ministériels" by the people.

IMPÔTS. Under the ancien régime, this referred to the charges of all sorts paid to the government to assure the smooth running of royal administration. They took the name, in 1789, of *contributions publiques*, the time at which the new system of duties and taxation came into force. The most fundamental change was the imposition of a universal form of taxation. All contributions which had previously been made by the nation without consent were declared to be illegal.

IMPRIMERIE NATIONALE. Established on March 1, 1793 to print and publish the laws, reports, addresses and proclamations which the Convention *(q.v.)* decreed. The whole range of materials which covered legislation in all its branches came from the Imprimerie, including all of the books covering the arts and sciences which had been published for the benefit of the Republic, under the directions of the Convention. All of the administrative departments of the Republic were required to send their reports to the Imprimerie, which could print materials only on its own premises.

INCORRUPTIBLE, L'. *See* **Robespierre.**

INCROYABLES. Young dandies and reactionaries of the Directory *(q.v.).* They wore exaggerated clothes and hairstyles and used the affectation of not using the letter *r*. "En véité, c'est incoyable!" was one of their well-known expressions.

INCURABLES, HOSPICE DES. Hospital situated in the Rue de Sèvres, founded in 1637 by Cardinal de la Rochefoucauld for the infirm of both sexes who were incurable. It held 446 beds. In 1790, the men and the women were separated, the men being moved to the suppressed Couvent des Récollets, and the women staying at the original hospice.

INDIGENTS. In 1788 and 1789 the number of needy persons in Paris grew alarmingly, to the point where it exceeded most previous levels. The usual, established support and charitable groups in the city found it impossible to support these people. On December 16, 1790 the Constituent Assembly *(q.v.)* voted the sum of 1,500,000 livres for the indigents, of which 80,000 livres went to each department for distribution. Each department was to open and support facilities for the working poor, to enable them to serve the republic.

INDIVISIBILITÉ. In the republican vocabulary, it is used repeatedly with "unity." These two principles were proclaimed by the Convention *(q.v.)* on September 25, 1792. The Girondins *(q.v.)* were accused of trying to break the unity and indivisibility of the republic, by pushing for a federalist system.

INFERNAL COLUMNS, THE (COLONNES INFERNALES). Name given to the mobile columns organized during the war in La Vendée by General Louis Marie Turreau de Linières (1756-1816). Fast-moving against their essentially partisan opponents, they practiced a scorched earth policy (i.e., burning, destroying and looting) against Royalist sympathizers.

INGENIEURS (ENGINEERS), **DES PONTS ET CHAUSSÉES.** Officials responsible for the management and supervision of travel by roads, bridges and canals. On January 19, 1791 the Constituent Assembly *(q.v.)* decided to appoint a chief engineer for each department. The engineers were paid for by the departments, while the chief engineers were funded by the national treasury.

INSTITUT NATIONAL. The Institut was founded by a decree of the National Convention *(q.v.)* in 1795. It met for the first time at the Louvre, on April 11, 1796, in the Salle des Suisses. It covered academic disciplines: physical sciences or mathematics, moral and philosophical sciences; literature and the beaux-arts. Its members received a salary of 1,500 francs per annum, and the Institut rapidly gained a European-wide reputation of excellence. At later periods of history it was known as "Royal," "Imperial" and again "National."

INTENDANTS. Royal representatives in the territorial departments until 1789 whose social and economic power over the population and other local authorities was virtually unlimited in law, though often these powers were, in fact, limited by the entrenched privileges of the nobility.

INVALIDES. Home for retired and semiretired soldiers similar to the Chelsea Hospital in London. Some of the inmates still carried out light duties and were, for example, part of the defense of the Bastille *(q.v.)* in 1789.

INVIOLABILITY OF THE HOME. The Convention *(q.v.)* passed an act, August 22, 1795, on the inviolability of citizens' homes during the night.

IONIAN ISLANDS. The Greek islands of Corfu, Cephalonia, Zante, Santa Maura, Ithaca, Cythera and Paxo. On the fall of the Venetian Republic in 1797, the Treaty of Campo-Formio *(q.v.)*, which gave Venice to Austria, annexed the islands to France. A Russo-Turkish force drove the French out in 1798 and in 1799 Corfu capitulated. In 1800 Czar Paul I erected the "Septinsular Republic," but anarchy ensued until the Treaty of Tilsit (1807) declared the islands to be an integral part of the French Empire. Later, the Treaty of Paris (November 1815) placed the islands under the exclusive protection of Britain and they became part of the Greek kingdom only in 1864.

IRELAND. *See* **Killala.**

ISNARD, MAXIMIN (1758-1825). Revolutionary and leading Girondist *(q.v.)*. He reproached Louis XVI for his lack of loyalty to the constitution, but was one of the deputies who, on June 20, 1792, went to help protect the king from the mob. In 1793 he presented, on behalf of the Girondist majority of the Committee of General Defense, a recommendation that a smaller committee of nine be established, and on April 6, 1793 this became the Committee of Public Safety *(q.v.)*.

JACOBINS. Dominicans were so called in France from the Rue St. Jacques, which was the location of their first religious house in Paris. The revolutionary Jacobin Club, founded at Versailles in 1789 as the Breton Club, moved to Paris and met in a former Jacobin convent, hence the name. Among the members of this most radical of revolutionary clubs, were Mirabeau, Robespierre, St. Just, Marat, and Couthon *(qq.v.)*. It controlled the country through its hundreds of associated societies in the provinces until the coup of 9 Thermidor (July 27, 1794) and was responsible for the Terror *(q.v.)*. The club was suppressed on November 11, 1794. Their badge was the Phrygian Cap of Liberty.

Bouloiseau, Marc, *The Jacobin Republic, 1792-94*, 1983.

Brinton, C., *The Jacobins*, reprinted 1961.

JACOBINS BLANCS. Term of decision used in the Constituent Assembly *(q.v.)* against the enemies of the Revolution.

JACOBINS, ENGLISH. Name refers to the French Jacobin Club. The government of Pitt the Younger regarded radicals, such as Thomas Paine *(q.v.)* and John Horne Tooke (1736-1812), and members of the London Corresponding Society (established January 25, 1792) as advocates of Jacobinism in England. The Corresponding Society was banned in July 1799, the government acting with increasing severity. Habeas corpus was suspended (1794-1801) and the Combination Acts (1799, 1800), which did not allow the "combining" of two or more people in order to gain better working conditions or increased wages, were introduced. The 1800 act was repealed only in 1824.

JACQUERIE. Peasant revolt. A peasant was commonly called a "Jacque."

JAMAICA. In 1795 there was an insurrection, fomented by black slaves. At the beginning of 1796 the French landed and seized the camp of Colonaire.

JANSENISM. Movement, prominent in the Catholic church in France, based on the religious principles of Cornelius Jansenius, archbishop of Ypres (1585-1638), laid down in his book *Augustinus* (1640). His work was a study of the teachings of St. Augustine, with a special view to 17th-century needs. It challenged the concept of free will. Jansenism strongly opposed the doctrines and ethical teachings of the Jesuits. Promoted in France through one of Jansenius's disciples, Antoine Arnauld, these ideas came into conflict with the Jesuits and the French state.

JARDIN DU ROI. The Jardin du Roi was created in 1635. It was not originally a botanical garden, but gradually was augmented by the various branches of natural history. By 1739, when George Louis Leclerc, comte de Buffon was named director, the Jardin had become an important center, although it had only slight collections and much of the area was uncultivated. Between 1792 and 1814 it was known as the Jardin des Plantes, the name it bears today.

JARDINS PUBLICS. During the Revolution, there were public gardens at the Tuileries, the Luxembourg and the Palais Royal, which became national properties and were supported by the Republic. The Parc Monceau, the Marbeuf and the Beaujon in the Champs Élysées, were hired out by the Convention for fêtes. There were also scientific gardens, like the Jardin du Roi (q.v.), later the Jardin des Plantes, the Botanical Garden, the Boutin, later the Tivoli, the gardens of the Arsenal and the Temple and, finally, those gardens designed for recreation, dances and sports of every kind.

JEANBON SAINT-ANDRÉ, ANDRÉ (1749-1813). Revolutionist. He became pastor at Monaubon. The proclamation of liberty of worship made him a supporter of the Revolution, and he was sent as a deputy to the Constituent Assembly (q.v.). He

sat on the Mountain (q.v.) until the death of Louis XVI, for which he had voted, and opposed the punishment of the authors of the September Massacres (q.v.). In July 1793 he was the president of the Convention (q.v.), a member of the Committee of Public Safety (q.v.), and was sent on a mission to the Armies of the East. Saint-André reorganized the military harbors of Brest and Cherbourg. He was arrested in May 1795 and later released. He was appointed as Consul at Smyrna and Algiers (1798) and he was imprisoned by the Turks for three years. Subsequently, he became prefect of the department of Mont-Tonnerre (1801) and commissary-general of the departments on the left bank of the Rhine.

JEFFERSON, THOMAS (1743-1826). American statesman, diplomat, author, architect and scientist. Jefferson arrived in Paris in 1785. He was appointed as Franklin's (q.v.) successor as minister to France and remained there until October 1789. He carried on the tradition of Franklin. Jefferson admired much of the French and their society but was distressed by the inequalities of social conditions; he came to think less than ever of royalty, nobility and priests. Like the early revolutionaries, Jefferson had a deep faith in the perfectibility of mankind and made a near-religious treatment of enlightenment.

Jefferson followed the course of the Revolution up until his departure. He suggested and submitted a proposed charter to Lafayette (q.v.), and a desirable course of procedure for the Assembly of Notables (q.v.). Lafayette arranged for a meeting of the leaders of the patriot party at Jefferson's house to arrive at a compromise on the question of the royal veto and the constitution of the Assembly (*q.v.*). Jefferson was intimate and sympathetic with the moderate reformers but deplored the later violence and retained the overall conviction that the Revolution had done far more good than ill.

JEMAPPES, BELGIUM. Battle won by the Republicans, under Dumouriez, in which 40,000 French troops drove out 19,000 Austrians, who were entrenched in woods and mountains, November 6, 1792. The number killed on each side was about 5,000. Following this victory, Mons, Tournai and Brussels opened their gates to the French and the Belgians declared their independence.

JEU DE PAUME. *See* **Tennis Court, Oath of.**

JEUNESSE DORÉE (GILDED YOUTH). A party name applied during the Revolution to certain young Parisians who sought to bring about a counterrevolution after the fall of Robespierre (*q.v.*), July 27, 1794. They were also called *petits-maitres, elegants and muscadines*, "scented darlings."

JEWS. In 1789 it was estimated that there were 50,000-60,000 Jews in France. In 1790 the Jews of Spain, Portugal and Avignon were declared to be citizens of France, and on September 27, 1791 Jews were granted emancipation.

JOSEPH II (1741-90). Holy Roman Emperor (1765-1790), son of Francis I and Maria Theresa and brother of Marie Antoinette. Until the death of his mother in 1780 he had limited power, but after that event he declared himself independent of Rome and stopped the publication of any new papal bulls without his agreement. He suppressed convents, reduced the number of clergy to 27,000, and in 1781 published the Edict of Toleration for Protestants and Greeks. He also abolished serfdom, reorganized taxation and reduced the privileges of the nobles.
Blanning, T.C.W., *Joseph II and Enlightened Despotism*, 1970.

JOUBERT, BARTHÉLEMY CATHERINE (1769-99). General. In 1793 he distinguished himself by the brilliant defense of a redoubt in the Col di Tenda, Italy, with only 30 men, against an Austrian battalion. In 1796 he was commanding under Augereau (*q.v.*) and attracted Bonaparte's attention, who had him made a general of division. In December 1796, Joubert was in charge of the retaining force at Rivoli and in 1799, during the invasion of Austria, he commanded the detached left wing of Bonaparte's army in Tirol, and fought his way through the mountains to rejoin his chief in Styria. Subsequent commands included Holland, the Rhine and Italy, where up to January 1799 he was commander in chief. He took over the Italian command again from Moreau (*q.v.*) in July 1799. The forces and odds were heavily against the French, and Joubert and Moreau were compelled to fight Suvarov. The result was the French defeat at the Battle of Novi and Joubert's death (August 15, 1799).

JOURDAN, JEAN BAPTISTE, COMTE (1762-1833). Marshal of France. Jourdan volunteered at the beginning of the Revolution and had a rise even swifter than that of Hoche and Moreau *(qq.v.)*. In 1793 he was a general of division, selected by Carnot *(q.v.)* to succeed Houchard as commander in chief of the Army of the North. Jourdan won the great Battle of Wattignies (October 15-16, 1793). Soon after he became suspect because of his moderate views and his concern for future conduct of war. He retired but was reinstated and, in 1794, became commander in chief of the Army of Sambre-et-Meuse. By his victory at Fleurus (June 26, 1794, *q.v.*), having earlier crossed the Sambre, Jourdan had extended the French sphere of influence to the Rhine, where he waged an indecisive campaign in 1795. In 1796 his army formed the left wing for the march into Bavaria. The advance suffered from a series of Austrian victories over Jourdan at Amberg and Würzburg, and the French were forced over the Rhine.

Jourdan, made a scapegoat by the government, was not employed for two years. He became a politician and framed the famous Conscription Law of 1798. In 1799 he was placed at the head of the army of the Rhine but was again defeated by the archduke Charles at Stockach (March 25). Handing over his command to Masséna, he resumed his political interests. An opponent of the 18 Brumaire coup *(q.v.)*, Jourdan was afterwards expelled from the 500. (*See* **Council of Five Hundred.**) He was, however, soon reconciled to the new régime, and accepted new civil and military employment from Bonaparte. In 1804 he was made marshal and was governor of Naples in 1806. In 1813 he was defeated by Wellington at Vitoria and in 1814 he transferred his allegiances to the Bourbons. He supported the 1830 revolution.

JOURNAL DE PARIS. Founded in 1777 by Cadet, Dussieux and Corancez, this was the first French daily newspaper, also known as the *Poste du Soir* and the *Poste de Paris*. It was regarded as one of the most dangerous of the antirevolutionary papers and was closed for three months in 1792.

JOURNAL DE PERLET, LE (1789-97). Newspaper founded by Charles Perlet (1765-1828), a bookseller with political and literary interests. It reported proceedings of the National Assembly and the Commune de Paris *(qq.v.)*, and took a moderate line. It was suppressed by the Directory *(q.v.)*.

JOURNAL DES DÉBATS, LE. A famous daily paper founded 1789. During the Revolution it was largely devoted to fearlessly ironic reports of discussions in the National Assembly and the Commune de Paris *(qq.v.)*.

JOURNÉES. Days of violence in Paris directed against the aristocracy. These include the fall of the Bastille *(q.v.)* on July 14, 1789, the October Days *(q.v.)*, October 5-6, 1789, the invasions of the Tuileries on June 20 and August 10, 1792, the overthrow of the Girondins *(q.v.)* on June 2, 1793, and 9 Thermidor *(q.v.)*, July 27, 1794.

JULIERS, BATTLE OF. A battle fought between the Austrians and the Armée de Sambre-et-Meuse on October 3, 1794, commanded by Jourdan *(q.v.)* on the banks of the Ruhr, the day after the Battle of Aldenhoven. There were considerable losses but it was a great victory for the French. It assured a point of entry to the Rhine, pushed the enemy over the river, opening the way to Holland, and assured good winter quarters.

JUNOT, GENERAL JEAN AN-DOCHE, DUC D'ABRANTES (1771-1813).   Soldier and close associate of Bonaparte. Junot was his secretary at Toulon and became his lieutenant aide-de-camp soon after. He served in Italy (1795-96) and was Bonaparte's senior assistant (1796-97). He followed Bonaparte to Egypt and later fought at Aboukir (*q.v.*), where he was captured by the English and later released. In 1805 he was ambassador to Portugal and was later governor-general. In 1812 he was in Russia and returned to France in January 1813. He became insane and killed himself.

JURANDES.   Meetings of the principal masters of the guilds, elected by all the members of corporations. Its chiefs were called "Syndics jurés et prud'hommes," and judged the disputes between its members as well as punished infringements of the corporation's rules and exacted fines and penalties. The Jurandes admitted the apprentices and administered the taxes of the industrial communities. They were briefly suppressed by Turgot (*q.v.*) in 1776 and abolished by the Constituent Assembly (*q.v.*) on March 2, 1791. On September 16, 1792 they were ordered to be reimbursed by the Legislative Assembly (*q.v.*).

JURIES.   The laws of September 16 and 29, 1791 established the system of juries. The Constituent Assembly (*q.v.*) decided that they could not hear criminal cases, and created juries in two sections. The first was the *jury d'accusation*, the second being the *jury de jugement*. The first jury declared whether the accusation should be admitted or rejected. The facts were examined by the second jury, and the punishment was decided by the criminal tribunal, using established law.

KAISERSLAUTERN, BATTLES OF. Town in the Rhineland-Palatinate, Germany, occupied by the French in 1794. Lost and retaken on several occasions in battles against the Austrians under Archduke Karl, it was decisively taken by the French in June, 1796.

KELLERMANN, FRANÇOIS É-TIENNE CHRISTOPHE, DUKE OF VALMY (1735-1820). Marshal of France. He was born in Strasbourg, served in the Seven Years' War and was a major-general at the outbreak of the Revolution. In 1792 he, with General Charles-François du Périer Dumouriez *(q.v.)*, repelled the Duke of Brunswick, and saved France from invasion by the "cannonade of Valmy." He was accused of treason and was imprisoned (1793-94) by Robespierre *(q.v.)*. Afterwards, he served in Italy, and under the Empire was made a marshal and duke. In 1815 he became reconciled to Louis XVIII *(q.v.)* and sat in the House of Peers.

KENZINGEN AND EMMENDINGEN, GERMANY. Battle won by Austria, fought October 19-20, 1796 between Austria, under Archduke Karl, and France, under General Jean Victor Moreau *(q.v.)*.

KILLALA, COUNTY MAYO, IRELAND. With the aim of keeping the British occupied in their own islands, a French force landed from three frigates under General Humbert at Killala on August 22, 1798. The invaders were joined by the Irish insurgents and marched 40 miles to the south. There was little support in Ireland, and after the victories at Castlebar and Coloony the French were defeated at Ballinamuck on September 8. The French troops were well disciplined, and given greater strength the outcome could well have been different, as the Irish militia were in great disorder. In September 3,000 more soldiers were sent from France with an escort. A naval battle was fought on October 11-12 off Tory Island, Donegal. The French lost a battleship and three frigates and the British, under Commander Warren, were victorious.

Jones, E. H. S., *An Invasion that Failed: The French Expedition to Ireland, 1796*, 1950.

KLÉBER, JEAN BAPTISTE (1753-1800). General of the revolutionary armies, he distinguished himself in the Vendée, at Fleurus *(q.v.)* and with the Army of the Rhine. Bonaparte left him in charge of the Army of the Orient in Egypt when he returned to France in 1799. Kléber defeated a greatly superior Turkish army at Heliopolis. He was assassinated in Cairo by a Moslem fanatic on June 14, 1800 while attempting to conclude a treaty with the Turks.

L

LACOMBE, CLAIRE ("RED ROSA") (1765-?). Actress and revolutionary. She played in theaters in Marseilles and Lyons with a traveling company of players. She went to Paris in July 1792, visited the Convention *(q.v.)* and Jacobin Club, and was named the "Heroine of August 10th" for her part in the storming of the Tuileries *(q.v.)*. In April 1793 she founded the Republican Revolutionary Society, an organization for working women, which became associated with a left-wing group known as the Enragés *(q.v.)*. Militant feminism was attacked by Robespierre *(q.v.)* in the Assembly and, although Lacombe defended its activities fiercely, the club was finally suppressed in November 1793. In March 1794 she was arrested and was in prison until 1795. Nothing is known of her from that date.

LAFAYETTE, MARIE JOSEPH PAUL YVES ROCH GILBERT DU MOTIER, MARQUIS DE (1757-1834). Soldier and politician. He entered the army, sailed for America in 1777 to help fight for independence, and became a friend of George Washington. He returned to France in 1779, encouraging the government to help the colonists. Returning to America he was in charge of the defense of Virginia and was at the Battle of Yorktown. As a liberal reformer he sat in the Estates-General *(q.v.)* and in the National Assembly *(q.v.)* of 1789, becoming commander of the National Guard *(q.v.)*. He tried to restrain mob rule in Paris and also tried to protect the king after the failure of the flight to Varennes *(q.v.)*. He became commander of the Army of the East in 1792; the military operation failed, he fled across the Rhine and did not return to France until 1799. Under Napoleon he took no active part in politics but after the emperor's fall he served in the Chamber of Deputies and was active in the revolution of 1830.

Buckman, Peter, *Lafayette,* 1977.

LA FORCE. House that became a debtors' prison in 1780. Political prisoners were kept here from 1792 and it was the scene of some of the September Massacres *(q.v.)*. The building was demolished in 1850.

LA GRANDE PEUR. *See* **Great Fear.**

LA JAUNAIE, PACIFICATION OF. The first peace treaty between the republicans and the Vendéans, negotiated by Hoche, for the government, and Charette and Cormatin, for the Vendéans. The meeting took place at the Chateau de la Jaunaie near

Nântes on February 15, 1795. The participants swore to recognize the indivisibility of the Republic and demanded that finances should be poured into the Vendée to restore commerce and agriculture, that the young men taken into the army should be allowed to serve in the area, that other citizens without any profession should be allowed to enter into the republican army and that 2,000 of them should be organized into territorial companies to protect the localities.

LAKANAL, JOSEPH (1762-1845). Educational reformer. A priest who, when his order was suppressed, subscribed to the Civil Constitution of the Clergy *(q.v.)* and was elected to the Convention *(q.v.)*, voting for Louis XVI's death. He was a member of the Committee of Public Instruction and in 1793 was author of a bill which planned national education. The plan was rejected, but after the fall of Robespierre *(q.v.)* some of his plans were implemented, including *écoles centrales*, which operated until the establishment of *lycées* in 1802. He was also responsible for the setting up of *écoles normales* for the training of teachers.

LALLY-TOLLENDAL, TROPHIME GÉRARD, MARQUIS DE (1751-1830). Politician and son of Thomas Arthur, comte de Lally, baron de Tollendal (1702-66), who was executed for surrendering to the British army at Pondicherry in 1761. He was joined with the Third Estate in the Estates-General *(q.v.)* in 1789, but soon allied himself with the king. He held the view that France should have two legislative chambers. He later fled to England. He wrote *Defence of the French Emigrants* (1794).

LAMETH, ALEXANDRE THEODOR VICTOR, COMTE DE (1760-1829). French soldier and politician. In 1789 Lameth was elected to the Estates-General. In the Constituent Assembly he formed (with Barnave and Adrien du Port) the association called the "Trimvirate," which was made up of approximately forty advanced leftist deputies. On February 28, 1789 Lameth made a strong speech at the Jacobin Club against Mirabeau *(q.v.)*. He served in the army under Lafayette *(q.v.)* and Lockner, but was accused of treason in August 1792. Lameth fled the country, was imprisoned by the Austrians but returned to France under the Empire. He is the author of *History of the Constituent Assembly* (1828-29).

LAMETH, CHARLES MALO FRANÇOIS (1757-1832). Brother of Alexandre Lameth *(q.v.)*, he served in America and the Estates-General. He eventually emigrated and joined the Bourbons.

LAMOIGNON, CHRÉTIEN FRANÇOIS DE (1735-89). Assistant of Loménie de Brienne *(q.v.)*, who was extremely unpopular. The two were burned in effigy. Lamoignon was later found dead, either from an accident or by suicide.

LAMOURETTE, ANTOINE ADRIEN (1742-94). Bishop of Lyons and member of the Legislative Assembly *(q.v.)*. On July 7, 1792 his speech brought about a temporary reconciliation of opposing factions. (*See* **Lamourette's Kiss**.) He was later executed.

LAMOURETTE'S KISS (BAISER LAMOURETTE). Signifying an insincere or short-lasting reconciliation. On July 7, 1792 Bishop Lamourette, in a strong speech in the Legislative Assembly (q.v.), caused the different factions to lay aside their differences, but the reconciliation proved to be ephemeral.

LANJUINAIS, JEAN DENIS, COMTE DE (1753-1827). Jurist and politician who believed in constitutional monarchy. A Girondist (q.v.), he bravely opposed the trial by the Assembly of Louis XVI. When the king was found guilty, he moved a motion, which was lost, that a two-thirds majority should be necessary to carry the death penalty.

LANTERNE, LA. Group of revolutionary extremists, followers of Robespierre (q.v.), among the Montagnards (q.v.). Denunciation of them by Danton and Camille Desmoulins (qq.v.), resulted in the execution of the Dantonists in April 1794. Also, street lamp of Paris useful for hanging aristocrats.

LA ROCHEFOUCAULD-LIANCOURT, FRANÇOIS ALEXANDRE FRÉDERIC, DUC DE (1747-1827). Social reformer. He established a model farm at Liancourt and founded a school of arts and crafts for the sons of soldiers, which became in 1788 the École des Enfants de la Patrie. In 1789 he was elected to the Estates-General and became president of the Assembly. When he was placed in command of a military division in Normandy, he offered Louis XVI a refuge and then assisted him with a considerable sum of money. After August 10, 1792 La Rochefoucauld fled to England, then to America, returning to France in 1799. Later governments recognized the value of his institutions at Liancourt. He was one of the first promoters of vaccination in France and was an active member of the Central Boards of Administration for Prisons.

LAROCHEJAQUELEIN, HENRI, COMTE DE (1772-94). From August 1792 he led the Royalists in La Vendée and was successful initially in repelling the republican armies. He was defeated on December 21, 1793 and was later killed at Nouaille.

LAROCHEJAQUELEIN, LOUIS DU VERGER, MARQUIS DE (1777-1815). Brother of Henri Larochejaquelein (q.v.). He left France when the Revolution began, returning in 1801. In 1813 he headed the Royalists in La Vendée. (See **Vendéan Rebellion**.)

LAROCHEJAQUELEIN, MARIE LOUISE VICTOIRE (1772-1857). Wife of Louis du Verger (q.v.) noted for her memoirs, which were published in 1815.

LA ROCHELLE. The chief center of the Département de la Charente-Inférieure. During the Terror (q.v.) there were massacres here, including the murder of four priests on the Île d'Oléron. A National Guard army from La Rochelle was signally defeated by an inferior Vendéan force at Chantonnay on March 17, 1793, resulting in the execution of Marcé, its commander.

LAST WORDS. See **Dying Sayings**.

LA TOUR DU PIN, HENRIETTE-LUCIE DILLON, MARQUISE DE (1770-1853). Courtier who was for a short period in the service of Marie Antoinette. Her memoirs give vivid descriptions of episodes in the Revolution, with fine character studies of the leaders of all sides.

LAUSANNE. Swiss city in the canton of Vaud. Many émigrés arrived here during the Revolution and in 1795 the administrators of the city established a bureau to correspond with the Bourbons. From here emigrés easily entered France, using forged passports. Lausanne was, therefore, a center for establishing disruptive actions, plots and subplots. In 1798 the French aided the inhabitants in their insurrection against the Berne government and the Republique Lémanique was proclaimed.

LAUZUN, ARMAND-LOUIS DE GONTAUT-BIRON, DUC DE, *LATER* DUC DE BIRON (1747-93). Soldier, he became a general in the revolutionary army. He was executed in the Terror (q.v.).

LA VENDÉE. *See* **Vendéan Revolt.**

LAVOISIER, ANTOINE-LAURENT (1743-94). Chemist. He did much work on the composition of air, and discovered oxygen. He held the office of fermier général (q.v.), the proceeds of which he used to finance his experiments. He was also a member of the commission established to obtain uniformity of weights and measures, which eventually led to the metric system. When former members of the Ferme Générale were arrested and tried, he was one of the 28 executed.

McKie, D., *Lavoisier: Scientist, Economist, Social Reformer*, 1952.

LAW, CHAPELIER'S (LOI DE CHAPELIER). Law enacted on June 14, 1791 banning meetings and associations of workers or employers and making strikes illegal. It was introduced into the Assembly by Isaac René Guy Le Chapelier (1754-94, q.v.), a Breton lawyer. Although over the next century there was some easing of the right to assemble and strike, complete freedom was not achieved until 1884.

LAW OF SUSPECTS. Law passed by the Convention on September 17, 1793, during the Terror (q.v.). All citizens suspected by conduct, association, talk or writings who had shown themselves enemies of liberty were to be placed in jail.

LE BRETON, ANDRÉ-FRANÇOIS (1708-79). Publisher of the *Encyclopédie* (q.v.).

LE BRUN, CHARLES-FRANÇOIS, DUC DE PLAISANCE (PIACENZA) (1739-1824). Statesman. He was an advisor to Chancellor Maupeou and shared in his downfall in 1774. After the Revolution he professed liberal views in the Constituent Assembly (q.v.), and proposed various financial laws. At the 18 Brumaire coup (q.v.), he was made third consul and took an active part in the reorganization of finances and in the administration of the departments. In 1804

Le Brun was the arch treasurer of the empire and in 1805-06, as governor-general of Liguria, he effected its annexation to France. (*See* **Ligurian Republic**.)

LECLERC, GENERAL CHARLES VICTOR EMMANUEL (1772-1802).

Soldier. He enlisted in 1791 and in 1793 was a staff assistant in the Army of Italy, advancing to become the chief of staff of a division under General Lapoype, serving before Toulon. He served in the Italian Campaign at Castiglione and Rivoli. In 1797 he married Pauline Bonaparte (*q.v.*). In early 1798 he was appointed chief of staff to the so-called Army of Ireland, and was later transferred to the same post in the Army of England. In August 1799 he became general of division and helped further Bonaparte's fortunes in the Brumaire coup (*q.v.*). In 1801 he was the commander-in-chief of the Saint-Domingue expedition. His army disembarked in Haiti in February 1802, and after fighting Toussaint L'Ouverture (*q.v.*) for several months, Leclerc died of yellow fever on November 2, 1802.

LEDOUX, CLAUDE NICOLAS (1736-1806).

Architect, trained in the baroque and neoclassical styles of the time. He worked to break away from traditionalism; his (unexecuted) projects for spherical, cylindrical and pyramidal houses have no parallel. In 1775-79 he built the factory buildings and workmen's houses of the Royal Saltworks, the Salines de Chaux, at Arc-et-Senans in the Franche-Comté. In 1775-84 the Theater of Besançon and in 1783 the office building of the Ferme Générale were built. Four of his Parisian toll houses (barrières, *q.v.*) have survived. He was imprisoned in 1793 as a suspected Royalist. He published *L'Architecture . . .* in 1804, in which he presented his advanced designs for futuristic cities.

LEFEBVRE, FRANÇOIS JOSEPH, DUC DE DANZIG (1755-1820).

Marshal of France, he was a sergeant in the Guards at the Revolution. He fought at Fleurus (*q.v.*), Altenkirchen and Stockach. In 1799 he was in charge of the Paris military area and helped Bonaparte in the overthrow of the Directory (*q.v.*). He won the Battle of Danzig and was created duke of Danzig in 1807. He also distinguished himself in the early part of the Peninsular War. He voted for Napoleon's abdication and was made a peer. He did, however, rejoin Napoleon during the Hundred Days.

LÉGION D'HONNEUR.

An order of distinction and reward instituted by Napoleon in 1802 for either military or civil merit. Orders of chivalry had been abolished by the Constituent Assembly (*q.v.*) in 1791.

LÉGIONS.

In 1792 the Legislative Assembly (*q.v.*) ordered the formation of six small army corps, to be called "Légions." Each was composed of two battalions of light infantry, a regiment of mounted light infantrymen and one company of artillery with support (four pieces).

LEGISLATIVE ASSEMBLY.

See **Corps Legislatif, Le**

LÉMANIQUE REPUBLIC.

See **Lausanne**.

LENORMAND, MARIE (1772-1843). Fortune-teller. In Paris she was known as "The Sybil of the Faubourg Saint-Germain." Her clients included Danton, David, Desmoulins, Marat, Saint-Just and Robespierre (qq.v.). She survived the Terror and found an equally profitable role under the Directory (q.v.) and then the Empire.

LEOBEN, PRELIMINARIES OF. Following the capture of Mantua, Bonaparte pressed the campaign into the Friou, forcing Archduke Charles back into the Semmering Pass, not far from Vienna. The French had occupied Leoben on April 7, 1797. The Austrians agreed to a five-day suspension of hostilities, subsequently extended three times. Without any official authority, Bonaparte launched into full-scale negotiations, and on April 18, on the point of having his bluff called by the Austrians, the enemy suddenly agreed to sign the Preliminaries. Later the terms were embodied, in a somewhat modified form, in the peace of Campo-Formio (q.v.).

LÉON, PAULINE (1758-?). Revolutionary and feminist. In 1791 she addressed the National Assembly (q.v.) on behalf of Parisian women, suggesting that a women's militia be formed. In July 1791 she signed the petition at the Champs de Mars. Léon was a founder of the Société des Révolutionaries Républicaines with Claire Lacombe (q.v.) and became its president in 1793. She married the leader of the Enragés (q.v.), Théophile Leclerc, and they were arrested and spent some time in the Luxembourg prison. Little is known about her subsequent career.

LEOPOLD II (1747-92). Third son of Francis I and Maria Theresa, he succeeded his father as grand-duke of Tuscany in 1765 and his brother, Joseph I, as Holy Roman Emperor in 1790. He was strongly influenced by the Enlightenment (q.v.). He wished to avoid war with the revolutionaries but in 1791 he was responsible, with the Prussians, for the Declaration of Pillnitz (q.v.) which aimed at restoring Louis XVI to the throne. The Declaration was a decisive factor for the outbreak of the revolutionary wars which broke out a few weeks after the emperor's death.

LEPELLETIER DE SAINT FARGEAU, LOUIS MICHEL (1760-93). President of the Paris Parlement and deputy of the nobility to the Estates-General. A conservative at the beginning of the Revolution, he later changed his views. On July 13, 1789 he demanded the recall of Necker (q.v.) and in the Constituent Assembly (q.v.) moved the abolition of the death penalty, galleys and branding, and the substitution of beheading for hanging. On June 21, 1790 he became president of the Constituent Assembly and voted for the trial of the king and for his execution. He was hated by the Royalists and was assassinated on January 20, 1793, the eve of the king's execution, by a member of the king's body guard. He was honored by the Convention with a magnificent funeral. David (q.v.) painted a representation of his death that was later destroyed by his daughter, who was "adopted" by the nation.

LE POSTE DU SOIR. See Journal de Paris.

LE PUBLICISTE PARISIEN. *See Ami du Peuple, L'.*

LE QUESNOY, BATTLE OF. Le Quesnoy, 9 miles southeast of Valenciennes, was placed under siege by the Austrians in 1793 and capitulated after a considerable resistance. In 1794 it was retaken by Schérer and Marescot. The news reached Paris within an hour, marking the first occasion on which the aerial telegraph was used to carry army news.

LÈSE-MAJESTÉ, CRIME DE. Under the ancien régime, this referred to all crimes against the monarch, his family or the kingdom. The punishment for attacking the monarch was dismemberment by the use of four horses. The law was abolished in 1791.

LÈSE-NATION, CRIME DE. Crimes against the state, or the interests, peace and well-being of the state. Those who were involved in the attempt to spirit Louis XVI and his family out of the country were arraigned on the charge of lèse-nation, as were the marquis de Favras, who had proposed the raising of a large army on the frontiers to oppose the new constitution, Deschamps, who had been accused of stealing grain and selling it for his own profit, and others. A meeting of the Comité des Recherches Publiques of the Paris Commune met, on November 30, 1789 to examine these and a variety of like charges.

LESSART, ANTOINE NICOLAS DE WALDEC (1741-92). Advocate, master of requests, controller-general and minister. Louis XVI instructed him, with the other commissioners as conciliators, to bring together the three orders of the Estates-General. At the end of 1790 he replaced Lambert in the contrôle général des finances and then went to the interior ministry in November 1791. He was opposed to the declaration of war against Austria, which made him unpopular, and his residence was surrounded by menacing crowds. Having been accused, he decided to present himself to his judges. Convicted before the national high court, he was massacred at Versailles during the transfer of Orleanist prisoners to Paris.

LETTRE DE CACHET. *See* **Cachet, Lettres de.**

LEVÉE. Morning reception. Before the Revolution the French monarch would receive visitors at the time of his *levée* (just after rising from bed).

LEVÉE EN MASSE. An enactment in the name of the Committee of Public Safety (*q.v.*) in August 1793, requiring compulsory enlistment for military service because of the possibility of foreign invasion and also to put down internal insurrections. There had been a levée of 85,000 men in July 1792, and it had risen to 300,000 in February 1793. Applying to all able-bodied males between 18 and 25, it introduced the principle of total mobilization of the population for national defense.

LIBRAIRIE, LA. In 1559 an edict of Henry II made it punishable with death to print without authority, or the "privilège," which was printed (usually at the end) in each published text. Originally, the University of Paris had claimed the right of licencing new theological texts, but this jurisdiction was vested in the crown by an ordinance of 1566. Offences against religion were severely punished by the secular authorities. In 1626 Cardinal Richelieu declared it a capital offence to publish a work against religion or the state.

In 1723 a regulation appeared which forbade any but licenced booksellers to deal in books. At the Revolution, all of these restrictions were abolished, and the Assembly declared it to be the right of any citizen to print and publish his or her opinions.

LIBERTÉ. First word of the republican motto.

LIGURIAN REPUBLIC. Name given to the Republic of Genoa in May 1797 after the French invasion had forced it to change its constitution, a measure opposed by its nobles and priests. In 1805 it requested to be united with France, forming the three new departments of Apennins, Gênes and Montenotte, and later became part of the Kingdom of Italy.

LILLE, SIEGE OF. Chief center of the Département du Nord in 1790. During a siege in 1792, Lille held off an Austrian army for ten days. The siege, which began on September 24, 1792, was lifted by the Austrians on October 3 because of the stout resistance.

LINDET, JEAN-BAPTISTE ROBERT (1746-1825). Lawyer and politician. A member of the Legislative Assembly (1791-92) and Convention (qq.v.). He was opposed to Louis XVI, and on December 10, 1792 he published *Rapport sur les crimes imputés à Louis Capet*. Later, as a member of the Committee of Public Safety (q.v.), he was in charge of economic matters and was the only member of the Committee who did not sign the order for the execution of Danton (q.v.) and his associates. He took no part in the fall of Robespierre (q.v.) on July 27, 1794. He was arrested in May 1795 and was defended by his brother Thomas (q.v.). It is likely that he would have been found guilty but for the amnesty of October 26, 1795. For a short period in 1799 he was minister of finance under the Directory (q.v.). He was proscribed by the Restoration government in 1816 and did not return to France until shortly before his death.

LINDET, ROBERT THOMAS (1743-1823). Cleric and deputy of the clergy to the Constituent Assembly (q.v.). Brother of Jean-Baptiste Robert (q.v.). He was appointed constitutional bishop of Evre. Lindet was publicly wed in November 1792 by a married priest. Reelected by his department for the National Convention (q.v.), he voted for the king's death. After having demanded the suppression of the episcopal vicars, he renounced his episcopal position on November 7, 1793 and submitted to the Convention the letters of resignation of 16 clerics of Evreux who had followed his example.

Lindet defended his brother when he was denounced as having been one of the authors of the May 20, 1795 insurrection. A member of the Council of Ancients, he left France in 1798, was banned by the law against regicides in 1816, and traveled in Switzerland and Italy, later returning to France.

LINGUET, SIMON NICOLAS HENRI (1736-94). Lawyer and journalist. Because of his political writings he was exiled from France twice before the Revolution. He settled in London and in 1777, he found and edited the *Annales politiques, civiles, et littéraires*. Returning to France, he spent 1780-82 in the Bastille. Back in London, he continued to edit his *Annales* there, and again in Paris (1790-92). He was executed in 1794 on the charge of "having flattered the despots of Vienna and London." His *Mémoires sur la Bastille* published in London in 1783 gives a vivid picture of life in the Bastille.

LIT DE JUSTICE. Session of a *parlement (q.v.)* convened to enforce by edict an ordinance or law to which it had previously denied consent. The monarch, when in attendance, was the fount of authority. The king rested on cushions (the "lit") surrounded by peers and officials, and the decree was then read, objections heard, and the bill declared law.

LIVRE ROUGE. Book of secret expenses incurred by Louis XV and XVI. It was published in an incomplete form by the government on August 10, 1792 during the time that Louis XVI was being held at the Temple. In 1793 the administrators of Versailles found in a secret cabinet three other red books that referred to

expenses during the reign of Louis XV, and they were taken to the Convention *(q.v.)* and published the following year. The books furnished proof that Louis XVI provided funds for a large number of the émigrés.

LIVRET D'OUVRIER. Type of passport used as a means of controlling workers. Every artisan was required to carry this document giving his work record, which was endorsed by successive employers. Without the endorsement a worker was not able to find another employer. It was introduced by Turgot *(q.v.)* about 1781 and abolished in 1869.

LIVRE TOURNOIS. Basic unit of currency before the Revolution, divided into 20 *sols*, each *sol* into 12 *deniers*.

LLANWNDA. *See* **Tate, William.**

LOI LE CHAPELIER. *See* **Law, Chapelier's.**

LOMBARDY. Lombardy was conquered by the Armée d'Italie in 1796. On May 24, 1796 the Cisalpine Republic *(q.v.)* was formed. Later, in 1799, the arrival of an Anglo-Russian army, commanded by Suvarov, forced the French to retreat. After the Battle of Marengo *(q.v.)* in 1800, power again returned to the French. In 1805 Lombardy became part of the new Kingdom of Italy and finally was under Italian rule in 1859.

LOMÉNIE DE BRIENNE, ÉTIENNE CHARLES DE (1727-94). Political ecclesiastic. Brienne had a distinguished church career and was named archbishop of Toulouse in 1763. He was a friend of Turgot *(q.v.)*, André Morellet and Voltaire *(q.v.)*, and became an academician in 1770. On three occasions Brienne was the head of the Bureau de Jurisdiction at the General Assembly of the Clergy, and took an interest in social and political questions. In 1787 he was the head of the Assembly of Notables *(q.v.)*, and attacked Calonne's fiscal policies. He had succeeded Calonne as head of the Conseil des Finances in May 1787. Once in power, Brienne moved against the Parlement's intransigence regarding its refusal to register edicts on the stamp duty and the new proposed general land tax. Brienne persuaded the king to hold a *lit de justice (q.v.)*. He fell when the Parlement refused to register an edict for raising a loan of 120 million livres. On May 8, 1787 the Parlement consented to an edict for its abolition, but only on the basis that the Estates-General should be called. Brienne was attacked from all sides. He was forced to suspend the Plenary Court, which had been set up to replace the Parlement, and to promise that the Estates-General would be called. On August 29 Brienne resigned. He was made a cardinal and went to Italy. After the start of the Revolution he returned to France, where he accepted the Civil Constitution of the Clergy *(q.v.)*. This action was repudiated by the pope. He died in prison.

LONDON REVOLUTION SOCIETY. The most important of the revolutionary societies, which met annually to celebrate the Glorious Revolution in Britain (1668-69). There was no fixed constitution in 1668 but the Society supported the Whig constitutional practices. Its members included the leading Whig reformers. On November 4, 1789 the Society initiated a debate on the Revolution, with Richard Price (1723-91) speaking on "The Love of our Country." Price welcomed the Revolution, urged the repeal of the Test Acts and demanded parliamentary reform in Britain. This occasion inspired Burke to write *Reflections on the Revolution in France* (1790).

LONGWY, BATTLE OF. Fortified town in the Moselle district, on the Belgian border, that had fallen to the Prussians on August 23, 1792. It was retaken by the French on October 22. The town's administrators were arrested for not having put forward a sufficiently strong defense against the enemy.

L'ORIENT. French flag-ship, *L'Orient,* blew up during the battle of the Nile on August 1, 1798. Admiral Brueys and about 900 men were killed.

L'ORIENT. Maritime town of the Département du Morbihan. It was a free port and named after the Eastern countries with which the French East India Company traded. A naval battle was fought on June 23, 1795 between Vice Admiral Lord Bridport (Great Britain) and Villaret-Joyeuse (France). Lord Bridport was the victor and there was considerable loss of French lives. It was used as a center of operations by Hoche *(q.v.)*, in his successful strikes against the attempted Anglo-émigré invasion of France through Quiberon Bay in 1795.

LOUIS XV (1710-74). Louis XV succeeded his great-grandfather to the throne at the age of 5, in 1715. For part of his reign he was guided by the able statesman André Hercule de Fleury but when Fleury died in 1743 Louis did not appoint a successor and proved to be unable to rule forcefully. The loss of Canada and other colonial possessions and the expense involved in the War of Austrian Succession (1741-48) and the Seven Years' War (1756-63) increased the country's economic difficulties, which led directly to the Revolution in 1789.

Gooch, George Peabody, *Louis XV: The Monarchy in Decline*, 1956.

LOUIS XVI (1754-93). Son of Louis, dauphin of France, and of Marie Joseph of Saxony; brother of Louis XVIII (*q.v.*) and Charles X (*q.v.*). He succeeded his grandfather, Louis XV, to the throne in 1774. He was reasonably well-intentioned but lacked the will to govern progressively and was dominated by his wife, the Austrian Marie Antoinette (*q.v.*), whom he married in 1770. Louis was faced with a legacy of a half-century's financial bankruptcy on a national level. He wavered between courses of action, in 1776 disposing of the able Turgot (*q.v.*), who might have discovered a reasonable solution to France's great economic problems. Louis led the country into involvement in the American Revolutionary War (*q.v.*) in 1778 and Necker (*q.v.*) had to finance this successful but ruinously expensive transatlantic venture.

The Estates-General was called in 1789, leading to revolution in June of that year. Louis was forced to reside at Paris. He trusted Mirabeau (*q.v.*) for a while, and then dropped him. His attempt on June 21, 1791 to flee with his family to the Austrian Netherlands cost him the respect and trust of his people, and his willingness to take the oath to the new constitution on September 9 impressed no one. In August 1792 the armies of the First Coalition marched into France and the Paris mob threatened to murder the royal family. On August 10 Louis was forced to seek sanctuary within the building of the National Assembly. The monarchy was declared suspended, and Louis was brought to trial for alleged treason against France. He refused to plead and was guillotined on January 21, 1793. The revolutionaries called him "Monsieur Veto" and "Louis Capet."

Fay, B., *Louis XVI, or, the End of a World*, 1968.

Padover, S. K., *Life and Death of Louis XVI*, Rev. ed. 1963.

LOUIS XVII (1785-95). Titular king of France 1793-95. Second son of Louis XVI, he became dauphin on the death of his brother in 1789. His death is rumored to have taken place on June 8, 1795 as a result of neglect and ill-treatment. Over 30 people subsequently claimed to be the dauphin. *See also* **Orphans in the Temple.**

Castelet, A., *Louis XVII*, 1960.

LOUIS XVIII (1755-1824). Brother of Louis XVI and Charles X. He escaped over the French frontier to Brussels in June 1791 and was a leader of the émigré army at Coblenz. After the execution of his brother, he reigned for two years as regent-in-exile for the imprisoned Louis XVII (*q.v.*). On the latter's death he was regarded by the supporters of the House of Bourbon as the rightful king of France. Louis established a small court at Verona, but moved to England after the death of his wife and while French armies conquered northern Italy. He hoped that Bonaparte would restore him to the throne. In April 1814 Louis returned to Paris as King and accepted the terms of the Treaty of Paris, which limited France to its 1792 boundaries, and attempted to gain his people's support. The situation was soon out of control due to vengeful, reactionary ex-émigrés, and Louis was forced back into Belgium in March 1815 as Bonaparte returned from Elba. Louis was restored after the Hundred Days and Waterloo, but was forced to accept the harsher terms of the Second Treaty of Paris.

LOUIS CAPET. *See* **Louis XVI.**

LOUISETTE. *See* **Guillotine, La.**

LOUISIANA Claimed for France by La Salle in 1682, it was named after Louis XIV and covered all land drained by the Mississippi and its tributaries. To avoid Louisiana falling to the British, it was ceded to Spain in 1762 by the Treaty of Fontainebleau. Spanish control was not complete until 1769. Bonaparte forced the retrocession of Louisiana to France in 1800. Renewed fears of a British invasion led to the Louisiana purchase, in which France sold the territory to the United States for $15 million in 1803.
Whitaker, A. P., *The Mississippi Question 1795-1803*. Reprinted 1962.

LOUIS LE GRAND, COLLÈGE.
Founded in 1550 by the Jesuits in the Rue de la Harpe, it was transferred 14 years later to the Rue Saint-Jacques in the old Hôtel de Langres under the title Collège de Clermont de la Société de Jésus. The Jesuits were expelled from France in 1594 and the Collège was closed until 1603. Joining with the Collèges de Marmoutier and du Mans (1641 and 1682), it became the Collège Louis le Grand, developing a brilliant reputation, until it was again closed in 1762. Voltaire (*q.v.*), Robespierre (*q.v.*) and Camille Desmoulins (*q.v.*) were students here. It was reorganized in 1792, when it became the Institut de l'Égalité.

LOUIS PHILIPPE (1773-1850). King of the French 1830-48. Eldest son of Philippe, duc d'Orléans (Philippe Égalité, *q.v.*). Louis Philippe fought at Valmy and Jemappes (*qq.v.*) but in 1793 went into exile, living in Switzerland, the United States and England until 1815. When Charles X was deposed in 1830 he was succeeded by Louis Philippe, who was known as the "Citizen King." This régime was known as the July Monarchy. When the barricades went up in February 1848, following Louis Philippe's ban on a meeting for franchise reform, he fled to England, where he died.
Haworth, T. E. B., *Citizen King*, 1961.

LOUVET DE COUVRAY, JEAN-BAPTISTE (1760-97). Politician and author. He was a member of the Convention and edited a wall newsheet *La Sentinelle*. When the Girondins (*q.v.*) were overthrown in 1793, he left Paris. Returning in 1794, he retook his seat in the Convention (*q.v.*). Under the Directory (*q.v.*) he was a member of the Council of Five Hundred (*q.v.*). He wrote the novel *Les Amours du Chevalier de Faublas* (1786-91).

LOUVRE. Former royal palace of the French kings in Paris. The present buildings were begun by Francis I in 1541. Since 1793 the greater part of the Louvre has been used for a national museum and art gallery. The private collections of the kings of France were the nucleus of the present collection of paintings.
Bazin, Germain, *The Louvre*, 1971.

LUNÉVILLE, TREATY OF. Treaty signed on February 9, 1801 in the town of the same name, which ended the European fighting in the War of the Second Coalition (*q.v.*). The French were represented by Joseph Bonaparte, the Austrians by the comte de Cobentzel. The treaty fixed one part of the limits of France, from the Rhine to the Alps. The Milanese stayed with the République Cisalpine, Tuscany was given to Ferdinand IV. The treaty was declared as equally applicable to the Batavian, Helvetic, Cisalpine and Ligurian republics (*qq.v.*), and their independence was recognized. Emperor Francis II (*q.v.*) received as indemnities only the Venetian states to the Adige, and the fortresses on the left bank of the Rhine, which were dismantled.

LUXEMBOURG, PALAIS DU. Palace on the left bank of the Seine in Paris, built by Salomon de Brosse in 1615-27 for Marie de' Medicis, widow of Henry IV. During the Terror (*q.v.*) it was converted into the largest political prison, holding 2,000 people, including Danton and Desmoulins (*qq.v.*). In 1795 the seat of government was moved from the Tuileries to the Luxembourg, and since 1799 it has been the usual seat of the upper house of the legislature, now the Senate.

LYCÉE. Type of secondary school.

LYCÉE DES ARTS. Society founded in 1792 to encourage the arts and useful sciences. Initially the society, established in the circus of the Jardin du Palais-Royal, provided free tuition for the young. Throughout the Revolution it aimed at solving practical problems in agriculture and manufacturing. The circus was burned down in 1799 and the society moved to the oratory and then to a room in the Hôtel de Ville, where, in 1803, it changed its name to Athenée des Arts de Paris.

LYONS. City of southern France of the department of the Rhône, 240 miles south-southeast of Paris and 170 north of Marseilles. In 1793 the Royalists and Girondists (*q.v.*) rose against the Convention (*q.v.*), but were forced to yield to Kellermann (*q.v.*) after a siege of seven weeks, ending on October 10. There were terrible retributions, with the city's name changed to Ville Affranchie, wholesale demolition of buildings, and those who had escaped the scaffold mown down with grapeshot. The city took back its old name after the fall of Robespierre (*q.v.*), and the terrorists were drowned in large numbers in the Rhône. Its swift recovery as an economic center was partly due to the invention here of the Jacquard loom in 1802.

MABILAIS, PEACE OF. A "suspension of hostilities," signed in the Château de la Mabilais on 3 Floréal, Year III, between the chiefs of the Vendéan army and the representatives Guezno and Guermeur, in an attempt to end the civil war.

MACHAULT-D'ARNOUVILLE, LOUIS CHARLES DE (1737-1820). Bishop of Amiens, he was famous for his charity but excessively conservative. In the Estates-General he voted consistently against every reform.

MACHINE INFERNALE, COMPLOT DE LA. A bomb attack on Bonaparte on December 24, 1800, when a cart loaded with explosives was detonated in the Rue de Richelieu, causing considerable destruction and loss of life. The first consul suffered no harm.

MACKINTOSH, SIR JAMES (1765-1832). Scottish writer. His *Vindiciae Gallicae* (1791) was written in response to Burke's *Reflections on the French Revolution*. It was less radical than Paine's writings and it represented Whig sympathies with the early stages of the Revolution. It had a wide circulation and went through three editions. Mackintosh was liberal but became disenchanted with the Revolution. As its secretary, he defended the Friends of the People against Pitt (*q.v.*), but moved away from radical events in France, seeing them as having rejected reason and talent.

MADAME ROYALE. Title given to Marie-Thérèse de France, the eldest daughter of Louis XVI and Marie Antoinette. Later, she became the duchesse d'Angoulème by her marriage to her cousin. Also, the title "Madame" was reserved for the eldest daughter of the king, the dauphin or the wife of the king's oldest brother, who was known as "Monsieur." "Mesdames de France" were the younger daughters of the king and they used the title "Madame" followed by their first name.

MADELEINE, ÉGLISE DE LA. It was first a chapel, founded in 1493, and created a Paris parish in 1639. It was too small for the growing population of the Faubourg Saint-Honoré, so the princesse d'Orléans constructed a large church in 1660. This was suppressed in 1790, sold, demolished and converted into a chantry. An even larger church had been started in 1754. In 1792 the Convention (*q.v.*) was installed in this second church. The present church was started in 1806 and was finished in 1842.

MADELONNETTES PRISON. Prison situated in the Rue Fontaine-du-Temple, in the old convent of the same name. Before the Revolution it served as a hostel for "les filles débauchées." In 1793 it was changed to a public prison. The abbé Barthélemy, Saint-Prix, Fleury and the other actors of the Comédie-Française were detained here.

MADEMOISELLE. Title of the first princess of the blood royal while unmarried, or of the daughter of the king's eldest brother, "Monsieur."

MAINMORTE. Literally "dead hand." A feudal condition under which a serf, who was tied in perpetuity to his land, could not change his domicile. On his death, if his children decided to move, all the possessions left went directly to his lord. It was abolished in 1789.

MAIRE DE PARIS. *See* **Mayor of Paris.**

MAÎTRES DES REQUÊTES. *See* **Masters of Requests.**

MALESHERBES, CHRÉTIEN-GUILLAUME DE LAMOIGNON DE (1721-94). Statesman. He acted as a tolerant censor of the press, and it was he who sanctioned the publication of the *Encyclopédie*. In 1771 he opposed abuses of the law by the king. In 1774 he again took office but resigned on the dismissal of Turgot *(q.v.)*. He defended Louis XVI before the Convention *(q.v.)* and was arrested in December 1793 and guillotined on April 22, 1794 together with his daughter and her husband.

MALLET DU PAN, JACQUES (1749-1800). French journalist and pioneer of modern political journalism. He was coeditor with H. S. N. Linguet *(q.v.)* in the production of *Annales Politiques* (1778-80), running the paper by himself while Linguet was in the Bastille (1781-83). He changed the title of his own publication to *Mémoires Historiques* in 1783. From this time, he incorporated this work with the *Mercure de France*, where he had been given responsibility for its political direction. At the Revolution, Mallet du Pan sided with the Royalists. From 1791 to 1792, he was in Frankfurt, where he had been sent by Louis XVI to try and gain the support of the German princes. He published violently antirevolutionary pamphlets, attacked Bonaparte and the Directory *(q.v.)*, and was exiled to Berne (1797). Mallet du Pan went to England, where he founded the *Mercure Britannique*.

MAILLARD, STANISLAS MARIE (1763-94). Born at Gournay, he was a clerk in the office of his brother, a bailiff at the Chatelet *(q.v.)*, and took part in the events of July 14, 1789. Under the rifle bullets, he arranged the surrender agreed by de Launay, the governor of the Bastille, and was made captain of the Company of the Vainqueurs de la Bastille. On October 5, Maillard was involved in organizing the mob, which was going to Versailles to force the royal family to return to Paris. Captain of the National Guard in 1790, Maillard was accused by Marat *(q.v.)* of espionage, but forced the latter to make a public retraction of these charges (January 21, 1791).

During the 1792 massacres *(q.v.)*, Maillard was at the Abbaye *(q.v.)* at the moment when the crowd was organizing to force the doors and gates in order to let out the prisoners. He died in 1794.

MALOUET, PIERRE VICTOR (1740-1814). Deputy for Riom in the Constituent Assembly *(q.v.)*, where he sat at the head of the constitutionalists. He founded the Club des Impartiaux or Club Monarchique, which were influential with the king, and they aimed to guide policy. Malouet voted for the reunion of the three orders and against the "Rights of Man" proceedings.

MALTA. Island in the Mediterranean, between the North African coast and Sicily, the headquarters of the ancient Order of Saint John of Jerusalem. On June 9, 1798 Bonaparte, with his expedition heading for Egypt, demanded entrance into the harbor of Valetta but this was refused by the Order because of their neutrality. Bonaparte entered and garrisoned the town, leaving on June 19. The British retook Malta on September 5, 1800 with the Peace of Amiens *(q.v.)* returning the island to the Order. The 1815 treaties then gave it to Great Britain.

MAMELUKES. Troops in the service of the Sultan of Egypt who held great power in the country, under the leadership of Mourad Bey and Ibrahim Bey, toward the end of the 18th century. They were tremendous fighters but were badly beaten at the Battle of the Pyramids (1798). Bonaparte formed a Mameluke company for his consular guard.

MANÈGE. Court adjoining the Terrace des Feuillants, where the Constituent Assembly *(q.v.)* and later the Legislative Assembly *(q.v.)*, held their meetings. Here the king and queen stayed on the night of August 10, 1792. The Convention was installed here on May 10, 1793 and the Council of Ancients worked from here toward the end of 1795.

MANNHEIM. A fortified town in the Palatinate, at the confluence of the Neckar and the Rhine, which served as a secure spot for émigrés (1791-92). It was occupied by the Austrians, helped by the elector Palatine. The Army of the Rhin-et-Moselle placed the fortress under siege, and it was forced to capitulate to Pichegru *(q.v.)* on September 19, 1795. It was attacked by the Austrians on February 8, 1798. In September 1799 it was the scene of an extended battle between the Austrians and the French, the French being forced to retreat to the left bank of the Rhine. The Treaty of Lunéville *(q.v.)* (1801) gave Mannheim to the Grand Duchy of Baden.

MANTUA. Fortified city, the chief center of the old Legation of the same name, in Venetia. It capitulated to Bonaparte after a siege, February 2, 1797, and this victory allowed him to engage all his forces against Archduke Karl of Austria.

MARAT, JEAN PAUL (1743-93). French revolutionary politician born near Neuchâtel, Switzerland. Marat traveled in Holland and Britain, where he obtained a medical degree at St. Andrews, Scotland. Before the Revolution he was physician to the guards of the compte d'Artois (q.v.) but from 1789 he gave up medicine and engaged in journalism, editing *L'Ami du peuple*, in which he continuously expressed his hate of all those in authority. He fled to England in 1790 and 1791, and even in Paris, on one occasion, he was forced to hide in the sewers. His writings were responsible for bringing about the atmosphere which caused the September Massacres (q.v.) in Paris. He was elected to the Convention (q.v.) in 1792 and supported the Jacobins (q.v.) in the bitter conflict with the Girondists (q.v.), who dominated the Convention. On July 13, 1793 he was murdered in his bath by a Girondist sympathizer, Charlotte Corday (q.v.).

Gottschalk, L. R., *Jean Paul Marat*, 1967.

MARC D'ARGENT. The sum of 54 livres demanded by royal decree of January 24, 1789 to qualify for election to the Estates-General. This amount was suppressed by decree, and on August 27, 1791 a charge of one livre was established.

MARENGO, BATTLE OF. A village near Alessandra in northwest Italy, Marengo was the scene of a considerable victory by Bonaparte over the Austrians on June 14, 1800. The Austrians were led by Baron Friedrich von Melas and it seemed that victory would be his, but General Desaix de Veygoux (1768-1800), who was killed in the battle, brought in more troops with the result there was a successful counterattack. The French dead totaled about 5,800 and the Austrians, 9,400.

MARIE ANTOINETTE (1755-93). Queen of France. Daughter of Holy Roman Emperor Francis I and Maria Theresa, in 1770 she married Louis, the dauphin, who became King Louis XVI in 1774. Generally disliked by her subjects, she was blamed for the state of French finances because of her opposition to plans for their improvement by Turgot and Necker (qq.v.). She was known as "Madame Deficit" and "Madame Veto." Although unjustly accused in the Diamond Necklace Affair (q.v.), her guilt was taken for granted because of her extravagance.

She proved to have a stronger and more determined will than Louis and became increasingly influential in royal councils, influencing the king's decisions to resist reforms. Her intrigues with Austria prompted the storming of the Tuileries (q.v.) in 1792, during which she and Louis were captured and accused of treason. Louis was executed in January 1793 and the Queen was placed in solitary confinement in the Conciergerie. She was tried as "Widow Capet" before the revolutionary tribunal on October 14 and guillotined on October 16. Her first son had died in 1789, her second son, who became Louis XVII, died in prison in 1795.

Bernier, Olivier, *Imperial Mother, Royal Daughter: The Correspondence of Marie Antoinette and Maria Theresa*, 1986.

Castelot, André, *Marie-Antoinette*. Translation, 1957.

Kunstler, Charles, *The Personal Life of Marie-Antoinette*. Translation, 1940.

MARSEILLAISE, LA. French revolutionary marching song and French national anthem (from 1870). The words and music were written by Claude Rouget de Lisle (1760-1835) on April 24, 1792. It was sung in Paris by troops from Marseilles on their entry into the city and hence its name.

MARSHAL OF FRANCE. High military officers were honored by this title. In 1788 there were 20 marshals of France. The title was suppressed in 1793 but revived by Napoleon in 1804.

MARTELLO TOWERS. Round towers formerly used for coastal defense standing about forty feet high. Many of them were built on the Southeast coast of England about 1803 against the threat of French invasion. They took their name from Mortella Point in Corsica, where a similar tower had proved extremely difficult to capture in 1794.

MARY-ANNE (MARIANNE). Its origins are not certain but it has been suggested that the name may have arisen during the Terror *(q.v.)*, when, at a fête at Montpellier, the Goddess of Reason was impersonated by a "Marianne," the local term for a woman of easy virtue. It was an antirepublican nickname and also the name given to the republic of 1792, to the guillotine, and to small statuettes of Liberty.

MASSACRES. *See* **Champ de Mars** (1791) and **September Massacres** (1792).

MASSÉNA, ANDRÉ (1758-1817). French soldier. He served in the army of Louis XVI and in the Revolution, and in 1793 became a general of division. He served in most of the battles and distinguished himself in the campaigns in upper Italy, gained his great victory at Zürich in 1799 and became marshal of the empire in 1804. Later he was created duke of Rivoli and prince of Essling.

MASSIAC, CLUB. Formed at the beginning of the Revolution by the colonists of Saint-Domingue, it was antirevolutionary and against the enfranchisement of the slaves.

MASTERS OF REQUESTS (MAÎTRES DES REQUÊTES). There were two offices, "Maîtres des Comptes" and "Maîtres des Requêtes de l'Hôtel du Roi." Both were top-ranking magistrates in the "Chambres des Comptes," originally judges with jurisdiction over officers of the royal household. The king took to using them for special investigations in all parts of the administration, on which they reported directly to him in his council. In 1787 the number of Masters of Requests was limited to 67.

MAURY, JEAN-SIFFREIN, ABBÉ (1746-1817). French prelate, ecclesiastical writer and politician. In 1789 he was a member of the Constituent Assembly *(q.v.)* and defended the monarchy and the church. He was rewarded by Pius VI by being appointed a cardinal in 1794 after he had left France. He returned in 1804 and was created archbishop of Paris by Napoleon in 1810.

MAXIMUM. Fixing of prices in 1793-94 by the National Assembly (*q.v.*), to control the highest prices at which a merchant could sell his products. It was brought in partly because of the general scarcity of goods throughout the country and because of pervasive fear of Royalist plots and profiteering. On September 28-29, 1793 a price-regulating decree was passed, covering a comprehensive list of goods and services. Each merchant was required to show clearly the highest prices being charged. If he was found to be overcharging, he was placed on the suspects' list and charged double the value of the goods that he had sold. The Maximum was felt to be contrary to the spirit of free commerce, and was suppressed by the Convention (*q.v.*) on December 10, 1794 (*q.v.*).

MAY EDICTS. Attempt by the monarchy to reduce the power of the magistracy. Loménie de Brienne (*q.v.*), archbishop of Toulouse, the successor to Calonne (*q.v.*, who had been dismissed from office on April 8, 1788) was charged with this responsibility. On May 8, 1788 Louis XVI held a *lit de justice (q.v.)* to enforce edicts designed by Lamoignon (*q.v.*), the keeper of the seals, to destroy the political power of the *parlements* (*q.v.*). The edicts established a plenary court for the registration of royal legislation, and 47 bailiwicks to take over much of the *parlements'* judicial work. It was, however, too late. The monarchy was shortly to be committed to calling the Estates-General, a move recommended by the notables, and now demanded by the assembly of the clergy, the public and the magistracy. Lamoignon's attempted reforms provoked the magistrates into stirring up provincial revolts and the reforms were suspended.

MAYENCE, BATTLE OF. A large fortified town in the province of Hesse-Rhenane, on the Rhine near the opening of the Main. It was placed under siege by Custine on October 19, 1792 and taken two days later. The king of Prussia, in turn, put the town under siege with a considerable force, from the end of March 1793 to July 24, 1793, when the French army were permitted to leave with honor. The treaty of Campo Formio gave Mayence to France in 1797, when it became the chief center of the Département du Mont-Tonnerre.

MAYOR OF PARIS (MAIRE DE PARIS). The first magistrate of the city of Paris, his powers were suspended on June 20, 1792. The Convention (*q.v.*) divided Paris into 12 municipalities, each with its own mayor. It was held that those who controlled Paris could, in fact, greatly influence or usurp the central government and this new system considerably reduced the powers of the mayor of Paris.

MAZARIN, COLLEGE. Founded in 1664 by Cardinal Mazarin for the instruction of gentlemen's children from Pignerolles, Alsace, Germany, the church state of Flanders and Roussillon. It was located on the left bank of the Seine and possessed a fine library. During the Revolution, it served as a prison for some time and the Committee of Public Safety (*q.v.*) held its meetings here in 1793-94.

MENU PEUPLE. Term used before the Revolution to describe minor, lesser, base or ignoble people, the rabble, or those who did not own property or were not of the robe or the sword, with no social position or power and no economic strength.

MÉRICOURT, ANNE JOSEPHE THÉROIGNE DE (1762-1817). Revolutionary. She was born in Belgium. After living in England and France she trained as a singer in Italy. In 1789 she returned to Paris and became a revolutionary organizer and leader. She was at the storming of the Bastille (q.v.) and led the women's march to Versailles in October 1789. In 1790 she was forced to leave France and she planned a revolutionary journal to be published in Liège but was arrested by the Austrians and was imprisoned at Kuffstein and later in Vienna. She returned to Paris in 1792 and organized women's clubs, with some opposition from the men, in the Faubourg St.-Antoine. In 1793 she became involved in party conflict, siding with the Girondists (q.v.), and lost popularity. She was publicly attacked and beaten by Parisian women. She was arrested in 1794, and although she was imprisoned for a short period it was found that her mind had become deranged and she was kept in an asylum for the last 20 years of her life.

MERLIN, "DE THIONVILLE", ANTOINE CHRISTOPHE (1762-1833). Politician and lawyer. During the Revolution he was called "of Thion" to distinguish himself from Merlin "of Douai." He studied theology and later law, and in 1788 was an *avocat* at the Metz parliament. In 1790 he was a member of the Legislative Assembly (q.v.) and on October 23, 1791 he moved and carried the institution of the Committee of Surveillance, of which he became a member. He proposed the law sequestrating the property of émigrés. He was a deputy to the National Convention (q.v.) and pressed for the execution of Louis XVI, but actually missed the trial because he was at that period on a mission to Mainz. He took part in the Thermidorean reaction following the fall of Robespierre (q.v.) and sat in the Council of Five Hundred under the Directory (qq.v.). He participated in the coup d'état of 18 Fructidor (September 4, 1797) where he demanded the deportation of some republicans. In 1798 he was appointed director general of posts and organized the Army of Italy. He retired completely from public life at the Consulate.

MERLIN, PHILIPPE-ANTOINE, COMTE (1754-1838). Jurist called "Merlin de Douai." He was a member of the Constituent Assembly (q.v.) of 1789 and was responsible for the drafting and passage of important legislation abolishing feudal and other rights of the ancien régime. He was a member of the Convention (q.v.) and voted for Louis XVI's death. He was one of the most active members of the Committee of Public Safety (q.v.) and drafted much of the legislation dealing with crimes and punishments that was enacted in 1795. He was minister of justice in 1795 under the Directory (q.v.) and on September 4, 1797 he became one of the five Directors, resigning in 1799. Although he did not help in the drafting of the Code Napoleon (q.v.) he was the leading lawyer to interpret it.

MERVEILLEUSES. Term applied to extravagantly dressed women of the period of the Thermidorian reaction who were the feminine counterpart of Muscadins (*q.v.*). (*See also* **Thermidor Revolution.**)

MESSIDOR. Harvest month, June 19 to July 18. See **Calendar, Revolutionary.**

MÉTAYAGE. Cultivation of land for an owner who receives a proportion of the produce. Under the ancien régime, not only were all direct taxes paid by the *métayer* (*q.v.*), the landowner being exempt, but these taxes were pitched according to the quantity of produce, thus dampening any incentive to increase the land's production. The farmer had no fixed tenure, and could be withdrawn at the landowner's pleasure.

MÉTAYER. Sharecropper.

METRIC SYSTEM. Before the Revolution there was no uniformity in French weights and measures. In 1790 the Constituent Assembly (*q.v.*), at the insistence of Talleyrand (*q.v.*), decreed that a single system of weights and measures was essential. Scientific bodies were given the task of measuring an arc of the meridian between Dunkirk and Barcelona, and from their calculations the *mètre*, which is equal to a ten-millionth part of the distance between the poles and the equator (3.2808 feet) was made the unit of length and the base of the system by law in 1795. The system was completed in 1799 and made compulsory November 2, 1801, to the exclusion of all other systems.

MICHAUD, JOSEPH FRANÇOIS (1767-1839). French historian and publicist. He worked in Lyon where he became antirevolutionary. In 1791 he went to Paris where he edited several Royalist journals. In 1796 he was the editor of *La Quotidienne* and was arrested. Michaud escaped and was sentenced to death by the military council. On the establishment of the Directory (*q.v.*), he resumed his editorship and was proscribed on 18 Fructidor (*q.v.*). He returned to Paris when the Consulate (*q.v.*) replaced the Directory (*q.v.*). He was briefly imprisoned in 1800 for pro-Bourbon sympathies.

MIRABEAU, ANDRÉ BONIFACE RIQUETI, VICOMTE DE (1754-92). Soldier and politician, son of Victor Mirabeau (1715-89), brother of Honoré Mirabeau (1749-91, *q.v.*). He fought in the American army (1780-85), and at the outbreak of the Revolution was elected to the Estates-General. He led a force of émigrés against the Republic but was accidentally killed at Freiburg-im-Breisgau.

MIRABEAU, HONORÉ GABRIEL RIQUETI, COMTE DE (1749-91). Statesman and great orator. Son of Victor Mirabeau (1715-89), his face was badly disfigured by smallpox, which contributed to his father's dislike of him. Wild and extravagant he was imprisoned more than once and was sentenced to death. He traveled abroad, sometimes as a secret agent, until he returned to France before the Revolution. When the Estates-General were convened he was rejected as a representative by the Provençal noblesse but was returned for the Third Estate (*q.v.*) for both Aix and Marseilles. He sat for the former, and was present at the opening on May 4, 1789. He wished to bring in a system similar to that of the English constitution. To Mirabeau is attributed the successful consolidation of the National Assembly *(q.v.)*. He saw the fall of the Bastille *(q.v.)* as being impractical, as were the reforms of August 4, believing that there was no point in destroying the old régime before a new one was constituted. On November 7, 1789 the Assembly decreed that no member could become a minister. This overturned all of Mirabeau's hopes to see government on the English model.

From May 1790 to April 1791 Mirabeau worked closely with the court but never became a Royalist. In the case of peace and war, he supported the king's authority and felt that the French had the right to conduct their own revolution without outside interference. He was elected a member of the Diplomatic Committee in July 1790, becoming its reporter, and was able to prevent the Assembly from doing much harm in foreign affairs. Mirabeau anticipated that much had to be done internally to break down Louis's distrust and to moderate and direct reforms. Otherwise, there would be catastrophic foreign interference. His health failed and he could not win the confidence of the king.

Welch, O. J. G., *Mirabeau: A Study of a Democratic Monarchist*, 1951.

MONGE, GASPARD, COMTE DE PÉLUSE (1746-1818). French mathematician and the inventor of descriptive geometry. In 1768 he was a professor of mathematics and in 1771 a professor of physics at Mézières. In 1780 he was presented with a chair of hydraulics at the lyceum in Paris. He became a member of the Academie,

and in 1785 he was appointed examiner of naval candidates. He disvered the ordinary differential equation of curvature, and related his discovery of the production of water by the combustion of hydrogen (1783), results anticipated by Henry Cavendish. He served on the committee examining the use of the metric system *(q.v.)* and in 1792 the Legislative Assembly *(q.v.)* gave him the office of minister of marine, which he held until April 1793. The Committee of Public Safety *(q.v.)* appealed to scientists to produce materials for the defense of France, and Monge's contribution was *The Art of Manufacturing Cannon* and *Advice to Iron Workers in Steel Production*. He went with the Egyptian expedition, 1798-1801. After the fall of Bonaparte, Monge was deprived of all honors and excluded from membership of the reconstituted Institute.

MONITEUR UNIVERSEL. Liberal newspaper, established in Paris by Charles Joseph Panckoucke (1736-98). It was a daily paper from November 24, 1789, and the organ of the government from December 28, 1799. It had a wide circulation and reproduced official documents, reported National Assembly business, home and foreign politics, and had sections on literature. It outlasted the Revolution by trimming its views to suit the government of the day. It closed in 1868 and was superseded by the *Journal Officiel* on January 1, 1869.

MONSIEUR. Under the ancien régime this was the form of address used to designate the oldest brother of the king. In its general sense it was accepted by all classes in the country, but by the end of 1792, "Monsieur" was replaced by "Citoyen," "Madame" by "Citoyenne." After 9 Thermidor *(q.v.)* it was less used, returning under the Directory *(q.v.)*. The title was attached to one's title or job-description, e.g., "Citoyen-Général," "Citoyen-Boucher."

MONSIEUR VÉTO. *See* **Louis XVI.**

MONTAGNARDS, LES. *See* **Mountain, The.**

MONT DE PIETE DE PARIS. Institution for loans given on receipt of a deposit, founded on December 9, 1777 and set up in the Rue des Blancs-Manteaux. It moved into its own buildings in 1786, modeled on the Monts-de-Piete of Italy. It quickly came into public favor and soon had a massive circulation of capital. Although the Mont was carefully supervised the initial moderate rates of interest had risen so high by 1793 that calls were made for the institution to be closed down. A Convention *(q.v.)* decree of January 22, 1794 tightened considerably the business practices of the Mont. By 1797, again under decree, the Mont was reorganized and placed under tighter scrutiny and control. In addition there were many Monts established between 1577-1781 outside Paris.

MONTMÉDY. Town near the Luxembourg border that was the objective of Louis XVI's escape from Paris on June 20, 1791, which ended in his apprehension at Varennes *(q.v.)*.

MONTMORIN DE SAINT HÉREM, ARMAND MARC, COMTE DE (1745-92). Statesman. Gentleman-in-waiting to Louis XVI when he was dauphin, then ambassador to Madrid and later governor of Brittany. In 1787 he succeeded Vergennes *(q.v.)* at the Ministry of Foreign Affairs. He was an admirer of Necker *(q.v.)*, whose influence at the court he helped to maintain. Montmorin retired when Necker was dismissed (July 12, 1789) but resumed his office when Necker was recalled after the fall of the Bastille *(q.v.)*, and held his position until October 1791. Montmorin also helped Honoré Mirabeau *(q.v.)* establish relationships with the court, concerning the latter's plan for the policy to be adopted by the court toward the new Estates-General. It was a strange relationship with the feeble and uncertain Montmorin holding the title and position, Mirabeau the real power. After Mirabeau's death (April 1791) and the flight of the royal family to Varennes *(q.v.)*, Montmorin was forced to resign, but he still advised Louis and was one of the close circle of the king's friends, known as the "Austrian Committee." His papers were seized and although nothing compromising was found, he was denounced, proscribed and called before the Legislative Assembly. He perished in the Abbaye *(q.v.)* prison during the September Massacres *(q.v.)*.

MOREAU, JEAN-VICTOR MARIE (1763-1813). General in the revolutionary army, he was born in Brittany. His father was a lawyer who had been guillotined. He fought on the Rhine and was the victor of Hohenlinden. He was later exiled for his part in Royalist plots (1804) against Napoleon and went to America, returning to Europe only in 1813 to fight for Russia against France, and was killed in action.

MORTIER. Ceremonial black velvet cap worn by parlementary presidents.

MOUNIER, JEAN JOSEPH (1758-1806). French politician and lawyer, Mounier took part in the struggle between the parlements (q.v.) and the court in 1788, and promoted the meeting of the estates of Dauphine at Vizille on July 20, 1788. He became the secretary of the Assembly (q.v.), and drafted the grievances and remonstrances that it presented to the king. Mounier was elected a deputy of the Third Estate to the 1789 Estates-General (q.v.). There he proposed the Tennis Court Oath (q.v.), assisted in the preparation of the new constitution and demanded the return of Necker (q.v.). He was elected as president of the Constituent Assembly (q.v.) in September 1789, withdrawing, however, in 1790 and taking refuge in Switzerland. He returned in 1801 and was named as prefect of the departement of Ille-et-Vilaine by Bonaparte, and in 1805 was appointed a councillor of state.

MOUNTAIN, THE. Members of the extreme revolutionary party in the Legislative Assembly and National Convention (qq.v.), so named because they sat on the highest benches on the left side of the parliament. Their leaders were, at various times, Danton, Marat, St. Just and Robespierre (qq.v.). They believed in the centralization of government. At first they were a small group but finally they numbered more than a third of the Convention. They overthrew the Girondins (q.v.), directed the policy of the Jacobins (q.v.), supported the execution of the king, initiated the Terror (q.v.), and finally brought down Robespierre, but were soon themselves victims of the Thermidorian reaction. (See **Thermidor Revolution.**)

MURAT, JOACHIM (1767-1815). French marshal and king of Naples, son of an innkeeper. He was an early associate of, and later aide-de-camp to, Bonaparte, helping to suppress the Vendemiaire Rising (q.v.) of October 1795. He served as a brilliant cavalry commander in the Italian Campaign and led the troops which executed the coup d'état of Brumaire (November 9, 1799, q.v.). He married Napoleon's sister, Caroline, in 1800. He was made king of Naples and a marshal of the Empire and fought in the Russian campaign. Following Napoleon's downfall, he tried several times to rally support for the Napoleonic cause. He was court martialed and executed in 1815, just after Waterloo, for attempting to raise a revolt in Calabria.

MUSCADINS. Name given to extravagant and affected young people, who dressed in fairly outrageous ways so as not to be confused with the sans-culottes (q.v.). They associated with the Incroyables (q.v.) and the male counterparts of the Merveilleuses (q.v.) in the period 1794-95.

NANTES. *See* **Drowning.**

NAPLES, KINGDOM OF. Kingdom which existed from 1138 until 1860, on the gulf of the same name, the ancient capital of the Two Sicilies and of Naples. On March 7, 1793 the Convention *(q.v.)* declared war on the kingdom and after a series of French victories, the capital was taken by Championnet on January 23, 1799, and the Parthenopean Republic was declared. The return of the monarch, Ferdinand IV, the same year resulted in terrible oppressions. Obliged to accept the French alliance in 1801 and 1802, by the Peace of Amiens *(q.v.)* he was replaced on his throne. The following year Bonaparte sent an army against him. In 1806 Joseph Bonaparte was named King of Naples, and was replaced by Murat *(q.v.)* from 1808 to 1815. Naples became part of the Kingdom of Italy in 1861.

NAPOLEON I (BONAPARTE) (1769-1821). Emperor of the French. His early reputation as a soldier began in 1793 in Toulon *(q.v.)*. He was in command, under Barras *(q.v.)*, in Paris at the insurrections of September 1795. The result of the crushing of this rising was a new Constitution and the first Directory *(q.v.)*. In 1796 Bonaparte was in charge of the Italian operations and, being successful, he managed to act independently of the Directory. After the Egyptian Campaign he returned to France in October 1799. The Directory was overthrown and power placed in the hands of three consuls—Bonaparte being the first consul and the other two being mere figureheads. Under Bonaparte's personal rule the campaign against the Austrians ended with the Battle of Marengo *(q.v.)* in August 1802, and he was appointed consul for life. In 1804 he declared himself "emperor of the French" and was crowned in the cathedral of Notre Dame in December 1804. Following the Battle of Trafalgar in 1805 he abandoned plans to invade Britain. The Battle of Austerlitz took place in 1805, after which the Confederacy of the Rhine was established, and in 1807 Napoleon defeated the combined Prussian and Russian forces.

The following years saw a decline in his achievements, first the attempt to annex Spain, second the invasion of Russia and finally the battle of Leipzig in 1813, which drove him back across the Rhine. After the Allies *(q.v.)* invaded France he abdicated in 1814 and retired to Elba. The Bourbons were returned to the throne. In 1815 he escaped from Elba, and at Waterloo he was finally vanquished. He abdicated and was exiled to St. Helena where he died.

Cronin, Vincent, *Napoleon,* 1971.

NAPOLÉON, CODE. *See* **Code Napoléon.**

NARBONNE-LARA, LOUIS MARIE JACQUES AMALRIC, COMTE DE (1755-1813). Soldier and diplomat. Minister of war 1791-92, he emigrated in 1792.

NATIONAL ASSEMBLY. *See* **Assembly, National.**

NATIONAL CONVENTION. *See* **Convention, National.**

NATIONAL GUARD. Citizen militia instituted in Paris on July 13, 1789 to prevent a complete breakdown of law and order. Membership was of prosperous citizens and the Guard's first colors were red and blue, to which white was added when Louis XVI gave his approval to its formation. The first commander was Lafayette *(q.v.)*. They were responsible for arresting Louis XVI and his family but also protected them from the fury of the populace.

NATION, THÉÂTRE DE LA. Initially a wooden structure granted by the duc d'Orléans to Gaillard and Dorfeuil during the time that they were rebuilding the Théâtre Français, which had burned in 1781. While the old theater was being rebuilt the directors established themselves here with the troupe of the Théâtre des variétés amusants, which they had directed at the Boulevard du Temple. The new theater opened on May 15, 1790.

NATURAL BOUNDARIES, THEORY OF. The Convention passed a decree on November 19, 1792 promising "freedom and assistance" to all people wanting to recover their liberty in answer to the Rhineland's petitions for French protection. As a result France was now committed to a policy of annexation. The Scheldt was reopened on November 23. In January 1793 Danton *(q.v.)* caused the Convention *(q.v.)* to pass the decree which claimed for France her "natural frontiers"—on the Rhine, the Alps and the Pyrenées. The intention was to set limits on revolutionary annexations, not to extend them.

NECKER, JACQUES (1732-1804). Statesman and financier. Born in Geneva in 1762, he established the London and Paris bank of Thellusson and Necker, amassing a large fortune. In 1777 he was appointed director-general of finance. His methods and integrity helped to better economic conditions. His constraints were disliked by Marie Antoinette, and his famous *Compte rendu* published in 1781 caused his dismissal, brought about by those who had suffered from his economic policies. He was recalled to office in September 1788 and recommended the summoning of the Estates-General. The king instructed him to leave France on July 11, but the fall of the Bastille *(q.v.)* on July 14 caused the king to recall him. He finally resigned in September 1790, disillusioned by events, and retired to his estate near Geneva, where he died. His daughter was Madame de Staël *(q.v.)*.
Chapuisat, E., *Necker: 1732-1804*, 1938.
Harris, Robert D., *Necker: Reform Statesman of the Ancien Régime*, 1979.

NEERWINDEN, BATTLE OF. Village in the province of Liège in Belgium, the scene of a battle on March 18, 1793 between the prince of Saxe-Cobourg and Dumouriez (*q.v.*). After his defeat, Dumouriez evacuated Brussels and went back over the frontier, to be denounced as a traitor by Marat (*q.v.*) in the Convention (*q.v.*).

NELSON, HORATIO NELSON, VISCOUNT, DUKE OF BRONTE IN SICILY (1758-1805). English seaman. He saw service in the East and West Indies in the early years of his naval career. When war with France was imminent he was in command of the *Agamemnon* in the Mediterranean under Admiral Hood. In 1794 he lost an eye when trying to reduce the French garrison at Calvi. He contributed to the British success at the battle off Cape St. Vincent in 1797. That year he was promoted to rear-admiral and also lost his right arm. In August 1798 he was successful at Aboukir Bay. (*See* **Battle of the Nile**.) On being promoted to vice-admiral in 1801, he was successful at the Battle of Copenhagen. He joined *Victory* in 1803 and commanded the fleet in the Battle of Trafalgar on October 21, 1805, when he was mortally wounded.
Warner, Oliver, *Nelson*, 1975.

NEWSPAPERS. From early times France concerned itself with control over the written word in its various forms. An edict of Henry II (1559) made it punishable with death to print anything without authority, while Cardinal Richelieu, in 1626, declared it to be a capital offence to publish works against religion or the state. In 1723 a regulation appeared which forbade any but licenced booksellers to deal in books. Many later regulations were directed against unlicenced presses and such things as the employment of more than a certain number of workmen. Allied to these centrally motivated and directed controls was the system of *censeurs royaux* (*q.v.*) charged with the responsibility of examining books that could not be published without the king's permission. It is noteworthy that newspapers were under the eye of many more special censors than, for example, architecture, which had only one examiner.

At the Revolution, all restrictions were abolished, and the Assembly (*q.v.*) declared it to be the right of every citizen to print and publish his opinions; this was included in the 1791 constitution, which declared that freedom of thought and opinion were natural and imprescribable rights. The rush of a variety of opposing newspapers into print, with the attendant proliferation of violent and scandalous rhetoric, not just political in nature, encouraged the new government to try and impose some forms of control as early as 1791, but no effectual restraint was imposed until the law of February 5, 1810. In 1795 the Directory (*q.v.*) had renewed the new principles of free expression, but the day after the coup d'état of 18 Fructidor (*q.v.*), the newspapers were subdued for one year, then for two, and subjected to police inspection and the right to prohibit publication. By Louis XVIII's charter, the liberty of the press was expressed in specific terms, but restrictions soon followed, a characteristic which ran throughout most of the last century.

Before the Revolution, readers had had to depend on foreign journals; illicitly circulated, their chief writers resorted to covert presses, disguises and various subterfuges in order to escape the censors. True political journalism began during this period, and it had a relatively brief life. By 1797 periodical publications were charged a stamp duty, and the inevitable clamping down by the central authorities was not long in coming.

The most frantic period of publication ran from about May 1789, with Mirabeau's *Lettres à ses Committants* (later the *Courier de Provence*), to September 1792. Most of the papers published over this period, with the exception of the *Moniteur* and Baudouin's *Journal des Débats*, were finished by the autumn of 1792 or by the fall of the Girondins *(q.v.)* in September 1793. On February 17, 1800 the consuls suppressed all but 13 Paris-based journals, partly as a result of the conservative backlash but also with quite clear memories of the extremism that had occurred earlier through the encouragement of the most inflammatory and radical political journalists.

Gilchrist, John T. I. and Murray, W. J. (eds.). *The Press in the French Revolution: A Selection of Documents taken from the Press of the Revolution for the Years 1789-94.* 1971.

Murray, William J., *The Right Wing Press in the French Revolution: 1780-1792,* 1986.

Popkin, Jeremy D. *The Right-Wing Press in France, 1792-1800.* 1980.

NICE. Dependency of the Kingdom of Sardinia, Nice was separated from France by the Var. It was taken by Anselme on September 28, 1792 and the area joined France on January 31, 1793 with the County of Nice forming the eighty-fifth department of the Alpes-Maritimes. On May 15, 1796, at the conclusion of the peace treaty between Sardinia and France, it was ceded to France. It was restored to Sardinia in 1814 and again ceded to France in 1860.

NILE, BATTLE OF THE (BATTLE OF ABOUKIR BAY). Battle fought on August 1, 1798 between a British fleet commanded by Nelson *(q.v.)* and the French force that had brought Napoleon to Egypt. Nelson succeeded in placing the French fleet, under the command of Bruyes, between two lines of British vessels and thereby achieved a striking victory. Nine of the French line-of-battle ships were taken, two were burnt, including *L'Orient (q.v.)*, and only two vessels escaped. The Egyptian expedition was thus cut off from France.

NINE SISTERS (NEUF SOEURS). Masonic lodge of Nine Sisters in Paris, founded by Joseph Jérôme Lefrançais de Lalande (1732-1897), astronomer. This was to be an *Encyclopedic* lodge, to bring together men of learning and talent. Originally thought of by Lalande and Helvètius, it was pursued by Lalande after the latter's death in 1771. The lodge was constituted in 1777, after some difficulty in getting permission. The membership was open only to those with specific talents in the arts and sciences, and to those who had already publicly demonstrated those talents. Voltaire *(q.v.)* was initiated in 1778 and the most illustrious writers, scientists, artists and political figures became members.

NIVÔSE. Snow month, December 21 to January 19. *See* **Calendar, Revolutionary.**

NOAILLES, LOUIS MARIE DE, VI-COMTE DE (1756-1804). Soldier. He served in America under Lafayette and was a deputy in the Estates-General. He emigrated to America and defended Saint-Domingue against the English in 1803.

NOBILITY. On June 18, 1790 the National Assembly decreed the abolition of the hereditary nobility. The titles of dukes, counts, marquises, knights, barons, excellencies, abbots, and others were abolished and all citizens took their family names. Liveries and armorial bearings were also abolished. Nobles enjoyed privileges which belonged to all members of the second estate as such. They were exempt from the corvée (q.v.) and the taille (q.v.). Nobility was granted by the monarch in return for money or other services, or because of the appointee holding an office which conferred nobility. The records of the nobility, 600 volumes, were burnt on June 25, 1792. A new nobility was created by Napoleon Bonaparte in 1808.

NOIRS. See **Blacks.**

NOIRS, SOCIÉTÉ DES AMIS DES. Society founded in Paris in 1787 committed to the abolition of slavery. Interested participants included Antoine Joseph Marie Pierre Barnave (1761-93), the marquis de Condorcet (1743-94), Brissot de Warville and Mirabeau (qq.v.). Public opinion was considerably influenced by antislavery writings, including Frossard on L'Ésclavage des Nègres, his letter on his voyage to the coast of Guinea, Abbé Grégoire's memoir in favor of the blacks and addresses to like societies in London and America on the emancipation of blacks. Also, Lafayette wrote on French Guinea regarding black liberty from a political point of view.

On May 15, 1791 the Assembly decreed that a man, whatever his color, is free and enjoys the rights of the active citizen. In August 1791 the insurrections in Saint-Domingue and the Cape, Martinique and Guadeloupe caused setbacks to the overall policy. On February 4, 1794 slavery was abolished in all French colonies but was later reestablished by Bonaparte.

NORTH, ARMY OF THE. On October 1, 1792 Joseph Servan, the minister of war, proposed to the Convention that French military forces be divided into eight armies: of the North, the Ardennes, the Moselle, the Rhine, the Vosges, the Alps, the Pyrenees and the Interior.

The Army of the North was under overall command of Charles François Dumouriez (1739-1823, q.v.). The Army covered the area from Dunkirk to Givet, and all of the territories occupied by the armies in Belgium to the Meuse. Appropriate frontiers were also covered.

Dumouriez was mainly responsible for the declaration of war against Austria on April 20, 1792, and for planning the invasion of the Low Countries. With the invasion of France by a coalition of Prussians, Hessians, Austrians and émigrés (q.v.) under the Duke of Brunswick, on August 19, Dumouriez's army moved into the Argonne to block access to Paris. On September 20, 1792 the "Cannonade of Valmy" forced the Duke to break off his attack, and ten days later the invading army began its retreat, eventually leaving French soil.

Dumouriez resumed his intended scheme for the invasion of the Netherlands; on November 6 he won the greatest victory of the war at Jemappes, near Mons. Advancing, he had overrun the entire country from Namur to Antwerp within one month. Yet, with the foundation of the First Coalition—England, Holland, Austria, Prussia, Spain and Sardinia—French fortunes began to change. While Dumouriez was beginning his invasion of Holland, Prince Josias of Saxe-Coburg, the new Austrian commander in the Lower Rhine, advanced with 43,000 men from the region of Cologne. Dumouriez stopped his advance into Holland and, on March 18, 1793 was decisively defeated by Josias at Neerwinden. All of the French forces retreated to Valenciennes, Dumouriez having unsuccessfully attempted to induce his army to go over to the Austrians. Picot, comte de Dampierre, began to reconstruct and revitalize the badly shaken and demoralized French army—France was, at this stage, totally defenseless, and it was some time before the army was capable of professionalism and success. As had been demonstrated by the defeat of Neerwinden, the old, professional soldiers' deep distrust of the conduct of the new, "patriot" battalions was well-founded.

NOTABLES. Under the monarchy, members of the privileged orders. The king could at will call for an Assembly of Notables (*q.v.*). The assembly of February 1787 refused to agree to proposals for taxation, and the crisis which followed led to the convening of the Estates-General of 1789.

NOTABLES, ASSEMBLY OF. *See* **Assembly of Notables.**

NOTRE-DAME DE PARIS. The cathedral of Paris. Archbishop Maurice de Sully initiated the building of Notre Dame, which started in 1133 and was finished in about 1263. It was the setting for numerous magnificent royal ceremonies and festivals. On August 5, 1789 a "Te Deum" was sung here, to celebrate the suppression of feudal rights. In 1793 the Paris Commune voted to demolish the cathedral, and there were a number of acts of vandalism. The Fête de la Raison (*q.v.*) was celebrated in the cathedral on November 10, 1793 and the cathedral became for a time, the "Temple de la Raison." On June 29, 1801 it was the setting for a National Council of Bishops and Deputies of the Clergy of the Second Order. On April 18, 1802 celebrations were held here to honor the signing of the Concordat. On December 2, 1804 Napoleon Bonaparte was crowned in the cathedral.

NOUVELLES À LA MAIN. News sheets circulated in manuscript.

NOYADES. *See* **Drowning.**

OCTOBER DAYS. Period following the fall of the Bastille *(q.v.)* and the adoption of the Principles of 1789 *(q.v.)* when Louis XVI, who was residing at Versailles, was avoiding commitments on constitutional legislation. On being pressed for action he called in troops and this provoked a march by the mob on October 5 and on October 6 the king agreed to move to Paris. Some weeks later the Assembly *(q.v.)* also moved to the capital. One of the first acts of the Assembly was to declare martial law on October 21, 1789 to avoid further disorders.

OCTROIS. Taxes levied at the gates of towns in France on articles of food entering the city. The Farmers General of Taxes managed the system. (*See* **Fermiers Généraux.**) In 1785 Calonne *(q.v.)* authorized them to build a ten-foot wall around the city of Paris, broken with gates *(barrières, [q.v.])* for collecting dues. This step was taken to counter smuggling and the evasion of taxes. It caused resentment among the people as, in times of bad harvests and the consequent rise in the cost of food, especially bread, the price of which was tightly regulated and pegged officially every day, the tolls put additional burdens on the people. On July 12-13, 1789, forty out of fifty-four of the gates in the customs wall were attacked and

destroyed. Those responsible for this act were those worst hit by the octrois—shopkeepers, wage earners and small tradesmen—and they were motivated because of the increased prices of wine, firewood and foodstuffs. It was, essentially, a food-riot, a precursor to the march on the Bastille *(q.v.).* Octrois were suppressed in 1791, reestablished in 1797 and reorganized in 1816.

OFFICES. Under the ancien régime, a term referring to the judiciary, the offices of the notary, the recorder and to those of finance. The major concern, up to the time of the Revolution, was the growth in the power and in the corruption of these offices. The number of offices had so increased that, by the end of the reign of Louis XV, the government was forced to suppress many of them in 1771. On August 4, 1789 the Legislative Assembly *(q.v.)* voted for the suppression of all privileges. Progressive decrees swept away many of the established offices and their rights, including that of allowing titular heads of offices to gain from the fees of enregisterment, and culminating in the abolition of bribery and corruption in the judicial offices on July 5, 1790. In 1791 municipal offices were abolished along with much of the administrative structure which had developed under the ancien régime.

OFFICIALITÉ, PRISON DE L'. Situated in a tower enclosed by the walls of the great sacristy of Notre Dame and the old chapel of the Archepiscopal Palace, it was designed for ecclesiastics and held secret dungeons. It was pulled down in 1795.

OGDEN, JAMES (1718-1802). Author born at Manchester, England. He wrote volumes of turgid verse and was known locally as "Poet" Ogden. His son, William (1753-1822), was an ardent radical reformer. Among his poems were "The Revolution: An Epic Poem" (1790) and "Sans Culotte and Jacobine: A Hudibrastic Poem" (1800).

OLÉRON, ILE D'. Island situated on the Gulf of Gascony near the mouth of the Charente in the Bay of Biscay; part of the district of Marennes in 1790. In 1787 the island reclaimed a direct representation to the Estates-General, the title to the place having previously been held by the monarchy. The island suffered from considerable economic deprivations because of floods and received financial assistance from the mainland. In 1799 it became a holding place for those sentenced to be deported after September 4, 1797 (18 Fructidor, *q.v.*).

ONZE, COMMISSION D'. Commission formed by the Jacobins on May 31, 1793 within the revolutionary committees for the forty-eight sections of the city of Paris. The Commission was charged with giving to the Hotel de Ville, in co-operation with the General Committee of the Commune, support for labor and public safety. Danton and Robespierre *(qq.v.)* were responsible for the establishment of this body.

OPINION, L' (OPINION). One of the *sansculottides* (*q.v.*), September 20.

ORANGE, COMMISSION OF. Established in 1794 by a decree of the Convention (*q.v.*) to suppress the conspirators and assassins of the Midi. The Committee of Public Safety (*q.v.*) established an extraordinary commission of five judges on May 10. Within the space of several weeks the commission executed 331 persons within the two departments that fell under its jurisdiction.

ORATEUR DU PEUPLE, L'. Newspaper founded and edited by Stanislas Fréron (1754-1802, *q.v.*), the son of the critic E. Fréron, published under the name of *Martel* from May 1790 until September 1792. It was more a pamphlet than a newspaper and had the same kind of violence as Marat's *L'Ami du Peuple* (*qq.v.*), although it did not speak of black plots and massacres by the aristocrats. The second series of his newspaper started on 25 Fructidor, Year II, under his name and title as a deputy to the National Convention (*q.v.*). The second series totaled 60, but was totally different in character from that of the first, and the newspaper became a reactionary organ. The paper closed on 25 Fructidor, Year III. Fréron left France for Saint-Domingue, where he died.

ORATORY, CONGREGATION OF THE. Established in Paris in 1611 by the Cardinal de Bérulle, the Oratorians were suppressed in 1792. Their church, or oratory, built between 1621 and 1630, served for some years as a place for the assemblies of the district and section of the Louvre quarter. Numerous societies used the facilities, which eventually became a Geneva church in 1802.

ORDERS. *See* **Estates.**

ORDERS OF CHIVALRY. The most ancient orders of chivalry were:
1. Orders of Saint-Lazare de Jérusalem and Notre Dame du Mont-Carmel: Brought together by Henri IV in 1608, the king was the grand master of this order, which consisted of 50 commandeurs and 100 knights.
2. Ordre de mérite militaire: Instituted by Louis XV for Protestant officers, who could not receive the Croix de Saint-Louis (4 commandeurs, an indeterminate number of knights).
3. Ordre de Saint-Michel: Instituted by Louis XI in 1469, it was composed of 36 members, all but a few nobility, the remainder drawn from the arts and sciences.
4. Ordre de Malte: In 1789 there were 220 Commanderies with enormous revenues. The order consisted of a grand master and 800 knights.
5. Ordre royal militaire de Saint-Louis: Instituted by Louis XIV, the order was available to members of both the army and the navy. As the Revolution approached, membership of this order increased considerably. In June 1790 an attempt was made, in the Constituent Assembly (*q.v.*), to abolish the orders of chivalry, but it was defeated. However chivalric orders were finally abolished on July 30, 1791.

ORDONNANCES. The laws, edicts, declarations and letters patent enacted by the Capetian kings of France previous to 1789. They began with "in the name of the king," and ended with "such is our good pleasure." The first in French is dated 1287, under Philip IV.

ORIENT, ARMÉE D'. *See* **East, Army of the.**

ORIFLAMME. Banner which, under the ancien régime, was carried at the head of their armies and which served as a rallying point during battle. It was a popular symbol during the Revolution. On July 14, 1790 at the Fête de la Fédération (*q.v.*), it was carried at the head of the procession which met at the Champ de Mars. It was placed between the deputies of the National Guard (*q.v.*) of the 42 first departments in alphabetical order, and the deputies of the troops of the line. After the ceremony, it was suspended from the ceiling of the Constituent Assembly (*q.v.*). On August 11, 1793, during the adoption of the new constitution, it was pulled down and torn to pieces and thrown around the Convention (*q.v.*).

ORLÉANS, LOUIS PHILIPPE JOSEPH, DUC D' (1747-93) (CALLED PHILIPPE-ÉGALITÉ). His early lifestyle was disapproved of by the court, especially after the accession of Louis XVI (1774). During the period of financial problems in 1787, he spoke against the king and was exiled to his estates. In June 1789 he led the nobles who seceded from their own order to join the Third Estate *(q.v.)*. All hereditary titles were abolished in 1792 and from then on he called himself Philippe-Égalité. He was a deputy to the Convention *(q.v.)* for Paris and voted for the death of the king. Later he fell under suspicion when his eldest son (who later became King Louis-Philippe, 1830-38, *q.v.*) joined the Austrian armies. He was arrested, tried and guillotined.

Scudder, E. S., *Prince of the Blood*, 1938.

ORPHANS OF THE TEMPLE. The dauphin, Louis-Charles de France, and his sister, Marie-Thérèse-Charlotte de France, children of Louis XVI and Marie Antoinette, were imprisoned with their parents in the Temple *(q.v.)* in 1792. After Louis XVI's execution Louis-Charles was taken from his mother and put in charge of a guard. He is said to have died in prison in 1795, but this was never proved and rumors has it that he escaped and another child substituted for him. There were later many pretenders—"faux dauphins." To many he was known as Louis XVII after his father's death. Marie-Thérèse was exchanged for eight French prisoners by the Austrians in 1795. In 1799 she married the duc d'Angoulême and left France with him after the 1830 revolution.

Castelot, A., *Louis XVII*, 1960.

OSNABRUCK. Situated on the River Hase, in Lower Saxony, Federal Republic of Germany, but formerly a duchy. In 1795 a large number of French and Dutch émigrés assembled here under the orders of the prince of Orange, but the king of Prussia refused to allow these gatherings and ordered their immediate evacuation because of French feelings.

OSTEND. The chief point of Western Flanders (Belgium), situated on the North Sea at the beginning of the Ostend-Brussels canal, the entrepôt of the coalition at the beginning of the war against Austria and a formidable Allied center. The Allies *(q.v.)*, under the duke of York, were defeated on June 26, 1794. The French earlier succeeded in causing Ostend to join France. Successive attempts were made to take the port from the French in May 1798, but it was held by them until the treaties of 1814.

OUEST, ARMÉE DE L'. *See* **West, Army of.**

PACTE DE FAMINE. One of the several examples of rumor, suggestion and panic that occurred before and during the Revolution. Between 1787 and 1789 there were a series of bad harvests with a consequent shortage of grain. The price of wheat doubled within two years in the main production areas of the north. The rise in the price of bread, other food commodities and fuel, and the rise in unemployment caused people to flood into Paris from the provinces.

Both the Pacte de Famine and the Great Fear *(q.v.)* of July 1789 ran almost concurrently. There were developing rumors of a royal/aristocratic reaction in the countryside that would be turned against the peasantry, and any of those who were sympathetic with or had participated in the recent reforms. The difficulties of getting enough food into Paris to feed the growing population, plus the high prices being charged, led to suggestions that speculators *(accapeurs)* were cornering the market in grain, either removing it from the city to sell at a profit elsewhere or inflating the price of the stocks that were in Paris. These speculators were thought to be either Royalists, aristocrats or people sympathetic to the old order.

On July 12-13, 1789 *barrières (q.v.)* in Paris were attacked and burned. Their exactions were bitterly resented by the shopkeepers, wine-merchants and general small consumers, who were being driven to the wall by the lack of materials and the resulting outrageous prices. The march on the Bastille *(q.v.)* followed immediately after this event. The same rumor occurred during the early years of the Revolution, when supplies were either simply not available or problems with transportation to the major centers led to low stocks.

PAINE, THOMAS (1737-1809). English radical. After many unsuccessful occupations and eventual dismissal as an excise officer for writing a pamphlet advocating higher pay to avoid corruption in the service, he sailed for Philadelphia in 1774. In 1776 his pamphlet *Common Sense* argued for complete independence of the American colonies. He served in the American army and was made secretary to the Committee of Foreign Affairs, but was dismissed in 1779 for divulging state secrets. Later he was appointed clerk of the Pennsylvania legislature, but in 1787 he returned to England, where in 1791-92 he published *The Rights of Man,* a reply to Edmund Burke's *Reflections on the Revolution in France.* Having been elected deputy to the National Convention *(q.v.)* for Pas-de-Calais, he left for Paris. Voting with the Girondins *(q.v.),* he proposed to offer the king an asylum in America, which displeased Robespierre *(q.v.).* In 1794 he was imprisoned but just before his arrest he published part of *The Age of Reason*, and a further part was written while in prison. His views were not accepted by many of his former friends. He was released from prison after eleven months and regained his seat in the Convention. In 1802, having become disenchanted with politics in France, he returned to America. He died in New York.

McKown, Robin, *Thomas Paine*, 1962.

Williamson, Audrey, *Thomas Paine: His Work, Life and Times*, 1973.

PALACE, ARCHBISHOP OF PARIS'S. The Archbishop's Palace, rebuilt in 1670, was situated close to Notre Dame. On leaving Versailles, the Constituent Assembly *(q.v.)* installed itself here on October 19, 1789, holding its meetings here until December.

PALAIS DE JUSTICE. Seat of the Paris parlement. Scene of the great trials of the Revolution held by the Revolutionary Tribunal *(q.v.)*.

PALAIS DES VARIÉTÉS, THÉATRE DU. Constructed in 1791 by the architect Lenoir in the Rue de la Barillèrie, on the site of the royal church and the parish of Saint-Barthélemy. The following year it changed its name to Cité-Variétés, and specialized in vaudevilles, drama, comedy and pantomime. It was closed in 1799.

PALAIS ROYAL, PARIS. Originally named Palais Cardinal, built for Cardinal Richelieu by Lemercier, 1620-36. Its name was changed by Louis XIII, to whom the cardinal gave it. It was confiscated by the Republic in 1793 after the execution of Philippe-Egalité, duc d'Orléans *(q.v.)* and it was used for public meetings during the Revolution.

PAMPHLETS. Before the Revolution there were few newspapers, and books were expensive, but pamphlets could be printed quickly, and generally it was possible to avoid the censor. Their contents, passed by word of mouth, reached the illiterate. An important pamphlet was "What is the Third Estate?" which appeared in January 1789 before the elections began. The author was Sieyès *(q.v.)* and its propaganda value was considerable.

PANTHÉON. In 1754 the church of the ancient Abbaye de Sainte-Geneviève, on the left bank of the Seine, was just a ruin, and Louis XV conceived the idea of replacing it. Construction started in 1757. In 1791 the Constituent Assembly *(q.v.)* designated it a secular burial place for the great men who were distinguished by their virtues, talents, and their services to the state. The building is constructed on the lines of a Greek cross and the finance was largely raised by a lottery. The bodies of Hugo, Mirabeau, Marat, Rousseau, Voltaire *(qq.v.)* and others are buried here.

PANTHÉON, CLUB DU. Situated in the old Couvent des Génovéfains, this club was initially composed of republicans, but degenerated into a meeting place for ultraradicals, malcontents and Royalists. On February 27, 1796 it was declared illegal and contrary to the public peace. The

Directory (*q.v.*) had its papers and correspondence sealed, and Bonaparte was charged with closing the club. Later, the panthéonistes formed inoffensive groups, based in the cafés, and eventually most of them departed to join the Club de Clichy.

PAOLI, PASQUALE DE (1725-1807). Corsican patriot. Son of Giacinto Paoli, who was the organizer of opposition to the Genoese rule of Corsica. The family were in exile until 1755, when Paoli was chosen as president of Corsica. France bought Corsica in 1768 and Paoli opposed the French authorities. Defeated, he fled to England. In 1791 he was appointed governor of Corsica by the French revolutionary government. In 1793 he broke with France and, aided by the British, Corsica became a British protectorate. He returned to England in 1795 and the pro-French islanders drove the British out.
Thrasher, Peter Adam, *Pasquale Paoli: An Enlightened Hero, 1725-1807*, 1970.

PAPACY. The Papal States were taken from the pope in 1798-99 when Bonaparte had conquered much of the Italian peninsula and were included in the Cisalpine and Roman republics (*qq.v.*). See also **Pius VI.**
Hales, E. E. Y., *The Revolution and the Papacy*, 1960.

PARIS. In 1771 there were 900 streets in Paris and 24,000 houses, of which about 3,000 were the property of the clergy and hospitals. There were 75,000 taxed families, 500 hotels, 65 fountains and 14-15,000 water carriers, 580 city bakers and 1,700 foreign bakers. In 1789 when the population was 600,000, the number of houses had increased by 1,000 and it was estimated that 70 million livres was produced from house rents.

PARLEMENTAIRE. Member of a parlement (*see* below) under the ancien régime.

PARLEMENTS. Sovereign court of justice at Paris and in 13 other cities and towns, where justice was administered in the king's name under the ancien régime. They were suppressed by Louis XV in 1771 but restored in 1774 by Louis XVI. In 1787 the Paris parlement demanded a meeting of the Estates-General (*q.v.*). In 1789 there were 13 parlements, Paris (1190), Toulouse (1443), Grenoble (1453), Bordeaux (1462), Dijon (1494), Aix (1501), Rouen (1515), Rennes (1553), Pau (1620), Metz (1634), Besançon (1674), Douai (1686), Nancy (1775). On November 3, 1789 the National Assembly ordered that all the parlements should remain on their vacation leave. Another decree promised strong measures against any who attempted to retard the execution of the new organization of judicial power. Although the parlements of Rennes, Metz and Rouen acted against the decree, they were soon forced to accede to it.

PARQUET. Room where the king's counsel held deliberations under the ancien régime.

PARTHENOPEAN REPUBLIC. Republic established following the French occupation of Naples on January 23, 1799. The republic was overthrown by the Allies (*q.v.*) in the following June. Parthenope was an early name for Naples.

PASSPORTS. The Constituent Assembly *(q.v.)* abolished passports, which were used for the free passage of merchandise as well as individuals. On June 25, 1792 it was declared that passports could only be demanded within ten leagues (about 30 miles) of the frontiers, but with the increase of emigration, the attempted flight of the king and his family, as well as other notables, plus the prohibitions on English goods, it became necessary to reinforce the original laws. By the following year, all travelers were required to have passports.

PATENTES. Under the ancien régime these referred to "lettres patentes" or commissions, brevets or lettres de maîtrise, which authorized the holder to practice a profession or industry. The Constituent Assembly abolished the "lettres patentes" in 1791, along with the guilds and the masters, replacing them with an equal tax for all citizens practicing a trade.

PATRIE. "Homeland" or motherland.

PATRIE EN DANGER. On April 20, 1792 France declared war on Austria. Following the invasion of the Tuileries *(q.v.)* by the mob on June 20, a decree of the National Assembly *(q.v.)* on July 11 proclaimed "la patrie en danger." The news spread rapidly and moves were made to encourage as many volunteers as possible to enroll in the army.

PATRIOTE FRANÇAIS, LE. Journal, founded by Brissot de Warville *(q.v.)*, which was published from April 10, 1789 to June 2, 1793. It carried reports of the debates in the National Assembly *(q.v.)* and aimed to be free, impartial and national. The *Patriote* provided a systematic history of the Girondins *(q.v.)*.

PATRIOTS. Name in 1789 for those who were devoted to the new ideals, as distinct from the aristocrats and the apologists for the ancien régime. In 1793 they took the name of *sans-culottes (q.v.)* and became a force of radical reaction against succeeding governments.

PAUME, JEU DE. Royal game of tennis. There were two types, that played on an inside court *(court paume)* and *longue paume*, played in the open. It was at Versailles in the Salle du Jeu de Paume that the Tennis Court Oath *(q.v.)* was signed in 1789.

PAYS D'ELECTIONS. Province governed by an *intendant (q.v.)* under the ancien régime.

PAYS D'ETATS. Provinces having estates (assemblies) and retaining their ancient rights to vote on taxation in them. Many assemblies had disappeared in the 17th century. However, the provinces of Brittany, Languedoc, Corsica and Burgundy retained effective assemblies until the Revolution.

PÉAGES. Tax under the ancien régime that the king and his seigneurs received for the passage of vehicles, animals, merchandise and provisions. It was suppressed on

March 9, 1790, along with similar rights, such as *passage, pontonnage, barrage* and others.

PELTIER, JEAN-GABRIEL (1765-1825). Pamphleteer and journalist, founder-editor of the Royalist publication *Les Actes des Apôtres*. In 1792 he moved to England, where he edited (1803-18) *L'Ambigu*, a journal which was at first antirevolutionary, but later violently anti-Napoleon Bonaparte.

PENTHIÈVRE, FORT DE. Situated in the Bay of Quiberon, it was the scene of a victory by the French led by Hoche *(q.v.)* over the émigrés and the British invaders on 3 Thermidor, Year III.

PÈRE DUCHESNE, LE. Revolutionary journal founded by Jacques René Hébert *(q.v.)* with a large circulation. "Le Père Duchesne" was originally a stock character of the Théâtre de la Foire.

PÉTION DE VILLENEUVE, JÉRÔME (1756-94). Leading revolutionary and writer. He was elected a deputy to the Third Estate *(q.v.)* in 1789, mayor of Paris in 1791 and first president of the Convention *(q.v.)*. He was a member of the Jacobin Club and a keen supporter of Robespierre *(q.v.)*. He was one of those who brought back the royal family from Varennes *(q.v.)*. He voted for the king's execution. Proscribed on June 2, 1793, he escaped, and after much wandering committed suicide.

PETIT BLANCS. *See* **Grand and Petit Blancs.**

PHILOSOPHES. Name given to the French thinkers in the prerevolutionary period who were the leaders of the Enlightenment *(q.v.)*, including Condorcet *(q.v.)*, Diderot *(q.v.)*, Montesquieu, Rousseau *(q.v.)* and Voltaire *(q.v.)*. The 1789 Revolution was held by many to be influenced by the writings of the Philosophes.

PHYSIOCRATS. Name given to a group of French economists and philosophers of the 18th century who based their theories on the assumption that all wealth was derived from the land; all commerce was sterile and the only fruitful labor was in agriculture. They were led by François Quesnay (1694-1774), and Turgot *(q.v.)* attempted to put their theories into practice.

PICHEGRU, JEAN-CHARLES (1761-1804). General who enlisted in 1783 and by 1793 was commander of the Army of the Rhine. With Hoche *(q.v.)* he played an important part in the conquest of the Austrian Netherlands and Holland. He was recalled by the Thermidorians *(q.v.)* to crush an insurrection in Paris. He turned against the Revolution and made contact with the émigrés, and by deliberately withdrawing support he allowed Jourdan *(q.v.)* to be defeated. He was elected president of the Council of Five Hundred *(q.v.)* in 1797. He became aligned with the Royalist deputies and was arrested and deported to Guiana. He managed to escape and reached London, thereafter living in Germany and England until the conspiracy of

Georges Cadoudal *(q.v.)* for the assassination of the first consul. The pair reached Paris in January 1804 but were betrayed, and Pichegru was arrested on February 28, 1804. Imprisoned in the Temple *(q.v.)*, he was found strangled on April 5.

PILLNITZ, DECLARATION OF. Declaration issued at Pillnitz, a village near Dresden, on August 25, 1791. Emperor Leopold II and King Frederick William II of Prussia met to decide how to assist various groups of French émigrés, and threatened the use of force against France. Their manifesto demanded the release of Louis XVI, the abolition of the Constituent Assembly, and the reestablishment of the German princes' feudal rights in Alsace. The result was a call-to-arms in France that raised 150,000 men. The declaration did much to bring about the Revolutionary Wars. (*See* **Wars, French Revolutionary.**)

PITIÉ, HÔPITAL DE LA. Situated on the site of the Jeu de Paume de la Trinité, between the Rues du Battoir and the Jardin des Plantes *(q.v.)*, this hospital was founded in 1612 for beggars. They were given accommodation but had to work to keep it. The beggars were later replaced by children, old women and "filles débauchées." The latter lived in a special quarter called the "refuge," which existed until the creation of Sainte-Pélagie in 1665. Up to the Revolution, the hospital was reserved strictly for children of both sexes, abandoned orphans or beggars, and they were employed in making sheets for the hospitals and the military. In 1790 the Pitié numbered 1,397 pensioners, who were named "élèves

de la patrie," and "orphelins du faubourg Saint-Victor."

PITT, WILLIAM (1759-1806). Known as "Pitt the Younger." Son of Lord Chatham, he entered the House of Commons in 1781 and in 1782 was chancellor of the exchequer. He became prime minister in 1783 and, having won the election of 1784, he was prime minister until 1801, covering the years of the French Revolution, and again 1804-06. After 1789 Pitt advocated a need for national security both internally and externally; otherwise, he felt that England would follow the same path as France. He subsidized the military coalitions against France in 1793 and 1798, but neither were particularly successful on land, although naval activity produced some dramatic victories.
Ehrman, John, *The Younger Pitt*, 1969.
Jarrett, D., *Pitt the Younger*, 1974.

PIUS VI, POPE (GIANNANGELO BRASCHI), **1775-99** (1717-99). At the outbreak of the Revolution, Pius saw the Gallican Church suppressed and the pontifical and ecclesiastical possessions in France confiscated, and himself burned in effigy at the Palais Royal *(q.v.)*. The murder of Hugo Basseville, the republican agent, in the streets of Rome (January 1793) created tensions. The French charged the pope with complicity. Pius joined the league against France, but in 1796 Bonaparte invaded Italy, defeated the papal troops and occupied Ancona and Loreto. Pius sued for peace, which was granted by February, 1797 at Tolentino. On December 28, 1797 General Duphot of the French embassy was killed in a riot, providing a good excuse for an invasion. Berthier entered Rome on February 13 proclaiming a republic and demanding that the pope renounce his temporal authority. The pope refused and was taken prisoner to Certosa near Florence. The French declaration of war against Tuscany caused him to be taken to the citadel of Valence, where he died six weeks later. He was succeeded by Pius VII.

PIUS VII, POPE (BARNABA GREGORIO CHIARAMONTI), **1800-23** (1742-1823). The candidate of the French Bishop Maury, Pius VII was elected pope on March 14, 1800. His attention was directed to the ecclesiastical anarchy in France: churches were closed, Jansenism (q.v.) and clerical marriages were on the increase, dioceses existed without bishops, and the people were hostile or indifferent. He was encouraged by Bonaparte's wish for the reestablishment of the Catholic religion in France. Pius negotiated the Concordat, which was signed at Paris on July 15, and ratified by him on August 14, 1801. In 1804 Bonaparte negotiated to secure, at the Pope's hands, his formal consecration as emperor. Pius performed the ceremony at Notre Dame and stayed in Paris for four months, but gained only a few small concessions. Irritation increased between France and Rome, and, in February 1808, Rome was again occupied.

PLACE DE LA CONCORDE. *See* **Place de la Révolution.**

PLACE DE LA RÉVOLUTION. Square in Paris formerly called Place Louis XV and since 1795 called Place de la Concorde. At a fireworks display to celebrate the marriage of the dauphin Louis to Marie Antoinette in 1770, 133 persons were accidentally killed there. In 1792 the statue of Louis XV was replaced by one of Liberty and the square renamed Place de la Révolution. Louis XVI was guillotined here on January 21, 1793. Others suffering the same fate in the square included Marie Antoinette, Charlotte Corday, Philippe-Égalité, Madame Elisabeth, Robespierre and the Girondins (qq.v.).

PLACE LOUIS XV. *See* **Place de la Révolution.**

PLACE LOUIS-LE-GRAND. *See* **Place Vendôme.**

PLACE VENDÔME. Square in Paris partly designed by Mansard for Louis XIV, it had a statue of the king in the center and was called the Place Louis-le-Grand. The statue was destroyed in the Revolution and replaced in 1806 by a column with a statue of Napoleon Bonaparte at the top.

PLAIN, THE. Girondists (q.v.) led by Danton (q.v.) were so called in the National Convention (q.v.) because they sat on the level floor or plain of the hall. Following their attempt to overthrow Robespierre (q.v.), this part of the house was called the *marais* or swamp.

PLUVIÔSE. Rain month, January 20 to February 18. *See* **Calendar, Revolutionary.**

POIDS ET MESURES (WEIGHTS AND MEASURES). Before 1793 there were something like 500 variants in weights and measures throughout France. The *parlements (q.v.)* tried to legislate some kind of universal balance, common to all areas, but without success. A decree of August 1, 1793 set out the principle of a uniformity of weights and measures, followed by another decree on April 7, 1795, which set the obligatory time when uniformity would have had to have been met. Eighteen decrees had been issued before; on December 22, 1795 the new system came into force based on the agreed metric system *(q.v.)*. In 1798 the "Bureaux des poids publics" was established.

POINT DU JOUR, LE. Edited by Barère *(q.v.)*, this journal started publication on June 19, 1789, ceasing publication on October 21, 1791. It is an invaluable record of the discussions and decrees issued by the National Assembly *(q.v.)*.

PONDICHERRY, CAPTURE OF. Capital of the French possessions in India on the Coromandel Coast. Taken by the British in 1778, it was returned to the French in 1783 by the Treaty of Versailles. It was again taken by the British on August 21, 1793 only to be restored to France by the Treaty of Amiens in 1802. (*See* **Peace of Amiens.**)

PONTS ET CHAUSSÉES. Bridges and Roads Administration.

POPULATION (1789).

France   27,000,000
  Paris 600,000   Nancy 33,500
  Amiens 43,342   Nantes 65,000
  Angers 28,000   Nîmes 48,500
  Bordeaux 82,500   Orléans 43,000
  Caen 32,000   Reims 30,500
  Dijon 22,000   Rennes 29,500
  Grenoble 25,000   Rouen 65,000
  Lille 63,000   Strasbourg 41,500
  Lyon 139,000   Toulouse[1] 53,000
  Marseilles 76,000 Tours 32,000
  Metz 46,500
Denmark[2]   929,000
Germany[3]   18,500,000
Great Britain and Ireland[3] 15,960,000
  England and Wales   9,210,000
  Ireland   5,250,000
  Scotland   1,500,000
  London[2]   801,129
Holland (United Provinces)[3]
                  2,078,000
Italy[1]   18,500,000
Poland-Lithuania
  before second partition 9,000,000[4]
  after second partition   6,000,000
Portugal[1]   2,750,000
Southern Netherlands (Belgium and Luxembourg)[3]   18,000,000
Spain[5]   10,541,000
Sweden - Finland[1]   2,281,137
Switzerland[3]   1,700,000
Turkish Empire[3]   11,450,000
[1] 1790; [2] 1801; [3] 1800; [4] 1793; [5] 1787.

PRAIRIAL. Pasture month, May 20 to June 18. *See* **Calendar, Revolutionary.**

PRAIRIAL INSURRECTION. Between May 20-22, 1795 the faubourgs *(q.v.)* rose against the Directory *(q.v.)* and were quelled by the military. There were famine conditions in Paris, White Terror *(q.v.)* in the south, and food-riots and Royalist demonstrations in the countryside. On May 1, 1795 legislation was passed against returning émigrés and priests, and against all who wished to restore the monarchy. The Paris poor wanted the immediate implementation of the 1793 constitution as the only answer. On May 19 a pamphlet, *The Insurrection of the People to obtain Bread and reconquer their Rights*, was circulating, and this called for bread, the immediate release of all patriots, the application of the 1793 constitution and the prompt calling of a new legislature. On May 20 people were called to arms, led by groups of women, and they converged on the Tuileries *(q.v.)*. The Assembly *(q.v.)* was besieged, the galleries packed with women calling for bread. Feraud, a deputy, was shot and his head waved before Boissy d'Anglas *(q.v.)*, sitting as president of the Assembly. On May 21 there was an attempt to establish a Committee of Insurrection at City Hall. An insurgent army numbering around 20-40,000 faced a more powerful army mustered by the Convention *(q.v.)* in the Place du Carrousel. The insurrection petered out as the people's delegates were unwilling to shed blood. Between May 22 and 23 the Faubourg Saint-Antoine was cleared, and later 36 rebels were hanged. On May 31 the Revolutionary Tribunal *(q.v.)* was abolished.

The repression which followed the end of the prairial rising is often seen as the end of the Revolution. The people were eliminated from the political scene and the bourgeois rule of the *notables (q.v.)* began. The social democratic movement of the Revolution was dead; politics and social power were in the hands of men of power; and the sans culottes were by then totally isolated.

PRAIRIAL, LAW OF THE 22ND OF (JUNE 10, 1794). Law passed by the Convention *(q.v.)* on June 10, 1794 by Robespierre *(q.v.)*. It permitted the Revolutionary Tribunal *(q.v.)* to hear no evidence in the defense of those brought before it. Now only two steps were possible: to order an acquittal, or the death sentence. This law was encouraged by the need to further build and consolidate a complete power base. The law intensified the Terror *(q.v.)*, causing an anti-Robespierre reaction in the Convention, where various groups, fearful of their own lives, moved together to destroy him. The fall of Robespierre followed seven weeks later.

PRÉFET. The executive head of a department, an office created in 1800 by Bonaparte. There is also a *sous-préfet* for each *arrondissement (q.v.)*.

PREMIER COMMIS DES FINANCES. Special assistant to the controller-general under the ancien régime.

PRÉSIDIAL. A tribunal or intermediate court of appeal which, under the ancien régime, dealt with civil and criminal affairs. Its tribunals were suppressed in 1790 when the judicial system was being reorganized. Its members were judges of appeal, hearing sentences sent to them by the bailiffs.

PRESS, LIBERTY OF THE. Before the 1791 constitution, which contained the principle of the freedom of the press and printing, was passed, papers were always subjected to considerable censorship. In 1797, periodicals were charged a stamp duty, although those dealing with the arts and sciences were exempted. On February 17, 1800 the consuls suppressed all but 13 of the Paris-published journals.

PRÉVÔT DES MARCHANDS DE PARIS. Head of the municipal government in Paris under the ancien régime. The title of Provost of the Merchants was established in 1190.

PRICE, RICHARD (1723-91). Welsh dissenting clergyman, one of the most cogent writers in defense of both the American and the French revolutions. He was a friend of Priestley *(q.v.)*, Franklin *(q.v.)*, John Adams, Adam Smith and John Howard. He knew Gabriel de Mably, Count de Mirabeau *(q.v.)* and others, and is best known for three treatises: *Observations on the Nature of Civil Liberty . . . and the Justice of the War in America* (1776), *Observations on the Importance of the American Revolution* (1784), and *Discourse on the Love of Our Country* (1789). Price was a spokesman for emerging democratic thought and saw freedom in politics as moral, its opposite being tyrannical and immoral. People were entitled to rebel against oppression. In the case of the traditional monarchies, rulers deserved obedience only insofar as they represented the people. It was the *Discourse* which prompted Burke *(q.v.)* to write his *Reflections*.
Hudson, W. D., *Richard Price*, 1970.

PRIESTLEY, JOSEPH (1733-1804). English chemist, natural philosopher, theologian, nonconformist minister. Many of the political tracts written by him were hostile to the attitude of government towards the American colonies. He was a Fellow of the Royal Society and had a growing scientific reputation. He was chosen Foreign Associate of the French Academy of Sciences.

In October 1794 he was in Paris, having accepted a post as librarian and traveling companion to Lord Shelburne. On July 14, 1791 the Constitutional Society of Birmingham arranged a dinner to celebrate the fall of the Bastille *(q.v.)*. A "church-and-king" mob burnt his chapel and sacked his house. By a decree of 1792 he was made a citizen of France and was elected to the National Assembly *(q.v.)*, but refused to take up the post because of ignorance of the language.
Gibbs, F. W., *Joseph Priestley: Adventurer in Science and Champion of Truth*, 1965.

PRIEUR DE LA MARNE (PIERRE LOUIS PRIEUR) (1756-1827). French politician and secretary to the National Assembly *(q.v.)*. The violence of his attacks on the ancien régime gave him the nickname of "Crieur de la Marne." In 1791 he was the vice-president of the Criminal Tribunal of Paris. Reelected to the Convention *(q.v.)*, he was sent to Normandy where he attacked the Federalists. (*See* **Federalism.**) Prieur was a member of the committees of Public Safety *(q.v.)* and National Defense, and was sent, in October 1793, to Brittany, where he established the Terror *(q.v.)*. In May 1794 he was president of the Convention. Counterrevolutionaries then drove him into hiding in May 1795.

PRIMARY ASSEMBLIES. Under the constitution of 1791 the legislature consisted of a single chamber of

745 members. Voting for the members was indirect and was restricted to men over twenty-five years of age who paid in direct taxation the equivalent of three days' wages. These men met in primary assemblies to elect one man per 100 who was chosen to act as an elector—he, to be eligible, had to pay direct taxes of at least ten days' wages. These assemblies lasted for several days and it was observed that poorer citizens could rarely afford the time to attend the election meetings, especially if they were held in a town some distance from their homes.

PRINCIPLES OF 1789. *See* **Rights of Man, Declaration of.**

PRISONERS OF WAR. In 1779 the Spanish, French, and American prisoners of war in England numbered 12,000; in September 1798 English prisoners in France were estimated at 6,000, and French prisoners in England at 27,000.

PRIVILEGES. Particular advantages or prerogatives attached to positions, kinds of work, social status, localities, churches and abbeys and their dependencies, often outside the common law. They could also apply to the right to travel within certain areas of a city to avoid being taxed on certain items. Privileges that were essentially feudal were abolished on August 4, 1789. *Les privilèges* is a generic term applied to the nobility and the higher clergy under the ancien régime.

PROCÈS-VERBAL. Official report, proceedings, minutes of a meeting under the ancien régime.

PROCUREUR. Attorney, legal representative or proxy. A *procureur du roi* acted as public prosecutor in a royal court of law. In the jurisdictions of private seigneurs, his equivalent was the *procureur fiscal*. In general, the *procureurs* were lawyers practicing like solicitors.

PROCUREUR-GÉNÉRAL. Chief (king's) prosecutor in sovereign court under the ancien régime.

PROCUREUR-GÉNÉRAL-SYNDIC. Executive officer chosen by the electors under the ancien régime. A *procureur-syndic* was a deputy of the *procureur-général-syndic*.

PROVENCE, LOUIS STANISLAS XAVIER DE FRANCE, COMTE DE (1755-1824). King of France as Louis XVIII (1815-24). *See* **Louis XVIII.**

PROVINCES. In 1789 France was divided into 32 provinces, or *gouvernements militaires* ("military governments"), which were administered by an *intendant-general* and a military governor, assisted by a lieutenant-general. (*See* **Intendants.**) The revolutionaries were convinced that the concept of provinces worked against national unity, and in 1789 took the first steps to reorganize the administration and thus created the *départements* (*q.v.*). There was considerable dispute concerning the territorial areas, but the dividing lines between the old provinces were generally respected.

PROVOCATIONS, LOIS CONTRE LES. Group of measures dictated by the different revolutionary assemblies. The law of July 18, 1791 set out a system of less or severe punishment, two years in prison or death, for those who had incited others to pillage, arson, disobedience of the law, manslaughter or, under the National Convention (*q.v.*), encouraged the reestablishment of the monarchy.

PUBLIC SAFETY, COMMITTEE OF. *See* **Committee of Public Safety.**

PYRAMIDS, BATTLE OF THE (July 21, 1798). French victory by Bonaparte over the Mamelukes (*q.v.*) and the fellahs of Lower Egypt on July 21, 1798, in the village of Embabeh, at the foot of the pyramids. This victory enabled Bonaparte to enter Cairo with little resistance.

Q

QUESTION PRÉALABLE. The use of torture on a convicted and condemned criminal to obtain from him the names of accomplices to his crime. It was abolished in 1789.

QUESTION PRÉPARATOIRE. The use of torture on an accused person in order to gain a confession. It was abolished by Louis XVI in 1780.

QUEUE DE ROBESPIERRE. Thermidorean term created for the Jacobin supporters of Robespierre (*q.v.*), who were attempting to rebuild his party after his fall. Later the expression was used generally by reactionaries or conservatives against any republican or "advanced" ideas.

QUIBERON. Peninsula in southwest Brittany. In July 1795 a party of émigrés landed with the help of a British naval force and was joined by rebels from the Vendée led by Cadoudal (*q.v.*). Republican forces drove them back to the sea. Hoche (*q.v.*), commanding the republicans, had orders to take no prisoners; the reembarkment was a disaster. Over 1,200 Royalists died. *See* **Vendéan Rebellion.**

QUINZE-VINGTS, CLUB DES. Club based in the Faubourg Saint-Antoine that believed in the principle of insurrection as a sacred right. It was strongly against the Convention, considering that the government should be abolished when it was popularly felt to have violated the rights of the people as enshrined in the constitution.

QUOTATIONS.
One must not be more Royalist than the king (Saying from the time of Louis XVI).

Anonymous.

Ça ira, ça tiendra ("That will be, that will last.") (Revolutionary song, based on a phrase of Benjamin Franklin's.)

Anonymous.

Let the revolting distinction of rich and poor disappear once and for all, the distinction of great and small, of masters and valets, of governors and governed. Let there be no other difference between human beings than those of age and sex. Since all have the same needs and the same faculties, let there be one education for all, one food for all.
Babeuf, François Noël (1760-97).

The tree of liberty only grows when watered by the blood of tyrants.
Barère de Vieuzac, Bertrand (1755-1841).

The Revolution is like Saturn—it eats its own children.
The guillotine is the best physician!
        Büchner, Georg (1813-37).

France was long a despotism tempered by epigrams.
The sea-green Incorruptible (Robespierre).
        Carlyle, Thomas (1795-1856).

I should like to see the last of the kings strangled with the guts of the last of the priests!
Chamfort, Sébastian Roch Nicholas
        (1740-94).

Show my head to the people, it is worth seeing. (Last words, addressed to the executioner.)
    Danton, Georges Jacques (1759-94).

How much the greatest event it is that ever happened in the world! and how much the best! (On the fall of the Bastille.)
        Fox, Charles James (1749-1806).

Go and tell those who have sent you that we are here by the will of the nation and that we shall not leave save at the point of bayonets (June 23, 1789).
Mirabeau, Honoré Gabriel Riquetti,
        comte de (1749-91).

In revolutions there are only two sorts of men, those who cause them and those who profit by them.
    Napoleon Bonaparte (1769-1821).

Louis XVI: *Is it a revolt?*
La Rochefoucauld-Liancourt: *No, Sire, it is a revolution.* (1789).
Rochefoucauld-Liancourt, François
        Alexandre Frédéric, duc de la
        (1747-1827).

One can't reign and be innocent.
Saint-Just, Louis Antoine Léon de
        (1767-94).

They have learned nothing, and forgotten nothing (of the Bourbons).
Talleyrand-Perigord, Charles Maurice,
    prince de Benavento (1754-1838).

R

RABAUT DE SAINT ÉTIENNE, JEAN PAUL (1743-93). Politician. Son of Paul Rabaut (1718-94), who was leader of the Huguenots. He served as president of the National Assembly *(q.v.)* in 1790 but was guillotined during the Terror *(q.v.)*.

RAMBOUILLET. Royal château about 25 miles from Paris. Francis I died here March 31, 1547 and here Charles X abdicated on August 2, 1830. After being owned by the comte de Toulouse and the duc de Penthièvre, it was purchased by Louis XVI in 1778 for 6 million livres. The Constituent Assembly *(q.v.)*, however, placed it on the civil list, as it felt that kings had no right to hold things personally.

RASTATT, CONGRESS OF. The congress opened at Rastatt in Baden on December 9, 1797 with the aim of rearranging German boundaries to compensate those princes whose territories, on the left bank of the Rhine, had been occupied by France. Negotiations continued throughout 1798 but the result was inconclusive and with the outbreak of war the congress ended. Of the three French representatives to the congress, two were murdered on leaving Rastatt. The motive was uncertain but it was thought that the Austrians were anxious that papers with damaging evidence on their plans for Bavaria should be returned. Other theories are that it was the work of émigrés or those in France in favor of war.

An earlier Congress in Rastatt (November 1713 to March 1714) worked out the terms ending the War of the Spanish Succession.

RAYNAL, GUILLAUME THOMAS FRANÇOIS, ABBÉ (1713-96). French historian. He was dismissed from his parish of Saint-Sulpice for some unexplained reason and devoted himself to society and literature. He wrote for *Mercure de France* and composed a series of popular works that he sold himself. His most important work was *L'Histoire philosophique et politique des Établissements et du Commerce des Européens dans les deux Indes,* which was published in Amsterdam in six volumes. Diderot *(q.v.)* was credited with writing a third of it but Voltaire *(q.v.)* saw it as "a stale declamation." It did, however, help to develop the intellectual climate of the times and was both anticlerical and anti-Royalist. It ran into many editions, revisions and translations. The book was banned in France in 1779 and the authorities ordered that it should be burned and the author arrested. Raynal escaped and traveled in Germany and Russia, returning to France only in 1787. He was elected to the Estates-General (q.v.) in 1789 but refused to take his seat because he was against violence.

In 1791 he argued, in a message that was read to the National Assembly (q.v.), for a constitutional monarchy based on the English model. As a result his property was confiscated.

REBELLES, LES. Federalist deputies who, after May 31, 1793, resisted the decrees of the Convention (q.v.). The Convention decreed severe punitive measures against any of the towns in the Republic that either received or helped the brigands. As a punishment for disobedience, entire villages would be leveled.

RÉCOMPENSES. Rewards given to those wounded at Nancy and the Bastille (q.v.), to those who had stopped the intended escape of the king, and to those who had helped the shipwrecked.

RÉCOMPENSES, LES. One of the sansculottides (q.v.), September 21.

RÉGIE DES POUDRES. In 1775, Turgot (q.v.) abolished the "Ferme des Poudres," which had been established for the manufacture of gunpowder within the kingdom. The principle was to establish a new system of carefully monitored and controlled production procedures in order to ensure the highest quality of gunpower produced.

In July 1794 the rivalry between the Agence des Poudres et Salpêtres, the old establishment that had rendered excellent service during the early years of the Revolution, and the new, revolutionary agency caused the Convention (q.v.) to amalgamate the two.

REIGN OF TERROR. *See* **Terror, Reign of.**

REIMS. Before 1789 Reims was a subdelegation of the intendancy of Châlons-sur-Marne, becoming the chief place in the district of the department of the Marne in 1790. Troubles broke out in 1791 and the "Sainte-Ampoule," containing the sacred oil for the unction of the king, which had been in existence since Philippe-Auguste (1165-1223), was broken on the pedestal of the statue of Louis XV.

REMONTRANCES. Under the ancien régime they were the rights of formal objection to the implementation of new ordinances, edicts, declarations, orders in council, or letters patent. The monarch assumed the right of final decision, without appeal, concerning legislation.

RENTES. Used sometimes to mean "rents," the term usually signifies annuities or interest-bearing bonds received in return for a loan or a capital investment. A *rente constituée* was derived from purchase of the right to draw the revenue, or part of it, from a piece of real property. *Rentes sur le domaine royal* were pensions paid out of the revenue from crown lands. *Rentes perpetuelles* were bonds and *rentes viagères* were annuities.

RENTIER. One who enjoys an income, in the form of regular cash payments from a *rente (q.v.)*; a bondholder or pensioner.

REPUBLIC, FIRST. The First Republic was proclaimed on September 21, 1792 as a result of the Revolution of 1789. It lasted until May 18, 1804, when Napoleon Bonaparte became emperor. It falls into three periods: the Convention, Directory and Consulate *(qq.v.)*.

RÉPUBLICAINES RÉVOLUTIONNAIRES, SOCIÉTÉ DES. Founded at the beginning of 1793, this society had as its president the actress Mademoiselle Lacombe. It was denounced by the Jacobins *(q.v.)* as being counterrevolutionary and disappeared by about September 1793.

REQUISITIONS. Generally, an order addressed to particular persons to place at the disposition and disposal of the state food supplies, horses and cattle, transport and other goods and services necessary for the public good. Requisitions were frequent during the Revolution, and controlled by a decree of April 26-29, 1792.

RESTIF, NICOLAS EDMÉ, (CALLED RESTIF DE LA BRETONNE, 1734-1806). French novelist. He worked as a journeyman printer in Paris, then produced about 200 works. Many of the books were designed and printed by him on a vast number of subjects. He experienced poverty and intrigues. He used his own experience for his books, which gave an excellent view of French society in the period just before the Revolution. In 1795 he was granted 2,000 francs from the government.

RETRAITE, MAISON DE. Situated at Petit-Montrouge, some distance from the Barrière d'Enfer on the main road to Orléans, this theater was started in 1781 and completed in 1783. It was first named the Maison royale de santé, and was designed for sick soldiers and poor ecclesiastics. During the Revolution it took the name of *Hospice national*, serving the inhabitants of Bourg-la-Reine and the communes nearby.

REVOLUTIONARY COMMITTEES. Name given to the clubs, or popular societies, which were founded throughout the kingdom toward the end of 1790, and which eventually came to be known as Comités de Surveillance. These comités, for which those of the electors of Paris served as a model, continued to be corresponding societies in the country, which kept in touch with the Paris center.
Sirich, J. B., *The Revolutionary Committees in the Departments of France*, 1943.

REVOLUTIONARY GOVERNMENT. This form of government existed the day after August 10, 1792, when Louis XVI was imprisoned in the Temple *(q.v.)* and while the Legislative Assembly *(q.v.)* set up the administration of a Conseil executif provisoire. The monarchical constitution of 1791 was virtually abolished, and replaced by the democratic constitution of 1793, but this last was never applied. The Assembly issued a second decree concerning the provisional revolutionary government, organizing and reorganizing the administrative bodies at all levels. After the fall of Robespierre *(q.v.)*, the Convention *(q.v.)* maintained the revolutionary government, but this disappeared in 1795, to be replaced by the Directory *(q.v.)* and the two councils *(q.v.)*. At this point the word *revolutionnaire* was placed on the index, and removed from all public establishments and administrative organizations.

REVOLUTIONARY TRIBUNAL.

The Revolutionary Tribunal was originally established in Paris on August 17, 1792 but had been suppressed the following November. However, on March 29, 1793 it was revived. Up to July 27, 1794, when Robespierre *(q.v.)* was deposed, it had put to death 2,774 persons, including Queen Marie Antoinette, Princess Elizabeth, and a large number of nobility and gentry, male and female. The oldest victim was Counsellor Dupin, aged 97, and the youngest, Charles Dubost, aged 14. From July 27 to December 15, 1794 only Robespierre and about 100 of his accomplices were brought before it.

REVOLUTIONS.

France experienced four major revolutions between 1789 and 1870: (i) the Revolution of 1789, which ended the ancien régime; (ii) the 1830 or July Revolution, which overthrew Charles X *(q.v.)*; (iii) the 1848 or February Revolution, which overthrew Louis-Philippe *(q.v.)*; (iv) the 1870 or September Revolution, which overthrew Napoleon III.

RÉVOLUTIONS DE FRANCE ET DE BRABANT, LES (NOVEMBER 1789

to JULY 1791). A weekly newspaper founded and directed by Camille Desmoulins *(q.v.)*. It was published as *La Semaine politique et littéraire* 1791-92, but the last issue by Desmoulins was July 18, 1791.

RÉVOLUTIONS DE PARIS, LES.

Title of a widely read weekly newspaper published by Louis-Marie Prudhomme (1752-1830) from July 12, 1789. It had a readership of more than 200,000. The most independent and penetrating of all the journals, it concerned itself dispassionately with the most important public questions of the day. It reported on the debates and decrees of the government, possessing a veracity and impartiality that few of its competitors had. Publication ceased on February 24, 1794.

RIGHTS OF MAN, DECLARATION OF.

Manifesto debated in the National Assembly (1789-91) embodying the principles and philosophy of the Revolution. It consisted of 17 articles and stated that all citizens are born equal and are equal in the eyes of the law, with rights to liberty, property, and security, and the right to resist tyranny. The nation is sovereign and laws are the expression of the general will. Every citizen has the right to freedom of opinion, speech, writing, etc. Later the Revolution did not honor these rights, as the Reign of Terror *(q.v.)* showed. It was published as the preface to the constitution in 1791. Some extracts from the Articles follow.

1. Men are born and remain free and equal in rights . . .

2. . . . These rights are liberty, property, security and resistance to oppression.

3. Liberty consists in the ability to do whatever does not harm another . . .

5. Law may rightfully prohibit only those actions which are injurious to society.

6. Law is the expression of the general will. All citizens have the right to take part, in person or by their representatives, in its formation. It must be the same for all . . . All citizens, being equal in its eyes, are equally admissable to all public dignities, offices and employments, according to their capacity, and with no other distinction than of their virtues and talents.

8. . . . no one may be punished except by virtue of a law established and promulgated before the time of the offence . . .

9. Every man being presumed innocent until judged guilty, if it is deemed indispensable to keep him under arrest, all rigors not necessary to secure his person should be severely suppressed by law.

10. No one may be disturbed for his opinions, even in religion, provided that their manifestation does not trouble public order as established by law.

11. . . . Every citizen may speak, write and print freely.

13. . . . for expenses of administration common taxation is necessary. It should be apportioned equally among all the citizens according to their capacity to pay.

14. All citizens have the right, by themselves or through their representatives, to have demonstrated to them the necessity of public taxes . . .

17. Property being an inviolable and sacred right, no one may be deprived of it except for an obvious requirement of public necessity, certified by law, and then on condition of a just compensation in advance.

RIVOLI, BATTLE OF. A considerable victory by the French, led by Bonaparte, over the Austrians, commanded by Alvinzi, occurred at Rivoli, Italy on January 14-15, 1797. Masséna (*q.v.*) provided a great deal of support, and this led to his being created duc de Rivoli. The success of this battle led to the capture of Mantua.

ROBE, LA. *La robe* referred, under the ancien régime, to people engaged in the administration of justice, many of whom were not nobles. The term *noblesse de robe* tended to mean nobles employed in the royal administration, who held their positions on the basis of hereditary right. It implied a function, not social status, and the *robe* (gown) was contrasted with that of the épeé (sword).

ROBESPIERRE, MAXIMILIEN FRANÇOIS MARIE ISIDORE DE (1758-94). Lawyer, leading revolutionist and orator. He was elected to the Estates-General in 1789. He made his mark as a radical and was an early member of the Jacobin Club (q.v.). In 1792 he became a Paris deputy to the Convention (q.v.), emerging as leader of the Mountain party (q.v.). In July 1793, having beaten the Girondists (q.v.), he became president of the Committee of Public Safety (q.v.) and launched the Reign of Terror (q.v.). By 1794 he had achieved almost limitless power, but was at last overthrown on July 27, 1794 and guillotined the same day.

Hampson, Norman, *The Life and Opinions of Maximilien Robespierre*, 1979.

Jordan, David P., *The Revolutionary Career of Maximilien Robespierre*, 1986.

Mathiez, A., *The Fall of Robespierre and other essays*, trans., 1927.

Rudé, Georges, *Robespierre-Portrait of a Revolutionary*, 1985.

Thompson, J. M., *Robespierre and the French Revolution*, 1952.

ROCHAMBEAU, JEAN BAPTISTE DONATIEN DE VIMEUR, COMTE DE (1725-1807).   General. He joined the army in 1742, was at the siege of Maestricht, and distinguished himself in other European conflicts. In 1780 he was sent to Newport, Rhode Island with 6,000 men to support the Americans, and in 1781 helped in the capture of Yorktown. He commanded the Army of the North (q.v.) in 1791. He was arrested during the Reign of Terror (q.v.) and avoided the guillotine.

ROHAN, LOUIS RENÉ ÉDOUARD, PRINCE DE ROHAN-GUÉMÉNÉE, CARDINAL DE (1734-1803). Rohan was politically ambitious, enjoyed high life and was indifferent to clerical duties. He had incurred the displeasure of Marie Antoinette and

of her mother, Maria Theresa, during his diplomatic trip to Vienna in 1777 when he made it quite clear that he was opposed to the Austrian alliance. In the Affair of the Diamond Necklace (q.v.), Rohan was duped by the comtesse de Lamotte, Cagliostro and others, and was led to believe that his attentions to the queen were welcome and that his arrangement by which she received the necklace was approved. Rohan was acquitted by the Parlement in 1786, to wild public acclaim. The judgment was regarded as being a victory over the court and the unpopular queen. In 1789 Rohan was elected to the Estates-General, and in January 1791 he refused the oath to the constitution and went into exile.

ROLAND DE LA PLATIÈRE, JEAN MARIE (1734-93). Politician. He was inspector of manufactures at Amiens (q.v.), when in 1775 he made the acquaintance of Marie Jeanne Philipon (1754-93, q.v.), whom he married in February 1780. During 1791 he and his wife became acquainted with leaders of the Girondists (q.v.) such as Brissot, Pétion and François Buzot (qq.v.). In March 1792 Roland became minister of the interior. Dismissed three months later by the king, he was recalled after the king's removal to the Temple (q.v.). He was hated by the Jacobins (q.v.) for his protests against the September Massacres (q.v.). He escaped arrest during the Jacobin coup d'état but his wife was arrested and eventually guillotined on November 8, 1793. Two days later he committed suicide.

ROLAND DE LA PLATIÈRE, MARIE-JEANNE PHILIPON (1754-93). Politician and admirer of the works of

Rousseau. Wife of Jean-Marie Roland de la Platière (*q.v.*). In 1789 they both became involved in revolutionary politics in Paris, where her salon, attended by Brissot, Pétion, Buzot (*qq.v.*) and Clavière, became the center of democratic discussion. She was very influential while her husband was minister of the interior. She hated Robespierre and Danton (*qq.v.*), and used her considerable influence in the Girondist (*q.v.*) cause. When they fell in May 1793 she was imprisoned, and was guillotined on November 8, 1793.

ROMAN REPUBLIC. *See* **Rome.**

ROME. Capital of the Kingdom of Italy, situated on the Tiber, entered by the French army under General Alexandre Berthier (1753-1815) on February 10, 1798. The Roman Republic was declared, in the Forum, on February 15, on which occasion the pontifical government was abolished. The Directory (*q.v.*) found Berthier to be too moderate in his treatment of the pope, the church and the people, and replaced him with Masséna (*q.v.*).

The Papal States remained under French military control. The pope took refuge in Tuscany, and the States and its people were savagely exploited. In 1799 Pope Pius VI was removed as a captive to France and died at Valence, seeming to indicate the end of the papacy. The creation of the Roman Republic was a clear breach of the Campo Formio (*q.v.*) settlement, and on November 25, 1798 a Neapolitan army of 50,000 took Rome. On December 15, 1798 French forces reoccupied Rome and on January 23, 1799 the French established a republic in Naples.

ROTURIER. Member of the Third Estate (*q.v.*). The non-nobles, derived from *ruptuarius* ("those who break the soil").

ROUGET DE LISLE, CLAUDE JOSEPH (1760-1836). Soldier, minor poet and composer. He wrote the words and music of the "Marseillaise" in 1792 and was imprisoned and cashiered during the Revolution.

ROUSSEAU, JEAN JACQUES (1712-78). Writer and philosopher. He wrote many of the articles on music and political economy for Diderot's *Encyclopédie* (*qq.v.*). One of his most important works, *Contrat Social*, published in 1762, had the following opening words: "Man is born free, but everywhere is in chains." His writings had great influence on the leaders of the Revolution.

Grimsley, Ronald, *Jean Jacques Rousseau*, 1983.

McDonald, J., *Rousseau and the French Revolution, 1762-91*, 1965.

ROYALTY, ABOLITION OF. *See* **Abolition of Royalty.**

ROYER-COLLARD, PIERRE PAUL (1763-1845). Lawyer, philosopher and political activist. He was elected member of the municipality of Paris. In 1792 he left Paris to escape the Jacobins (*q.v.*), but in 1797 served for a few months on the Council of Five Hundred (*q.v.*). He became professor of philosophy in Paris from 1810 and exercised an immense influence on French philosophy.

SAINT-CLOUD. Royal chateau built by Louis XIV. Louis XVI and Marie Antoinette resided here, but public opinion forced them to return to Paris. After the execution of the king in 1793 the property was confiscated. The Convention *(q.v.)* decided that it should be saved and used by the people for recreation and to form useful establishments for agriculture and the arts. The coup d'état 18 Brumaire *(q.v.)* took place at Saint-Cloud, where the Council of Ancients and the Council of Five Hundred were meeting.

SAINT-CYR. Town near Versailles famous for the institution for young noblewomen of indigent families founded by Madame de Maintenon. The house, opened in 1686, was named the Institut de Saint-Louis, or the *filles de Saint-Louis.* It became, eventually, a regular convent and was suppressed in 1770. In 1803 the Military School of Fontainebleau was transferred to Saint-Cyr.

SAINT-DENIS. Town near Paris on the right bank of the Seine. Its early Gothic basilica was restored after the Revolution. In August 1793 the revolutionists destroyed many of its royal tombs. In October bodies were taken from their coffins and cast into a pit; the coffins' lead was melted. Gold and jewels were taken to Paris. Louis XVI and Marie Antoinette are buried in the crypt. By a decree of Bonaparte dated February 20, 1806, the church, which had been turned into a cattle market, was ordered to be cleaned and redecorated as "the future burial place of the emperors of France." On the return of the Bourbons, more restorations took place.

SAINT-EUSTACHE, CHURCH OF. Church situated in the Rue Trainée and the Rue de Jour, constructed in 1532 on the site of a chapel dedicated to Saint Agnes. On April 3, 1791 the body of Mirabeau *(q.v.)* was deposited here. In 1793 the church was used for non-Christian purposes when celebrating the Fête de la Raison *(q.v.).*

SAINTE-GENEVIÈVE, CHURCH OF. Built on the site occupied by the Lycée Henri IV, the original church was burnt by the Danes in 857 and rebuilt in 1175. The tomb of Sainte-Geneviève was here, and the relics of this patroness of Paris, placed in a golden casket, were publicly burnt in the Place de Grève in 1793. The church was demolished in 1807.

SAINT-JUST, LOUIS ANTOINE LÉON FLORELLE DE (1767-94). Revolutionary and fanatical aide of Robespierre *(q.v.)*. At 19 he went to Paris, taking some of his mother's property. He spent some months in a reformatory at his mother's request. His essay *L'Esprit de la révolution* was published in 1791. He was elected to the Convention *(q.v.)* in 1792 and attracted notice because of his attacks on the king. Robespierre sent him on missions to the armies of the Rhine and the Moselle. His speeches started the attacks on Hébert *(q.v.)* that eventually sent him and Danton *(q.v.)* to the guillotine. He was feared by many during the Terror *(q.v.)* but was arrested on July 27 and was executed, with Robespierre, by the guillotine on July 28, 1794.

Curtis, E. N., *Saint Just, Colleague of Robespierre*, 1935.

SAINT-LAZARE, PRISON DE. Prison in Paris. In 1632 the Congregation of the Mission (Vincentians or Lazarists) established themselves in Paris and cared for lepers. During the Revolution the mission was sacked, the Vincentians were persecuted and the buildings used as a prison for suspects. It was demolished in 1935.

SAINT-SIMONISM. Political system based on the teachings of Claude Henri, comte de Saint-Simon (1760-1825), the founder of French utopian socialism. The system was based on large-scale industrial production controlled by benevolent industrial leaders. It aimed to improve the living standards of the poorest. State ownership and the abolition of hereditary privileges were key principles of the system, but workers were to receive rewards according to their abilities rather than an equal division of the wealth created.

ST. VINCENT, CAPE OF. Promontory in Algarve province, Portugal, off which a naval battle was fought on February 14, 1797 between Britain, the victor, under Admiral John Jervis (later Earl St. Vincent, 1735-1823) with Nelson as his commodore, and a Spanish fleet.

SALLE DES MENUS PLAISIRS, VERSAILLES. Known also as "Salle des Menus." Grand hall at Versailles constructed for the Assembly of Notables *(q.v.)* in 1787 and 1788.

SALONS. Informal social gatherings in the houses of high society where art, literature, religion and politics were discussed. They were generally presided over by the lady of the house and took place once or twice a week. During the Revolution the discussions at salons tended to be mainly political. One such salon was that of Madame Roland *(q.v.)*.

SALPÊTRIÈRE, HOPITAL DE LA. Hospital built in 1656 as a home for aged and insane women on the site of an arsenal and saltpeter works. In 1684 a criminal wing was added. During the Revolution political prisoners were kept in the part of the buildings known as La Force and it was the scene of some of the worst of the September Massacres *(q.v.)*.

SALUT. In the Revolution the former greeting of *salut* was replaced by *salut et fraternité*.

SAMBRE-ET-MEUSE, L'ARMÉE DE. Army, under Jourdan *(q.v.)* that defeated the united Austrian and Netherlands armies at Fleurus *(q.v.)* in June 1794.

SANS-CULOTTES (WITHOUT BREECHES). Radical republicans who, to signify that they were manual workers, wore trousers rather than the knee-breeches of the prerevolutionary aristocrats. Originally a term of reproach, but the revolutionaries assumed the name with pride and applied it to themselves as "patriots." In 1792-94 it was applied to a specific group that was pressuring the Convention *(q.v.)* by mobilizing local clubs and assemblies.

Rose, Robert B., *The Making of the "Sans-Culottes": Democratic Ideas and Institutions in Paris, 1789-92*, 1983.

Rudé, George, *The Crowd in the French Revolution*, 1959.

Soboul, A., *The Parisian Sans-Culottes in the French Revolution 1793-1794*, 1964.

————. *The Sans-Culottes: The Popular Movement and the Revolutionary Government, 1793–94*. 1981.

SANS-CULOTTIDES. The five complementary days (six in a leap year) left over to balance the 12 months of the revolutionary calendar, each month being made to consist of 30 days. The days were named in honor of the sans-culottes *(q.v.)*, and were observed as national festivals and holidays. The name was produced by Fabre d'Eglantine *(q.v.)*. See **Calendar, Revolutionary.**

SANSON, CHARLES (1740-93). Official executioner in Paris during the Revolution. He beheaded Louis XVI; his son, Henri (1767-1840), was also an official executioner and beheaded Marie Antoinette.

SANTERRE, ANTOINE JOSEPH (1752-1809). Brewer who, in 1789, had a command in the National Guard *(q.v.)* and took part in the storming of the Bastille *(q.v.)*. He was in charge at the king's execution. On being appointed general of division in 1793 he fought the Vendéan Royalists but was defeated. He was called back to Paris and imprisoned.

SARDINIA, KINGDOM OF. In 1789 Sardinia was composed of the marquisates of Saluces and Montferrat, Savoy, Piedmont, Nice and the island of Sardinia. The kingdom was deprived of its mainland territories by Bonaparte in 1796 but they were reinstated, with Genoa, by the Congress of Vienna.

SAUMUR, BATTLE OF (June 10, 1793). The chief center of the district of the department of Maine-et-Loire. This town was attacked and taken by a Vendéan army on June 10, 1793, held for eight days and then abandoned.

SAVANTS (SCHOLARS). In 1790 it was decided to provide pensions for scholars, artists and men of letters. The value of the pensions was to be 3-6,000 livres. On January 3, 1795 the Convention provided 300,000 francs for dispersal to a long list of the deserving.

SAVENAY, BATTLE OF. Town in Loire-Inférieure that was the scene of a battle on December 23, 1793 between the Vendéans and the army led by General Kléber (*q.v.*) and Moreau (*q.v.*). The Vendéan army was totally destroyed, with some survivors being executed at Angers.

SEA-GREEN INCORRUPTIBLE, THE. So Carlyle called Robespierre (*q.v.*), said to be of sallow, unhealthy complexion, in his *French Revolution.*

SÉANCES ROYALES. Formal audiences where the sovereign proceeded in great splendor to the opening of the Estates-General and the Assemblies of Notables (*qq.v.*), where he enforced by edict an ordinance or law. *See* **Lit de Justice.**

SECOND COALITION (1799). *See* **War of the Second Coalition.**

SECTIONS. Divisions, of Paris, numbering 48, created to replace the districts as decreed by the Constituent Assembly (*q.v.*), May 21, 1790. All citizens with voting rights formed the assembly of each section. The administration of the section was drawn from the elected members of the Assembly.

SEDYMANN, BATTLE OF. Village in the Fayoum Valley in Middle Egypt noted for being the scene of Desaix's (*q.v.*) victory over the Mamelukes (*q.v.*) under Murad Bey on October 7, 1798.

SEIGNEURIE. The *seigneurie* (manor) normally consisted of two different kinds of property. The *domaine*

proche was an area of land of which the seigneur usually cultivated a part for his own use with paid labor and let out the rest to tenant farmers or sharecroppers. (*See* **Metayage.**) The *domaine utile* was an area inhabited by peasant farmers who had to render feudal dues for the use of the land.

SEMAINE POLITIQUE ET LITTE-RAIRE, LA. *See* **Revolutions de France et de Brabant, Les.**

SEMAPHORE. *See* **Chappe, Claude.**

SENATE. The Senate was created by the constitution promulgated December 24, 1799 to watch over the administration of the laws. The number of senators was raised gradually from 60 to 137. The Senate was replaced by the Chamber of Peers in 1814.

SEPTEMBER MASSACRES. Indiscriminate slaughter by a mob, directed at the Royalists and "suspects" confined in the Abbaye and other prisons, lasting from September 2-5, 1792 in Paris. Between 1,200-4,000 were massacred with revolting brutality. It was caused by popular hysteria aroused by Marat's *L'Ami du Peuple* (*q.v.*), the fall of Verdun to the Prussians and rumors of Royalist and counterrevolutionary treachery.

SEPTEMBRISTS. Those taking part in the September Massacres of 1792 (*q.v.*).

SERVITUDES COLLECTIVES. Obligations enforced by the village communities on all cultivators of land under the open-field system. These included the obligation to sow the same crops as one's neighbors and to leave a proportion of land fallow. But there were also communal rights, in particular the right to *vaine pâture* *(q.v.)*.

SHARE-CROPPING. *See* **Metayage.**

SIEYÈS, EMMANUEL-JOSEPH, COMTE (ABBÉ SIEYÈS, 1748-1836). Statesman. Just before the meeting of the Estates-General in 1788-89 he published three pamphlets, *Vues sur les moyens d'execution* (1788), *Essai sur les privilèges* (1788) and *Qu'est-ce que le Tiers État?* (1789), and these publications caused him to be well-known throughout France. He was elected deputy for Paris and he proposed that the Third Estate *(q.v.)* assume the title of "National Assembly." Later he was also influential in the decision to divide France into *départements* *(q.v.)*.

From 1793 he gradually withdrew from public life, and when asked how he managed in the Terror *(q.v.)* he replied "J'ai vécu" (I remained alive). He returned to public life after the downfall of Robespierre *(q.v.)*. Sieyès served on the Committee of Public Safety *(q.v.)* and was elected to the Council of Five Hundred *(q.v.)*. Later he was one of the five members of the Directory *(q.v.)*, and with Bonaparte, Fouché and Talleyrand *(qq.v.)* brought about the coup d'état of November 9, 1799. He became a consul and drafted the new constitution, which was radically altered by Bonaparte allowing him to become first consul. Sieyès gave up his consulship. He was exiled at the Restoration and lived in Belgium (1814-30), returning to Paris where he died.

Clapham, J. H., *The Abbé Sieyès*, 1912.

Van Deusen, Glydon G., *Sieyès: His Life and His Nationalism*, 1932.

SIX EDICTS. Series of edicts issued by Turgot *(q.v.)* in January 1776, providing for the suppression of duties on grain in the markets, harbor dues, statutes of apprenticeship and incorporation, the *corvée (q.v.)*, and for the reduction of market dues. The edicts met with great opposition and were not registered without recourse to a *lit de justice (q.v.)* in March 1776, while they eventually led to Turgot's downfall. The two edicts which caused the greatest displeasure were those suppressing the corvée and the Jurandes *(q.v.)* and Maîtrises, the privileged guilds.

SLAVERY IN THE FRENCH COLONIES. On February 4, 1794 the Convention abolished slavery in the French colonies. The decree was not enforced in Martinique, which was occupied by Britain, and it was ignored in Mauritius. However, in Guadeloupe and Haiti slavery was abolished. Bonaparte, following pressure from sugar planters, reintroduced slavery in 1802, and it was not until 1848 that it was finally abolished in the French possessions.

SOCIÉTÉ DES ÉGAUX. Club with the aim to instigate a final revolution when elected officials would collect the produce of the land and place it in storehouses and then distribute it. It was agreed that May 11, 1796 was to be the day of action. Some of the plans provided that: literature, art and religion would be abolished; children would be brought up in common; towns would be destroyed; all citizens would wear the same type of clothing. The club was closed by the Directory (q.v.) in February 1796 but it continued to flourish in private houses and cafés.

SOCIÉTÉ NATIONALE. In 1792 Condorcet (q.v.) presented his report on the general organization of education. The Revolution had destroyed much of the educational system of the ancien régime. Condorcet produced a plan for a national system of education that was well in advance of its times and reflected the philosophy of "careers open to talents." It was coeducational and saw the importance of science and physical training. The Société was to be an autonomous body, supervizing this national system of education.

SOCIETY OF THIRTY. Society consisting of leading members of the liberal aristocracy in 1789.

SORBONNE. Society founded for indigent scholars in Paris by the theologian Robert de Sorbonne in 1252. The Sorbonne soon attained a European reputation as a faculty of theology, and although conservative they were favorably disposed towards the Encyclopedists. The Sorbonne was abolished by the Constituent Assembly (q.v.) in 1790 and was reestablished and reorganized in 1808.

SOU. Copper alloy coin with a value of between 12 and 15 deniers or one twentieth of a livre. (*See* **Livre turnois.**)

SOVEREIGN COURTS. Over 30 courts reported directly to the king under the ancien régime, the dozen *parlements (q.v.)* being the most influential. They exercised political and judicial functions and registered the king's edicts.

SOVEREIGNTY OF THE PEOPLE. The Constituent Assembly (q.v.) on February 28, 1791 stated that sovereignty resides in the nation as a whole, not within any single person or partial group.

(SPEYER) SPIRES, BATTLES OF. Town in Rhineland-Palatinate, Germany on the river of the same name, near the Rhine. It was taken by Custine (q.v.) on September 30, 1792, and retaken by the Armée de la Moselle in July 1794. It acted as the entrepôt for the artillery magazines for the Austrian armies. In 1796 Spires was the chief center of the district of the department of Mont-Tonnerre.

STAËL, ANNE LOUISE GERMAINE NECKER, MADAME DE (BARONNE DE STAËL-HOLSTEIN) (1766-1817). Writer and only child of Jacques Necker (q.v.). Before the Revolution she had a salon (q.v.) that was frequented by the liberal aristocracy. Her initial enthusiasm for the Revolution changed and she left Paris. Returning only in 1795, she reopened her salon, which, during the Consulate (q.v.), became a meeting place for those opposed to Bonaparte. By 1804 she was banned from France and lived in Switzerland, returning to Paris in 1814 after Napoleon's abdication.
Herold, J. C., *Mistress to an Age: A Life of Madame de Staël*, 1958.

SUPREME BEING (ÊTRE SUPRÊME, L'). In a decree of May 7, 1794 the Cult of the Supreme Being was instigated by Robespierre *(q.v.)*. His aim was to replace both Christianity and the worship of Reason. A Fête of the Supreme Being *(q.v.)* took place on June 8, at which the hymn of the supreme being was sung, an effigy of Atheism burned and a tree of liberty planted. The cult died with the fall of Robespierre.

SUSPECTS, LAW OF. *See* **Law of Suspects**

SWISS GUARDS. In 1481 Louis XI engaged the Swiss Guards, who formed an élite corps that replaced the Francs-archers. Their treaties of service were renewed over the years. By 1614 they had been organized into regiments and by 1791 there were 11, totaling 973 men. They defended Louis XVI at the Tuileries *(q.v.)* on August 10, 1792 and left shortly afterwards, not staying to have their licenses renewed. They returned under the Restoration and were in service until the July 1830 revolution.

SYMBOLS, REVOLUTIONARY. Examples include the sun, the eye of vigilance, the fascicles of union, Mercury. The president of the Revolutionary Tribunal *(q.v.)* had two crossed axes on a red background as a symbol of office. Later the entrance cards carried by senators bore a snake, the symbol of Prudence.

T

TABOR, BATTLE OF MOUNT.
Battle during the siege of Acre.
Kléber *(q.v.)* encountered 35,000
troops of the pasha of Damascus near
Mount Tabor. On April 15-16, 1799,
outnumbered 17 to 1, the French
formed two small squares and fought
desperately. After eight hours Bonaparte appeared at the head of his
guides and General Bon's division,
which he had marched up overnight
from Acre, 25 miles away. The Turkish force, the only one available to
attempt the relief of Acre, was driven
off.

TAGLIAMENTO, BATTLE OF.
River in north Italy. Here Bonaparte
defeated the Austrians on March 16,
1797. Masséna *(q.v.)* fought another
battle here on November 12, 1805.

TAILLE. Tax in France that took
two forms, personal and "real," and
provided the greater part of all taxation under the ancien régime. Personal *taille*, a direct tax levied from the
15th century to 1789, was assessed on
personal possessions at a rate that
was arbitrarily determined by the tax
collector. In practice it fell almost
entirely on the peasants because the
First and Second Estates and many of
the Third Estate were exempt. (*See*
Orders.) "Real" *taille* was levied over
a similar period in the Midi and
southwest of France and fell on common land. Less arbitrary than personal taille, it raised more revenue.

**TALLEYRAND-PÉRIGORD,
CHARLES MAURICE DE, BISHOP
OF AUTUN, PRINCE DE BENA-
VENTO** (1754-1838). Diplomat
with a genius for personal survival
that saw him through numerous
changes of power. In 1788 he became
bishop of Autun. He represented the
Second Estate at the Estates-General
(q.v.). In 1790 he accepted the Civil
Constitution of the Clergy *(q.v.)* and
resigned his bishopric in 1791 to take
up politics. From 1792 he was sent on
a number of diplomatic missions to
London and the United States, thus
escaping the Terror *(q.v.)*. He returned to France in September 1795
after periods spent in Holland and
Germany. Talleyrand was appointed
as minister of foreign affairs in July
1797, but he then transferred his
opportunistic loyalties to Bonaparte.
It was Talleyrand who encouraged
Bonaparte's ambitious expansionist
dreams. He was made grand cham-
berlain of the empire in 1804, prince
of Benavento in 1806, as well as arch-
chancellor and grand-elector.
Cooper, Duff, *Talleyrand*, 1947.

TALLIEN, JEAN LAMBERT (1767-
1820). Revolutionary journalist. He

became famous in 1791 by publishing his Jacobin broadsheet, *L'Ami des citoyens.* He was present at the attack on the Tuileries (*q.v.*), and behind the September Massacres (*q.v.*). Elected to the Convention (*q.v.*) in 1792, he voted for the execution of the king. He was elected to the Committee of General Security (*q.v.*) and played a part in the downfall of the Girondists (*q.v.*). He was sent to Bordeaux to organize army recruiting in the southwest and to put down a rebellion. He halted this opposition with the use of the guillotine. He married Comtesse Thérèse de Fontenay, born Jeanne Marie Ignace Thérèse Cabarrus (1773-1835, *q.v.*), in 1794 after saving her from the guillotine. He became president of the Convention in March 1794 after his return to Paris. He led the moderates and helped the fall of Robespierre (*q.v.*) in 1794. His influence was reduced under the Directory (*q.v.*), though he accompanied Napoleon to Egypt. On the return voyage he was captured by an English cruiser. He eventually died in Paris in poverty.

TALLIEN, THÉRÈSE CABARRUS, MME (1773-1835). Daughter of a Spanish financier, she was married to the marquis de Fontenay, whom she later divorced. She then married the journalist Jean Lambert Tallien (*q.v.*), one of Robespierre's (*q.v.*) opponents. She became known as "Notre-Dame de Thermidor." Having divorced Tallien, she became the mistress of Barras (*q.v.*) during the Directory (*q.v.*) and in 1805 married the comte de Caraman, later prince de Chimay.

TATE, WILLIAM. In February 1797 French frigates landed some 1,400 men at Llanwnda in Fishguard Bay, Wales, under the command of William Tate, an American who had fought as an officer against the English during the American Revolution. The invaders soon capitulated to the local militia, with few shots being fired.

TAXES. Direct taxation consisted chiefly of the *taille* (*q.v.*), mainly on land; *capitation*, which was a poll tax; *vingtième* a form of income tax; *octroi*, a local tax on commerce; and the *corvée* (*q.v.*), which was an obligation to provide labor for such tasks as road work. Indirect taxation consisted of the *gabelle* (*q.v.*) on salt, *aides* on wine, *tabac* on tobacco.

TAXES RÉVOLUTIONNAIRES. Arbitrary, selective taxation against very rich citizens who were usually Royalist reactionaries. One reason for this selective imposition was the suspicion that those who could afford to pay were falsifying their abilities to do so.

TEMPLE. Thirteenth-century monastery in Paris. One of its towers was used as a prison for Louis XVI and his family from August 10, 1792 until their execution. The name was also given to churches in Paris and elsewhere from 1793, when the Convention (*q.v.*) abolished Catholicism.

Some of the temples were:

Temple de l'Agriculture—The Church of Saint-Eustache (1793).

Temple de la Bienfaisance—The Church of Saint-Jacques du Haut-Pas.

Temple de la Paix—The Chapelle de Saint-Thomas-d'Aquin. After the suppression of the convents in 1790 this became a center of the Théophilantropes (q.v.).

Temple de la Piété Filiale—Church of Saint-Étienne-du Mont.

Temple de la Raison—Notre-Dame-de-Paris.

Temple de la Reconnaissance—Church of Saint-Germain-l'Auxerrois (1793).

Temple de la Victoire—Saint-Sulpice. In 1793, the Théophilantropes held their meetings here, and on November 9, 1799 a great dinner was held here for Bonaparte.

Temple de l'Hymen—Church of Saint-Nicolas-des Champs (1793).

Temple de l'Immortalité—The Panthéon, especially in the Sepulchre of Great Men.

Temple de l'Industrie—In September 1789 the first Public Exhibition of French Industrial Products was held in the Champ de Mars (q.v.), running for five days.

Temple de Mars—Chapelle des Invalides.

Temple de Terpsichore—Name given to the theater in the Rue de la Chaussée-d'Antin in the hotel of the celebrated Mlle Guimard, danseuse de l'Opéra. It was built by Ledoux at the end of the reign of Louis XV. The hotel and theater were bought in 1796 by the banker Peregaux.

Temple du Génie—Church of Saint-Roch (1793).

Temple du Travail—Church of Saint-Médard.

TENNIS-COURT OATH. Dramatic action by the Third Estate (q.v.) and a step towards Revolution that took place on June 20, 1789 when the deputies of the Third Estate found that they were locked out of their usual meeting hall. They adjourned to the royal tennis court on the other side of the palace of Versailles. There the deputies took an oath which claimed authority by the Commons of France. Louis XVI eventually gave way and on June 27 ordered the nobles and clergy to join together with the Third Estate in the National Assembly.

The Tennis Court Oath is as follows:

> The National Assembly, considering that it has been summoned to establish the constitution of the kingdom, to effect the regeneration of public order, and to maintain the true principles of monarchy; that nothing can prevent it from continuing its deliberations in whatever place it may be forced to establish itself; and, finally, that wheresoever its members are assembled, *there* is the National Assembly;
>
> Decrees that all members of this Assembly shall immediately take a solemn oath not to separate, and to reassemble wherever circumstances require, until the constitution of the realm is established and consolidated upon firm foundations; and that, the said oath taken, all members and each one of them individually shall ratify this steadfast resolution by signature.

The oath was taken individually and orally by all but one of the members present.

TERRAY, JOSEPH MARIE, ABBÉ (1715-78). Controller-general of finances under Louis XV. His administration contributed to the general dissatisfaction with the tax system which eventually led to the Revolution.

TERROR, REIGN OF. The Terror occurred from September 5, 1793 until July 27, 1794, when absolute authority lay with the Committee of Public Safety and the Jacobins (*qq.v.*), dominated by Robespierre, St. Just and Couthon (*qq.v.*). During this period 300,000 people were arrested and about 17,000 were put to death. Many more died in prison or without trial. Robespierre had stated that "in times of peace the springs of popular government are in virtue, but in times of revolution, they are both in virtue and terror." He used the threat of foreign invasion and Royalist plots to unleash the Terror.

Greer, D. M., *The Incidence of the Terror during the French Revolution*, 1935.

Loomis, Stanley, *Paris in the Terror, June 1793-July 1794*, 1964.

Lucas, Colin, *The Structure of the Terror*, 1973.

TEXEL. Island off the Zuider Zee, Holland. In January 1795 Pichegru (*q.v.*) entered Amsterdam and French cavalry captured the Dutch fleet, which was frozen in the Texel River at Zeeland. As a result the Stadholder fled to England.

THÉOANDROPOPHILES. Sect which reintroduced certain practices of the Magi. It was regarded as being a forerunner of the sect of the Théophilantropes (*q.v.*).

THÉOPHILANTROPES. Members of a sect formed in 1796. The main articles of the sect's creed were belief in God, in virtue and immortality; it rejected Roman Catholicism as superstition. The sect was dissolved in 1802 following the Concordat of 1801.

THÉOT, CATHERINE (?-1794). Religious visionary, she called herself "The Mother of God." Locked up as insane before the Revolution, towards the end of it she preached the worship of the Supreme Being (*q.v.*) and announced that Robespierre (*q.v.*) was the forerunner of The Word. She called him her well-beloved son and chief prophet. She died in prison in 1794.

THERMIDOR. Hot month, July 19 to August 17. *See* **Calendar, Revolutionary.**

THERMIDOREANS. Revolutionaries who passed the decree of accusation against Robespierre (*q.v.*) and his followers on 9 Thermidor 1794 (July 27, 1794). Until the Directory (*q.v.*) was established, the Thermidoreans ruled through the Convention (*q.v.*) and ended the Terror (*q.v.*) and the Jacobin dictatorship. They achieved the ascendancy of the middle classes by breaking the power of the sans-culottes (*q.v.*) and the Paris Commune (Commune de Paris, *q.v.*), but under the Directory proved to be in favor of maintaining the decrees against the clergy, the émigrés and the nobility.

Lefebvre, Georges, *The Thermidoreans*, 1964.

Woronoff, Denis, *The Thermidorean Régime and the Directory, 1794-1799*, 1984.

THERMIDOR REVOLUTION. On the 9th Thermidor of Year II (July 27, 1794), the Convention deposed Robespierre (*q.v.*), and on the next day he and 22 of his partisans were executed, ending the Jacobin (*q.v.*) dictatorship and the Terror (*q.v.*).

THIERS, LOUIS ADOLPHE (1797-1877). Statesman and historian noted for his *Histoire de la Révolution française*, published between 1823 and 1827.

THIRD ESTATE (TIERS ÉTAT). The Commons or the third group of the Estates-General.

TIERS ÉTAT. *See* **Third Estate.**

TOCSIN. The bell that in normal times was sounded on the occasion of the birth or death of the sovereign, or members of the royal family, a fire or an uprising. During the Revolution it was used as an alarm preceding insurrection.

TOLENTINO, TREATY OF. Treaty signed in the town of Tolentino, Italy on February 19, 1797 between Bonaparte and Pope Pius VI *(q.v.)*. The latter renounced all claims to Avignon and the County of Venaissin, and ceded to the Republic, Bologna, Ferrara and the Romagna. Ancona stayed with France. Compensation for the murder, in January 1793, of Basseville *(q.v.)*, secretary to the French legation, was also demanded.

TONE, THEOBALD WOLFE (1763-98). Irish republican. He founded the Society of United Irishmen and organized three abortive invasions of Ireland in an attempt to throw off English rule. After the government suppressed the Dublin chapter of the society, Tone left Ireland for America. Arriving in Philadelphia, he received letters of introduction to the Committee of Public Safety *(q.v.)* in Paris. On 12 February 1796 he met Carnot *(q.v.)* and Delacroix, who favorably received his plans for a French invasion of Ireland. General Hoche *(q.v.)* was appointed to command the invasion. In December 1796 he sailed from Brest with 43 ships and 14,000 men, but the invasion failed because of bad weather and was forced back to France. In 1798 he again attempted invasion but his fleet was intercepted off Donegal, and after a fight Tone was captured and sentenced to death. He wished to die by firing squad rather than hanging, but his request was refused and he cut his own throat.

Boylan, Henry, *Theobald Wolfe Tone*, 1981.

TOQUE. Headgear of blue-violet silk adopted by the Directory, the Council of Ancients and the Council of Five Hundred *(qq.v.)*.

TORY ISLAND. *See* **Killala.**

TOULON, SIEGE OF. Seaport and naval base on the Mediterranean. In 1792 the Royalists of the town sought the support of the English and Spanish fleets. The inhabitants opened their harbor to the enemy and in 1793 the republicans laid siege. The siege ran from September 7 to December 1793. The émigré troops and a force of Spanish and British were under the command of Admiral Lord Hood. Bonaparte made his name as a soldier here. The forts commanding the town were taken by the French, and the English ships retired, having first set fire to the arsenal.

Thirty-eight out of a total of 56 ships were destroyed. Under the Directory *(q.v.)* Toulon became the most important military fort on the Mediterranean. The Egyptian expedition embarked from here.

TOUSSAINT L'OUVERTURE, PIERRE DOMINIQUE (c. 1743-1803).   Haitian patriot. Born a slave, he emerged as a leader during the black rising in the French colony of Saint-Domingue on the island of Hispaniola *(q.v.)*. For a brief period in 1793 he joined the Spanish forces on the eastern half of the island, gaining the sobriquet "L'Ouverture" (opening) for his ability to break through enemy forces. When France abolished slavery in its possessions in 1794, Toussaint became its ally and was made commander in chief of French forces in Saint-Domingue. In 1801 he controlled all of Hispaniola and established a black republic nominally allied to France. Seeking to reestablish French control over the island and the reintroduction of slavery, Bonaparte sent 40,000 troops in February 1802. Led by his brother-in-law, General Leclerc *(q.v.)*, they precipitated Toussaint's downfall. Toussaint was arrested and, with his family, was sent to France, where he died at Fort-de-Joux in the Jura Mountains.
James, C. L. R., *The Black Jacobins: Toussaint L'Ouverture and the San Domingo Revolution,* 1963.

TRAITS D'HÉROISME.   Decree of 1793 ordered the publication of details of specific heroic actions by revolutionary heroes, which were published throughout the country.

TRANSPADANE REPUBLIC.   After his 1796 victory at Lodi, Bonaparte worked quickly to organize Lombardy as the Transpadane Republic. In March 1797 the Republic consisted of Milan, Bergamo, Brescia, and Crema, which had revolted against Venice. In June 1797 this republic joined with the Cispadane *(q.v.)* to form the Cisalpine Republic *(q.v.)*.

TRAVAIL, LE (LABOR).   One of the *sans-culottides (q.v.),* September 19.

TREASON.   There were several classifications of high treason under the ancien régime based, primarily, on lèse-majesté. Later they were those acts that placed the country in peril, whether threatening the interior or the exterior of the state. On January 2, 1792 it was suggested that the names of traitors against their country be engraved on tablets of bronze for posterity to note and this was passed by the Legislative Assembly *(q.v.)*. On April 13, 1793 there was a decree of Non-intervention and Treason issued by the Convention *(q.v.)*, which stated that the death penalty would be inflicted on any who negotiated or treated with enemy powers that had not recognized the independence of the French nation.

TRENTE JOURS (THIRTY DAYS). Expedition during which Bonaparte crossed Great Saint Bernard Pass, entered Milan, won the battles of Montenotte and Marengo *(q.v.)*, and returned to Paris between May 6 and June 2, 1800.

TRIBUNE OF THE PEOPLE. *See* **Babeuf.**

TRICOLEUR (TRICOLOR). French national flag of three vertical stripes of blue, white and red, blue and red being the colors of the city of Paris and white the Bourbon color. It was invented by Lafayette (*q.v.*) and adopted on July 17, 1789. *Tricoleur* is used to describe any emblem in the national colors, i.e. cockade, flag, or rosette.

TRICOTEUSES (KNITTERS). Name given to Parisian women who zealously attended political meetings and executions in 1792, doing their knitting (tricotage) at intervals. Also known as Les Tricoteuses de Robespierre and Les Furies de la Guillotine.

TUILERIES. Royal residence in Paris, started by Catherine de'Medici in 1564, continued by Henri IV and completed by Louis XIV. It was destroyed by fire in 1871. The Tuileries Gardens is the site of the old palace. Louis XVI and his family were moved to the Tuileries after the October Days (*q.v.*) of 1789. It was stormed twice during the year 1792. After the republic was proclaimed it was used by the Convention and the Committees of Public Safety and General Security (*qq.v.*).

TUILERIES, THÉATRE DES. One of the great theaters of Europe, it was the scene of a tremendous reception for Voltaire (*q.v.*) on March 20, 1778. Voltaire's bust was, at the end of the evening, crowned with a circle of laurel. It was used by the Convention (*q.v.*) for its meeting on May 10, 1793.

TURGOT, ANNE-ROBERT-JACQUES, BARON DE L'AULNE (1727-81). Administrator and economist. He was appointed controller-general by Louis XVI on August 24, 1774, and during his period in office he attempted to tackle some of the problems arising in the financial system. His Six Edicts (*q.v.*) were received with considerable opposition and he was dismissed in 1776. Dakin, Douglas, *Turgot and the Ancien Régime*, 1939.

TURIN COMMITTEE. In 1790 the émigrés gathered around the comte d'Artois (later Charles X, *q.v.*), at Turin, where they plotted a strike on Lyon, but this project was discovered. Charles Alexandre de Calonne (1734-1802, *q.v.*), who had left France in 1787 as one of the most severe critics of the Constituent Assembly (*q.v.*), was adviser to the comte d'Artois.

TUSCANY. Grand Duchy from 1569 with the chief town at Florence. Before passing to the Habsburgs in 1737 it was governed by the Medicis. During the Revolution attempts were made to remain neutral in order to avoid foreign invasion, but in 1799 a French force entered Florence and the grand duke fled. A counterrevolution took place and the French were expelled. However Bonaparte, after his success at Marengo (*q.v.*), reentered Florence in October 1800. By the Treaty of Lunéville (*q.v.*) Tuscany became part of the Spanish dominions as the Kingdom of Etruria.

TWELVE, COMMISSION OF. Formed by the Girondins *(q.v.)* May 18, 1793 to investigate the Commune's decision to form a revolutionary army and to arrest suspects. The Commission was suppressed on 27 May at the suggestion of Danton *(q.v.)* following the arrest of four sans-culottes *(q.v.)* and when the mob invaded the hall where the Convention was sitting. The following day the Girondins obtained the Commission's restoration, but the prisoners were released and the Convention soon after disavowed the Commission.

U

ULTRAMONTANISM. Religious principle which claims absolute papal authority and supremacy, in contrast to Gallicanism *(q.v.)*, the principle and practice of French Roman Catholics, which maintains the claims of the French church to be, in certain respects, self-governing. Contrasting claims of jurisdiction have been at the heart of controversies throughout French history.

During the Revolution a religious-political faction existed, which wished to reverse the principles of the Revolution. It was prominent during the reign of Charles X *(q.v.)*, and one of the causes of the fall of the Bourbons.

ULTRAS, LES. Parties and individuals who held exaggerated political opinions. In 1793 they were the ultrarevolutionnaires. Danton *(q.v.)* encouraged the people to act against them.

UNE ET INDIVISIBLE (ONE AND INDIVISIBLE). Part of the name of the Republic in 1793.

UNITÉ. Part of the first article of the 1793 constitution. 1793 was the year of the celebration of the Fête de l'Unité et de l'Indivisibilité, of which David *(q.v.)* was the master of ceremonies.

UNITED IRISHMEN, SOCIETY OF. Society formed in October 1791 by Theobald Wolfe Tone (1763-97, *q.v.*). It was located, initially, in Belfast, and was along the lines of French democratic representative societies. Headed by a secret committee of eleven middle-class businessmen who were Presbyterians, it was committed to obtain an impartial and adequate representation of the Irish nation in Parliament by securing the cooperation of Irishmen of all religious persuasions. Ostensibly interested in Catholic emancipation and parliamentary reform, it was anti any form of violence. Its paper, *The Northern Star* (first issue January 4, 1792), was pro-French, independence and Catholicism.

Another branch of the society, headed by James Napper Tandy, was founded in Dublin. Tone became secretary of the General Committee of the Catholics. In May 1794 the British government suppressed the Dublin chapter, forbidding public assembly and any open discussion or fraternization of its members to generate reform. The members considered armed insurrections and conspiracy to be radical agitation.

UNITED PROVINCES OF THE NETHERLANDS. Also known as the Dutch Republic, which existed 1579-1795. The invasion by France and a Dutch democratic revolution caused the republic's collapse in 1795.

UNIVERSITY OF PARIS. The university was suppressed on September 15, 1793 by a decree of the Convention. Only under the Empire, in 1808, was it reconstituted, under Napoleon's plan for state education, as the University of France.

USHANT. Naval battle fought June 1, 1794 between Admiral Lord Howe of Great Britain and Villaret Joyeuse of France. Lord Howe was the victor. *See* **Glorious First of June.**

V

VAINE PÂTURE. Rights of French villagers to pasture their animals on common land, including the open fields after the harvest, the meadows after the first hay harvest and the fields left fallow. Enclosures represented the main method of obtaining improvement in agriculture in France and *vaine pâture* was the chief obstacle to realizing this aim.

VALENCIENNES, FRANCE. City (Roman Valentianae) taken by Louis XIV in 1677 and ceded to France in 1678. It was besieged from May 23 to July 28, 1793, when the French garrison surrendered to the Allies under the duke of York. It was retaken by the French August 27-30, 1794.

VALMY, BATTLE OF. Village in the Argonne, France, where on September 20, 1792, the French under General François Dumouriez and General Charles François Kellermann *(qq.v.)* halted the allied advance. This army consisted of Prussian, Austrian, Hessian and French émigrés commanded by Karl Wilhelm Ferdinand, duke of Brunswick. This was the first great victory of the revolutionary armies *(q.v.)* and it was of immense moral advantage to them. Kellermann was created duke of Valmy in 1808.

VALOIS, CLUB DES. A right-wing and short-lived political club based in Paris.

VAR, ARMY OF. This army operated to defend Provence and, on occasion, provide contingents to reinforce the Army of Italy.

VARENNES, FLIGHT TO. Flight from the Tuileries *(q.v.)* by Louis XVI and his queen, sister and two children on June 21, 1791. Louis hoped to suppress the Revolution by joining Austrian troops across the border, then appealing to European rulers to intervene. The monarchy never recovered from the plan's failure, and the royal family returned to Paris as prisoners. It was agreed that the king would join François Claude Amour, marquis de Bouillé (1739-1800, *q.v.*) at Metz, but the *procureur-syndic* of Varennes became suspicious of the royal party and refused to let them proceed.

VAUCLUSE. Name of a department that in 1793 replaced the former papal enclave (ceded 1229) made up of the counties of Avignon and Venaissin.

VENDÉAN REBELLION. La Vendée in western France on the Bay of Biscay was a center of resistance to republican France from 1793-96, following the execution of Louis XVI. The first revolt, caused mainly by the Revolution's moves against the Roman Catholic church that were not accepted by the mainly peasant population, lasted from March to October 1793. The peasants' leaders were Jacques Cathelineau, Gaston Bourdic and Jean-Nicolas Stofflet, and they were joined by Royalist nobles, forming a 50,000-strong army. On their defeat, severe punishments were meted out, including the killing of prisoners. Discontent continued and another insurrection flared up in the summer of 1795. Rebel bands, known as Chouans (q.v.), which received assistance from Royalist agents from Britain, started an ill-fated second revolt in 1795. Peace did not come to the region until 1800, when Bonaparte sent an expedition to La Vendée and also offered freedom from conscription, liberty of worship and some compensation. Deaths in the Vendéan rebellions far exceeded those of the Terror (q.v.)
Ross, Michael C., *Banners of the King: The War of the Vendée, 1793-4*, 1975.

VENDÉMIAIRE. Vintage month, September 22 to October 21. *See* **Calendar, Revolutionary.**

VENDÉMIAIRE, RISING OF. On 14 Vendémiaire (October 5, 1795) Barras (q.v.) and Bonaparte suppressed a Royalist revolt against the Convention. *See* **Day of the Sections.**

VENTÔSE. Wind month, February 19 to March 20. *See* **Calendar, Revolutionary.**

VENTÔSE LAWS OF. The Laws of Ventôse were published by the Convention (q.v.) in February and March 1794. They provided for the confiscation of the property of those opposed to the Revolution and its redistribution between patriots. These extreme measures contributed to the reaction of Thermidor (q.v.).

VERDUN. Capital of Verdunois and chief center of the department of Meuse. It was attacked by the Prussians on September 1, 1792 after the taking of Longwy, and fell to them after fifteen hours due to Royalist treachery and pressure within the city. Part of the Prussian army occupied the city, while the majority fought at Valmy (September 20, q.v.). It was occupied until the Prussian retreat began on October 13. The Convention (q.v.) reacted savagely to those who had cooperated with the enemy, executing a number as collaborators.

VERGENNES, CHARLES GRAVIER, COMTE DE (1717-87). French statesman. At the accession of Louis XVI he became foreign minister. His hatred of England and his desire to avenge the disasters of the Seven Years' War, led him to support the Americans. In 1777, he informed the American commissioners that France acknowledged the new republic, and was willing to form an offensive and domestic alliance. Vergennes intrigued against Necker (q.v.), seeing him as a dangerous innovator, a republican, a foreigner and a Protestant. In 1781 he was chief of the Council of Finance, and in 1783 he supported Calonne (q.v.) as a nominee for the post of controller-general. Vergennes died before the meeting of the Notables (q.v.) that he is said to have suggested to Louis XVI.

VERDETS, LES. Name given to volunteer Royalists functioning in the Midi after 9 Thermidor (*q.v.*), fighting both the terrorists and the moderate republicans. They wore a green ribbon around their arms, following the example of the Guard (*q.v.*) of August 10, 1792.

VERGNIAUD, PIERRE VICTUR-NIEN (1753-93). Politician and orator. He was elected to the Legislative Assembly (*q.v.*) and became leader of the Girondists (*q.v.*). He voted for the king's death in the Convention (*q.v.*), and as president announced its decision. When the Girondists clashed with the Jacobins (*q.v.*) over the direction of the Revolution, Vergniaud and 28 other leaders of the Girondist party were arrested and guillotined on October 31.
Lintilhac, Eugene, *Vergniaud*, 1920.

VERONA. Town in the Lombard-Venetian kingdom on the Adige. In 1797 it was under the control of the Venetians, until it was occupied by the French on April 24, 1797. On March 30, 1799 Schérer was beaten by the Austrian general Kray. It was seized by the Austrians in the same year and held by them until 1801, being returned to the French by the Treaty of Pressburg, later being restored to the Austrians in 1815.

VERSAILLES. Originally a hunting lodge built by Louis XIII but enlarged into a palace by Louis XIV. The chief residence of the French monarchy twelve miles southwest of Paris. The royal family's preference for living there made Parisians suspicious of the king's attitude toward the city.

VERTUS, LES (VIRTUES). One of the *sans-culottides* (*q.v.*), September 17.

VETERANS. Under Louis XV this referred to old decorated soldiers. A battalion of this name was founded in 1789 by Callière de l'Étang. A law of May 16, 1792 instituted the Veterans, who were placed in regiments for military service in fortified places, coastal batteries or in protecting commerce. In 1799 they numbered some 14,000.

VETO. Louis XVI and Marie Antoinette were called Monsieur and Madame Veto by the republicans because the Constituent Assembly (*q.v.*) (1791) allowed the king to retain his power to refuse assent to legislation. He abused this power, which increased his unpopularity.

VICTIMS BALL. After 9 Thermidor (*q.v.*) a Bal des Victimes took place in the Hôtel Thelusson, Rue de Provence, Paris. Only those who had lost a member of their family on the scaffold were admitted. The dancers wore a red line around their necks, to signify the contact of the guillotine. The invited wore a red shawl and flour-powdered hair. There was a similar ball in the Faubourg Saint-Germain. The women in the streets carried *bonnets à l'humanité* and *corsets à la justice*, while the young people adopted a cap *à la victime*, their hair tressed and tied back like that of those going to the guillotine.

VICTOIRES NATIONALES, THÉATRE DES. Founded in Paris in 1798 in the Rue de Bac, on the site of an old convent that had been changed under the Revolution into a bakery storehouse. It put on a variety of performances, a number of which were forbidden, and was closed on at least three occasions.

VIENNA. Situated on the right bank of the Danube, capital of the Austrian Empire. The city was threatened by Bonaparte in 1797, when the Preliminaries of the Treaty of Leoben halted the French advance. The French ambassador, Bernadotte *(q.v.)*, had been insulted on April 14, 1798, when the locals mounted celebrations to honor the arming of the Imperial Volunteers in 1796. Bernadotte's counter-celebrations, designed to commemorate a French victory over the Austrians, resulted in his household being sacked, the French flag torn down and burned.

VIEUX CORDELIER, LE. Journal founded, written and edited by Camille Desmoulins (1760-97, *q.v.*). From December 1793 to January 1794, it was published every five days, consisting of seven editions. The journal had considerable influence and, in fact, cost Desmoulins his life. The aim of the journal was to appeal for moderation in an effort to curb government excesses and further bloodshed. While correcting the proofs of the seventh edition Desmoulins was arrested. This edition ended with the words *Les Dieux ont soif* (The gods are thirsty). He was executed before publication.

VIEUZAC, BERTRAND BARÈRE DE (1755-1841). Member of the Committee of Public Safety *(q.v.)* known as "Anacreon of the Guillotine."

VIGÉE-LE BRUN, MARIE ELISABETH LOUISE (1775–1842). Painter. She executed 20 portraits of Marie Antoinette between 1779 and 1789, and also painted numerous portraits of other members of the royal family. She left Paris for Italy at the outbreak of the Revolution, traveled throughout Europe and returned to Paris in 1802.

VINCENNES, DONJON DE. A large state prison set up by Louis XI. In the years just before the Revolution it held 470 persons. Mirabeau, Diderot *(qq.v.)*, Crébillon fils and others had spent time there. In 1784 it was suppressed as a state prison, becoming in the following year, under Louis XVI's direction, a bakery. In 1788 the demolition or sale of the chateau was ordered, but it was never carried out. In 1790 by a Convention *(q.v.)* decree, repairs were made to enable the prison to be used as a branch of the Paris prisons and it became known as a new Bastille.

VINDICIAE GALLICAE. See **Sir James Mackintosh.**

VINGTIÈME. A tax, mainly on land, nominally of one-twentieth, imposed in 1749. Its aim was to replace the *taille (q.v.)* and subject all landowners to equality in taxation matters. The attempt failed because of administrative difficulties.

VOLTAIRE, FRANÇOIS MARIE AROUET DE (1694-1778). French philosopher and author. He was imprisoned in the Bastille *(q.v.)* in 1717 for writings wrongly ascribed to him, and it was after his release that he assumed the name Voltaire. He dedicated his life to the ideals of tolerance, justice and freedom. His writings and ideals helped to foster the Revolution.

Ayer, Alfred J. *Voltaire*, 1986.

Mason, Haydn T., *Voltaire: A Biography*, 1981.

W

WARS, FRENCH REVOLUTIONARY
WAR OF THE FIRST COALITION

On August 2, 1791 in the Declaration of Pillnitz, Frederick William II of Prussia and the Emperor Leopold II of Austria declared themselves ready to join other European powers in restoring the authority of the French monarchy, and on December 14, 1791 the French formed three new armies for the defense of their northern and eastern frontiers.

1792	February 7: Alliance between Austria and Prussia, later joined by Sardinia. April 20: French Assembly declared war on Austria and the French Army of the North advanced into the Austrian Netherlands, but was thrown back by the duke of Saxe-Teschen. July 24: Prussia declared war on France. Allied army under the duke of Brunswick assembled at Koblenz for invasion of France. August 19: Brunswick's army crossed the French frontier, capturing Longwy on August 23 and Verdun on September 2. September 20: Brunswick's infantry halted by accurate fire from 54 French guns in the "Cannonade of Valmy." The Allies withdrew into Germany, evacuating Verdun and Longwy. The French under Custine (q.v.) took the offensive, capturing Mainz and Frankfurt. However, Brunswick drove Custine back to the Rhine, retaking Frankfurt on December 2. In the north the Austrians failed to capture Lille and were defeated by Dumouriez (q.v.) at Jemappes on November 6. Dumouriez entered Brussels on November 14, and the Austrians evacuated the country. November 19: The French declared themselves ready to help all peoples against their kings, and proclaimed the Scheldt an open river. In the south

French forces seized Nice and Savoy from the king of Sardinia.

1793   January 21: Louis XVI executed, and when England expelled the French ambassador, France declared war on England and Holland on February 1 and on Spain on March 7. Belgium was declared to be incorporated into France.

March 1: Allied offensive opened, as Austrian army of 40,000 men under the prince of Saxe-Coburg advanced into Belgium.

March 18: Dumouriez attacked Coburg at Neerwinden but was routed.

March 21: After a further defeat at Louvain. Dumouriez opened negotiations with the enemy and deserted to the Austrians on April 5. Coburg captured Condé on July 10 and Valenciennes on July 29.

July 23: Brunswick retook Mainz on the Rhine.

August 23: With the situation now desperate for France, the Committee of Public Safety (q.v.) ordered the conscription of the entire male population, the levée en masse (q.v.).

August 28: Hood seized Toulon (q.v.), but was forced to evacuate it on December 18.

September 6: Houchard attacked the duke of York (q.v.), who had invested Dunkirk, driving him back with the loss of his siege artillery.

September 13: Houchard defeated the prince of Orange at Menin, but was guillotined for his failure to follow up the victory.

October 16: Jourdan (q.v.) defeated the Austrians at Wattignies, forcing them to raise the siege of Maubeuge. On the Rhine, Hoche (q.v.) was victorious over the Austrians and Prussians at Fröschwiller on December 22 and Geisberg on December 26.

1794   May 18: The Army of the North (q.v.), temporarily commanded by Souham, defeated the Austrians, British and Hanoverians under Coburg at the Battle of Tourcoing.

May 22: A French attack on the Allied entrenched camp at Tournai was repulsed.

June 17: The French defeated an Austrian attempt to relieve Ypres at the Battle of Hooglede.

June 26: Battle of Fleurus (q.v.); Coburg, advancing to the relief of Charleroi, which had already fallen, was defeated by Jourdan, in command of the newly formed Army of the Sambre and Meuse.

July 10: The French entered Brussels, and Antwerp on July 27. The Austrians withdrew across the

Rhine, while the British retreated into Holland and on into Germany. The French under Pichegru *(q.v.)* invaded Holland.

1795 January: The French entered Amsterdam. Holland was renamed the Batavian Republic *(q.v.)* on May 16.

April 5: Treaty of Basle; peace treaty between France and Prussia, establishing neutrality of Prussia and northern states of Germany. Spain signed a peace treaty on July 22, and by the end of 1795 France had also made peace with Saxony, Hesse, Naples and Parma.

June 27: Landing of French émigrés and British troops at Quiberon. Hoche defeated these forces on July 16-20, and the British were evacuated.

September 5: Jourdan crossed the Rhine and advanced on Frankfurt, but was defeated by the Austrians under Count von Clerfayt. Clerfayt then attacked Pichegru, commanding the Army of the Rhine and Moselle, defeated him on October 29 and invaded the Palatinate.

December 31: Pichegru concluded an armistice with the Austrians.

Campaign in Germany

1796 May 20: The Austrians denounced the armistice of December 31, 1795.

June 10: Jourdan, commanding the Army of the Sambre and Meuse, crossed the Rhine to draw the Austrians northwards. He was defeated by Archduke Charles on June 16 at Wetzler, and retreated across the Rhine.

June 24: Moreau *(q.v.)*, commanding the Army of the Rhine and Moselle, crossed the Rhine at Strasbourg. After an indecisive battle at Malsch on July 9, Archduke Charles retreated across the Danube.

June 28: Jourdan again crossed the Rhine. The archduke marched north and decisively defeated Jourdan at Amberg on August 24. But on the same day Moreau defeated Latour at Friedberg.

September 3: The archduke defeated Jourdan at Würzburg, and again on the River Lahn at Biberach on October 2, but was beaten at Emendingen on October 19. He recrossed the Rhine on October 26.

1797	Hoche, who had succeeded Jourdan, crossed the Rhine and defeated General Werneck in the Battle of the Lahn on April 18. On April 21 Moreau fought his way across the Rhine near Kehl. The Austrians fell back to Rastatt.

Campaign in Italy

1796	Bonaparte appointed to replace Schérer as commander of the Army of Italy. He took command on March 27 of an army consisting of 37,000 effectives.

April 10: The Austrians under Beaulieu captured Voltri.

April 12: Seizing the initiative, Bonaparte drove a wedge between the Austrian and Piedmontese armies at the Battle of Montenotte. The French then captured Dego on April 13 and held it against Austrian attacks. Bonaparte then attacked the Piedmontese army under Baron Colli, driving it from Ceva on April 18 and defeating it at Mondovi on April 22.

April 28: The Piedmontese signed the Armistice of Cherasco.

May 7: Bonaparte crossed the Po at Piacenza. Beaulieu retreated eastwards.

May 10: Bonaparte took the vital bridge over the River Adda at Lodi.

May 15: Bonaparte entered Milan. King Victor Amadeus signed a treaty surrendering Savoy and Nice to the French.

May 30: Bonaparte broke Beaulieu's line on the Mincio at Borghetto, and as the Austrians retreated over the Adige he besieged Mantua, which was defended by 12,000 men and 316 guns.

July: The Austrians began their first attempt to relieve Mantua. By dividing their forces into three, however, they enabled Bonaparte to attack them in turn.

August 3: Bonaparte defeated Quasdanovich at Lonato.

August 5: The Austrians under Würmser were defeated at Castiglione and retreated into the Tyrol. The siege of Mantua was renewed on August 24.

French forces now marched northwards and defeated Davidovich at Roveredo on September 4. Learning that Würmser had resumed the offensive, Bonaparte pursued the main Austrian army and defeated it at Bassano on September 8. Würmser withdrew into Mantua on September 12.

A new Austrian offensive was now mounted by Baron d'Alvintzi. After an unsuccessful attack at Caldiero on November 12, Bonaparte defeated the Austrians in the Battle of Arcola on November 15-17. D'Alvintzi was forced to retreat.

1797   January 14: A fourth Austrian attempt to relieve Mantua ended when d'Alvintzi was defeated at Rivoli.

February 2: Würmser surrendered Mantua to the French.

March: Archduke Charles replaced d'Alvintzi. Bonaparte launched an offensive. The archduke was defeated by Masséna (q.v.) at Malborgetto on March 23, and Bonaparte advanced on Vienna. While maintaining his advance, fears about his lines of communication led him to offer an armistice.

April 7: Armistice of Leoben concluded.

May 16: The French occupied Venice.

October 17: Treaty of Campo Formio (q.v.); Austria recognized French possession of Belgium and the Rhine frontier, and acknowledged the independence of the Cisalpine Republic; in return, Austria was compensated with Venetian territory.

Egyptian Campaign 1798-1801

1798   April 12: Army of the Orient created with Bonaparte as commander.

May 19: Bonaparte sailed from Toulon with 36,000 troops, secured the surrender of Malta on June 12 and landed in Egypt on July 1.

July 2: The French captured Alexandria and advanced on Cairo.

July 21: Bonaparte routed the Egyptian army at the Battle of the Pyramids (q.v.), and occupied Cairo on the following day.

August 1: Nelson (q.v.) destroyed the French fleet at the Battle of Aboukir Bay, isolating the French army in Egypt.

1799   January 31: Bonaparte invaded Syria with 13,000 men. Jaffa was captured on March 7 and Acre invested on March 17.

April 17: An attempt by the Turks to relieve Acre

was defeated at the Battle of Mount Tabor. Nevertheless, Acre continued to resist, supported by an English squadron under Sir Sydney Smith. When plague broke out in his army, Bonaparte was forced to raise the siege on May 20 and retreat to Egypt.

July 25: Bonaparte defeated a Turkish force which had been landed from Rhodes at Aboukir.

August 22: Leaving Kléber (q.v.) in command, Bonaparte sailed for France, landing at Fréjus (q.v.) on October 9.

1800

January 21: Kléber agreed to evacuate Egypt by the Convention of El Arish, but Britain refused to ratify the agreement.

March 20: Kléber defeated the Turks at Heliopolis.

June 14: Assassination of Kléber.

1801

March 8: British troops under Abercromby (q.v.) landed at Aboukir Bay.

March 13: A British attack on Alexandria failed, but a French counterattack was beaten off on March 21, though Abercromby was fatally wounded. His successor, Hutchinson, advanced on Cairo, which the French agreed to evacuate on June 28.

August 31: French forces remaining in Alexandria surrendered.

WAR OF THE SECOND COALITION, 1798-1801

In December 1798 Austria, Britain, Naples, Portugal and Turkey reached agreement on cooperation against France.

Operations in Italy, 1798-1800

1798

November 29: A Neapolitan army under General Mack captured Rome.

December 15: The Neapolitan forces were driven out by the French under Championnet, who then took Naples on January 24, 1799 and proclaimed the Parthenopean Republic (q.v.).

1799

March 12: Austria declared war on France. Schérer, commanding the Army of Italy, moved against the Austrians under Kray, hoping for an early victory.

March 26: Schérer was repulsed at Verona and defeated at Magnano on April 5. Suvarov, who now succeeded Kray, pursued the French, defeating them at Cassano on April 27 and entering Milan on April 28.

June 17-19: Macdonald, who had marched north with the French forces in southern Italy, was defeated at Trebbia. He retreated to join Moreau, who had replaced Schérer, at Genoa. Moreau was himself replaced by Joubert (q.v.) on August 5.

August 15: Joubert attacked Suvarov at Novi, but was defeated and killed. Suvarov was then ordered to take 20,000 Russian troops into Switzerland.

November 4: Suvarov's successor, Melas, defeated Championnet at the Battle of Genoa, and the French retreated across the Alps.

1800

January 7: Bonaparte, now first consul of France, ordered the formation of an Army of Reserve around Dijon.

April 6: Masséna, commanding the Army of Italy, was defeated and besieged in Genoa by the Austrians under Ott, supported by the British navy. Genoa finally surrendered on January 4.

May 14-24: Bonaparte crossed the Great St. Bernard Pass with the Army of Reserve, seized Milan and Pavia and threatened Melas' lines of communication. Melas moved east and ordered a concentration at Alessandria.

June 9: Ott, marching north from Genoa, encountered French forces under Lannes at Montebello. He was driven towards Alessandria.

June 14: Melas advanced from Alessandria and attacked the French at Marengo (q.v.). After early reverses, Bonaparte was joined by Desaix's (q.v.) 9,000-strong corps and counterattacked. The Austrians were defeated and Melas was forced to ask for an armistice on June 15.

Russo-British Expedition to Holland, 1799

1799

August 27: British troops under Abercromby landed at the Helder. The Dutch navy in the Texel surrendered on August 30.

On the arrival of 9,000 Russians, the combined force, commanded by the duke of York, planned to advance on Amsterdam.

September 19: Battle of Bergen; lack of coordination resulted in a defeat for the Allies by Franco-Batavian forces under Brune.

Further attacks on enemy positions on October 2 and October 6 made little progress.

October 18: By the Convention of Alkmaar the Allies agreed to evacuate Holland, but retained the Dutch fleet.

1799	March 1: Jourdan's Army of the Danube crossed the Rhine at Kehl and advanced against Austrian forces under Archduke Charles.
	Jourdan was defeated at Ostrach on March 21 and Stockach on March 25. He retreated to the Rhine and resigned his command.
	Meanwhile, Masséna, commanding the Army of Helvetia, had crossed the Rhine near Mayenfeld and captured 7,000 Austrians around Chur. Masséna then took over Jourdan's army as well as his own.
	June 4: Masséna repulsed an Austrian attack at Zurich, but when he attempted to advance he was defeated on August 14.
	Austria then ordered Archduke Charles to move north to observe Allied progress in Holland.
	September 25: Masséna defeated the weakened Allied army under Korsakov at Zurich.
1800	The French under Moreau defeated Kray at Stockach on May 3, Moskirch on May 5, Ulm on May 16 and Hochstadt on June 19.
	An armistice was effective from July 15 to November 13.
	December 3: Moreau defeated Archduke John, who had replaced Kray, at Hohenlinden. Moreau then advanced on Vienna, while Macdonald invaded the Tyrol and Brune moved towards the Julian Alps.
	December 25: The Austrians sued for peace.
1801	February 9: Peace of Lunéville (q.v.) between France and Austria, confirming the terms of the Treaty of Campo Formio.
1802	Britain remained at war until the Peace of Amiens (q.v.).

Blanc, Oliver, *Last Letters: Prisons and Prisoners of the French Revolution,* 1987.

Roger, A. B., *The War of the Second Coalition: 1798-1800: A Strategic Commentary,* 1964

WARVILLE.   Another name for Girondists (*q.v.*). *See also* **Brissot de Warville.**

WATCH.   Police force organized from the Chatelet (*q.v.*) to keep law and order at night, but proved to be rather inefficient.

WEIGHTS AND MEASURES.   *See* **Metric System.**

WEST, ARMY OF THE.   Republican army raised to fight in the Vendée and the neighboring departments against the insurgent Royalists, from 1793 to the pacification, and then up to the pacification of the Chouannerie about 1800. (*See* **Chouans**.) Known, initially, as the Armée des Sables-d'Olonne.

WHITE TERROR (LES BLANCS). Name given by republican soldiers to Royalist soldiers in the Vendée, against whom they were fighting (1793-96). It refers to a white cockade which the Royalists wore on their hats.

WICKHAM, WILLIAM (1761-1840). English politician. In 1795 he was appointed as English minister to the Swiss cantons, where he gained much valuable information concerning the condition of Provence and the Royalist movements in the Vendée. He was, in fact, the government's principal spy on the continent. His success was so great that, in 1797, the Directory (*q.v.*) formally demanded his expulsion, as a fomentor of insurrections. In 1799 he returned as envoy to the Swiss cantons and to the Austrian and Russian armies, entrusted with considerable negotiating powers, covering treaties and arranging supplies for antirevolutionary forces. He returned to England in 1802.

XYZ

'XYZ' AFFAIR, THE. Diplomatic incident which occurred 1797-98. Three Americans, John Marshall (1755-1835, chief justice of the U.S.), Charles Cotesworth Pinckney (1746-1825), and Elbridge Gerry (1744-1814), were sent to France by President John Adams to negotiate a treaty relating to neutral trade and anti-privateering.

Talleyrand *(q.v.)* detached Gerry, who was pro-French and desperate to obtain reconciliations, from the other two. Gerry agreed to keep this fact secret from his colleagues, but all became public in April 1798. The others left France but Gerry remained because Talleyrand said that France would declare war if an understanding was not reached through Gerry. Though recalled he was allowed to leave France only when Talleyrand had given up trying to inveigle him into a beneficial settlement.

''XYZ'' was a substitution of letters for names of French agents used in the publication of dispatches that contained insulting demands made by Talleyrand and his colleagues. The agents suggested a bribe of $250,000 to Talleyrand and a loan of $10,000,000. The United States was put on a war footing but war was not declared and the matter was finally settled in 1800.

YORK DUKE OF (1763-1827). Son of George III and Queen Charlotte, he entered British and Hanoverian armies and studied military science in Germany. In 1793 he commanded the British army in the coalition armies fighting the French revolutionary forces in Flanders with mixed results. He was made a field marshal in 1795 and 1789-1809 was commander in chief of all British armies.

As a military leader he had limited abilities; his real qualities lay in administration and army reforms. He helped to establish the Royal Military College at Sandhurst, England.

YOUNG, ARTHUR (1741-1820). English agricultural writer and traveler. In 1767 he began a series of tours that yielded accounts of farming in England, Ireland and France. From 1784-1809 he edited the monthly journal *Annals of Agriculture*. When Pitt *(q.v.)* established the Board of Agriculture in 1793, Young was appointed secretary. With the president, Sir John Sinclair, he organized, prepared and published valuable reports on agriculture of the English counties. He took three tours of France: (1) May-November 1787, (2) July-October 1788, (3) 1789. *His Travels in France 1787-1790* is useful as a clear guide to France just before and in the months of the Revolution. He went on to Italy, returning to England on January 30, 1790. Shrewd, and perceptive, he gave great attention to close detail and was an excellent actual observer.

In 1801 by order of the Directory *(q.v.)* his writing was translated into French under the title *Le Cultivateur anglais* in 16 volumes.

Gazley, John G., *The Life of Arthur Young*, 1973.

ZURICH, SWITZERLAND. Place where two battles were fought, the first on April 4, 1799 between Archduke Karl (Austria) and Masséna *(q.v.)* (France). Archduke Karl was the victor. The second was fought September 25, 1799 between Masséna (France) and Korsakov (imperial Russia). Masséna was the victor.

CHRONOLOGY

1769	August	15	Birth of Napoleon Bonaparte.
1770	May	16	Marriage of the dauphin (later Louis XVI) and Marie Antoinette of Austria.
1774	May	10	Death of Louis XV. Succeeded by his grandson, Louis XVI.
	August		Louis XVI recalls *parlements*.
	September		Turgot reintroduces free trade in corn in France, suspended since 1766, but again abolished in 1776.
1775	April-May		Famine in Paris.
1776	January	6	Abolition of the *corvée*.
	February	5	Abolition of the Jurandes, or privileged corporations.
		12	Turgot dismissed for attempting to make further financial reforms. Necker appointed director of finances.
	July	4	American declaration of independence.
	August	11	*Corvée* and corporations restored in France.
	September		Free trade in corn (reintroduced 1774) abolished.
	October		Jacques Necker appointed finance minister.
1777	April		Marquis de Lafayette's French volunteers arrive in America.
	June		Necker, director-general of finance.
1778	February	6	Commercial, defensive and offensive treaty between France and U.S. Britain declares war on France.
	July	8	Comte d'Estaing's French fleet arrives off Delaware.

	September	4	French seize Dominica.
	November		British force under Admiral Samuel Barrington takes St. Lucia, in the West Indies, from the French.
1779	May		France abandons Gorée, West Africa, to Britain.
	July	4	French force takes Grenada, West Indies.
1781	April	29	de Grasse captures Tobago. French fleet under Suffren prevents Britain from seizing Cape of Good Hope.
	May	19	Louis XVI dismisses Necker.
	September	30	Washington and Lafayette cut Cornwallis's communications, beginning siege of Yorktown, Virginia.
	October	19	Cornwallis capitulates at Yorktown with almost 8,000 men and the British evacuate Charleston and Savannah and land operations are virtually over.
1782	February	13	French take St. Christopher, West Indies.
	May	9	Thomas Grenville is sent to Paris to open negotiations with Comte de Vergennes and Benjamin Franklin for a peace.
1783	July	17	Parliament of Besançon demands that the Estates-General be convened.
	September	3	Peace of Versailles between Britain, France, Spain and U.S.A. Britain recognizes independence of U.S.A. and recovers its West Indian possessions; France recovers St. Lucia, Tobago, Senegal, Gorée and East Indian possessions; Spain retains Minorca and receives back Florida; France may fortify Dunkirk.
	November	10	Charles Calonne appointed French controller-general.
1784	October		Joseph II breaks off diplomatic relations with Holland when two Austrian vessels, ordered to navigate the Sheldt, are fired on by the Dutch. Louis XVI offers to mediate.
1785	August	15	Arrest of Cardinal de Rohan in Diamond Necklace Affair.
	November	8	By treaty of Fontainebleau, Holland recognizes Joseph II's sovereignty over part of

			River Scheldt, Joseph abandons his claim to Maestricht, renounces his right to free navigation of Scheldt outside his dominions and receives 10 million guilders.
		10	Alliance between France and Holland.
1786	September	26	Commercial treaty between England and France lowers duties on English clothes, cotton and iron goods, and on French wines, soap and olive oil.
1787			The Edict of Versailles grants religious freedom and legal status to French Protestants.
	February	22	Assembly of Notables meets at Versailles (until May 25) and rejects Charles de Calonne's proposals for financial reform.
	April	17	Calonne is banished to Lorraine, succeeded as minister of finance by Cardinal Étienne de Brienne, Archbishop of Toulouse.
	July	6	Parlement of Paris opposes Étienne de Brienne and demands the summoning of the Estates-General.
	August	14	Parlement of Paris is banished by Louis XVI to Troyes but recalled to Paris on September 24.
		17	Riots in Paris.
	November	20	Louis XVI declares that the Estates-General will be summoned in July 1792.
1788	January	20	Parlement of Paris presents a list of grievances.
	May	9-10	Riots in Rennes.
	June	11	Riots in Dijon.
		19	Riots in Pau.
	August	8	Louis XVI summons the Estates-General for May 1789.
		25	Loménie de Brienne, who announced national bankruptcy on 16, is dismissed.
		27	Jacques Necker recalled as minister finance.
1789	May	5	Estates-General open in Versailles.
		20	Clergy renounce their financial pr followed by the nobility on 23.

June	17	Third Estate constitutes itself the National Assembly.
	20	Third Estate takes Tennis Court Oath, undertaking not to dissolve until a constitution is drawn up.
	23	Louis XVI rejects resolutions by the Third Estate.
	27	Louis XVI orders the nobility and clergy to sit with the Third Estate.
July	9	National Assembly declares itself a constituent assembly.
	11	Necker dismissed.
	14	Destruction of the Bastille.
	16	Recall of Necker.
	17	Jean Bailly becomes mayor of Paris and the marquis de Lafayette commander of the National Guard.
July-August		The Great Fear.
August	4	National Assembly decrees equality of taxation, abolition of feudal rights and privileges, and the sale of offices.
	23	National Assembly decrees freedom of religion, and on 24 of the press.
	27	National Assembly adopts Declaration of the Rights of Man.
October	5-6	Paris mob, mainly female, marches on Versailles, and forces Louis XVI to return to Paris with the royal family.
November	2	Church property nationalized.
	7	Exclusion of deputies from ministerial office. National Assembly forbids any member to accept office under Louis XVI.
	9	National Assembly moves into the Manège.
December	21	*Assignats* issued.
January	15	83 *départements* established.
February		In British Parliament Edmund Burke condemns and Charles James Fox welcomes the developments in France.

	13	National Assembly decrees the abolition of monastic vows and on 15 the abolition of all feudal rights.
June	9	National Assembly abolishes the civil list of Louis XVI and his queen and suppress titles, liveries and armorial bearings.
July	12	The Civil Constitution of the Clergy. Jews in France are admitted to civil liberties.
	14	Feast of the Federation in the Champ de Mars. Louis XVI accepts the constitution.
September	10	Jacques Necker resigns.
November		Edmund Burke publishes *Reflections on the French Revolution*.
December	26	Louis XVI gives his consent to the civil constitution of the clergy.
1791		Inflation of French currency by immense issue of *assignats*.
January	30	Mirabeau elected President of the French Assembly.
April	4	Death of Mirabeau.
	13	The Pope condemns the civil constitution of the clergy in bull *Charitas*.
	18	Louis XVI is prevented by a riot from going to St. Cloud, demonstrating that he was a prisoner.
May	31	Guillotine introduced.
June	20 (-25)	Louis XVI flight to Varennes.
July	6	Leopold II of Austria issues letter calling on the powers to support Louis XVI. Comte d'Artois makes Coblenz the headquarters of French émigrés.
	9	National Assembly orders all émigrés to return to France within two months.
	17	Rioters in Birmingham, Britain, attack Joseph Priestley's house because of his support of French Revolution.
August	27	By the declaration of Pillnitz, Austria and Prussia say that they are ready to intervene in French affairs with consent of other powers, but William Pitt announces Britain will

remain neutral. France interprets the declaration as a threat.

September	3	France becomes a constitutional monarchy.
	4	France annexes the counties of Avignon and Venaissin.
	13	Louis XVI accepts new constitution.
	30	National Assembly dissolves after decreeing that none of its members is eligible to serve in the Legislative Assembly.
October	1	Legislative Assembly assembles.
November	9	Louis XVI vetoes a decree of the Assembly demanding the return of the émigrés under pain of death.
1792		Religious orders are dissolved and civil marriage and divorce is instituted. Government adopts Claude Chappe's system of semaphore.
February	7	Austro-Prussian treaty of Berlin against France.
March	24	Jean Roland and Charles Dumouriez form ministry.
April	20	War of the First Coalition begins.
	24	"La Marseillaise" by Rouget de l'Isle.
June	20	Mob invades Tuileries.
July	1	Petition of 20,000 against the events of June 20.
	14	Third Festival of the Federation.
August	10	Mob invades Tuileries, killing the Swiss Guard.
	10-12	Louis XVI imprisoned with his family in the Temple.
	10	Call for a national convention from the National Assembly.
	19	Defection of Lafayette.
	30	The Assembly attempts to dissolve the Commune.
September	2	Longwy and Verdun fall to the Prussians.

	2-6	Paris mob assassinates 1,200 persons, including 100 priests detained in prison for political reasons.
	20	French defeat the Prussians at Valmy.
	21	First session of the Convention. Last session of the National Assembly and first of the National Convention, which declares royalty abolished and proclaims republic.
	22	Year I of the first republic proclaimed and the revolutionary calendar comes into force.
October	10	Brissot is expelled from the Jacobin Club. Convention decree forbids the use of *Monsieur* and *Madame*, replacing them with *citoyen* and *citoyenne*.
November	5	Robespierre defends Paris and the Montagnards.
	6	Charles Dumouriez defeats Austrians at Jemappes, takes Brussels and conquers Austrian Netherlands.
	8-12	French take Tournai, Ghent and Charleroi and by 30 most of present-day Belgium.
	19	Convention offers assistance to all peoples striving to recover their liberty.
	20	Discovery of the secret cupboard in the Tuileries.
December	5	Trial of Louis XVI begins.
	11	Interrogation of the king by the Convention.
	18	Paine is tried in his absence for publishing *The Rights of Man*.
1793		The Louvre, Paris, becomes a national art gallery. Compulsory public education in France from the age of 6. Jacques Hébert edits *Père Duchesne*, advocating atheism.
January	17	Louis XVI condemned to death.
	21	Louis XVI guillotined. Émigré princes declare the dauphin king of France.
	22	Resignation of Roland.

February	1	The Convention declares war on England and Holland.
	13	First Coalition against France is formed by Britain, Austria, Prussia, Holland, Spain and Sardinia.
	25	Food rioting in Paris.
March	7	France declares war on Spain and the Spanish invade Rousillon and Navarre.
	16	Beginning of the revolt in Vendée.
	18	Charles Dumouriez is defeated at Neerwinden, leading to the liberation of Belgium.
	26	Holy Roman Empire declares war on France. Royalist revolt in La Vendée.
	28	Civil war in La Vendée.
April	4	Charles Dumouriez and Louis Philippe desert to Austrians.
	6	Committee of Public Safety established in France with dictatorial power (until 1795), dominated by Danton.
	13	Impeachment of Marat.
May	10	The Convention moves to the Tuileries.
June	2	Final overthrow of Girondins and arrest of Jacques Brissot begins Reign of Terror.
	24	The Convention accepts the constitution of 1793.
July	10	Fall of the fortress of Condé. Danton leaves the Committee of Public Safety.
	13	Jean Marat is stabbed and killed by Charlotte Corday.
August	1	Decimal system adopted in France.
	23	*Levée en masse.*
	27	Surrender of Toulon to the British.
September	5	"Hébertist" rising in Paris.
	17	Law of Suspects decreed.
	22	Beginning of the Year II.
	25	The Committee of Public Safety survives attack in the Convention.

	29	The General Maximum in restraint of prices and wages.
October	3	Impeachment of Brissot and 44 other deputies.
	5	Revolutionary calendar established (from September 22). Christianity is abolished in France.
	9	Recapture of Lyons by the forces of the Convention.
	10	Decree sanctioning Revolutionary government for the duration of the war.
	16	Queen Marie Antoinette condemned to death and guillotined.
	17	Vendéans defeated at Cholet.
	24-30	Trial of Brissot and 20 other deputies.
	31	Execution of the Girondists.
November	10	Worship of goddess of reason in Notre Dame.
	12	Philippe Égalité (Duke of Orléans) executed.
December	4	The Law of Revolutionary Government (14 Frimaire).
	5	First issue of the *Vieux Cordelier* initiates a campaign against the Hébertists.
	15	Third issue of the *Vieux Cordelier* challenges the Terror.
	19	Toulon retaken by the French.
	25	Robespierre's speech on the Principles of Revolutionary Government.
	30	The Festival of Victory.
1794		École Normale founded in France. Foundation of the École Polytechnique at Paris. First telegraph Paris-Lille.
January	12	Arrest of Fabre d'Eglantine.
February	4	Convention proclaims all blacks to be free, and the abolition of slavery in the colonies.
	5	Robespierre speaks on the Principles of Political Morality.

		15	Tricolor adopted as the French national flag.
	March	4	Attempted insurrection at the Cordeliers Club.
		5	Execution of partisans of Jacques Hébert (Hébertists).
		14	Arrest of the Hébertists.
		24	Execution of the Hébertists.
		30	Arrest of Danton.
	April	5	Execution of Danton and Camille Desmoulins.
		19	Treaty of the Hague between Britain, Prussia, and Holland, against France.
	May	7	Robespierre introduces the worship of the Supreme Being.
	June	1	Lord Howe defeats French in the English Channel.
		8	Festival of the Supreme Being. Robespierre presides over the Feast of the Supreme Being in Paris.
		10	Law of 22 Prairial increases the power of the Revolutionary Tribunal, leading to mass executions.
		25	Austrians defeated at Fleurus and lose Belgium. French troops take Charleroi.
	July	27-28	Fall of Robespierre and the Mountain. End of Reign of Terror (9 Thermidor).
		30-31	Reorganization of the Committee of Public Safety.
	September	28	Britain, Russia and Austria form the alliance of St. Petersburg against France.
	Novermber	11	Jacobin Club, Paris, is closed.
	December	8	Surviving Girondists are admitted to the Convention.
		24	Abolition of the Maximum. A new issue of *assignats* further depreciates the French currency.
1795	January	30	Dutch fleet, caught in the ice, taken by French hussars.

	February	15	Peace of La Jaunaie whereby the Vendéans come to terms with the French government.
		19	Peace treaty between France and Tuscany.
		21	Freedom of worship in France.
	May	16	Peace with Holland. Treaty of Peace and Alliance between France and Holland. Batavian Republic established in Holland.
		20	White Terror in Paris (through June).
	June	8	Death of the dauphin (Louis XVII), son of Louis XVI, announced: Comte de Provence assumes title of Louis XVIII.
	July	21	Hoche destroys the émigré forces at Quiberon
	August	23	Third French constitution, which establishes the Directory and becomes effective on November 3.
	October	5	Bonaparte's "whiff of grapeshot" crushes insurrection.
		26	Dissolution of the Convention.
	November	1	Directory formed, with Senate, Council of 55, and an Executive Directory of 5 members.
1796	February	23	Bonaparte given command of army in Italy.
	March	9	Bonaparte marries Joséphine de Beauharnais.
		19	Freedom of the press in France.
		29	Rebellion in La Vendée ends.
	May	10	Failure of François Babeuf's plot to restore French constitution of 1793. Bonaparte defeats Austrians at Lodi.
		15	Bonaparte enters Milan.
		16	Lombardic Republic established.
	August	5	Franco-Prussian treaty of Berlin.
		19	Treaty of San Ildefonso.
	October	16	Cispadane Republic established.
		22	English evacuate Corsica.

	November	15-17	Bonaparte defeats Austrians at Arcola.
	December	15	French fleet with 15,000 men embarks at Brest to attack Ireland.
		19	Directory refuse further negotiations with Britain.
1797	January	14	Bonaparte defeats Austrians at Rivoli.
		29	Trento occupied by the French.
	February	2	Mantua surrenders to the French.
		9	Ancona taken.
		19	Pius VI by Treaty of Tolentino cedes the Romagna, Bologna, and Ferrara to France, and Napoleon Bonaparte advances through Tyrol to Vienna.
	April	18	Preliminary peace between France and Austria signed at Leoben.
		20-23	Armistice on the Rhine.
	June		Franco-Dutch fleet, with 14,000 men, embarks at Texel to attack Ireland.
		6	Bonaparte founds the Ligurian Republic in Genoa.
		28	France occupies the Ionian Islands.
	July	9	Cisalpine Republic established.
		15	Cispadane and Cisalpine republics united.
	September	4	Coup d'état of 18 Fructidor.
	October		Treaty of Campo Formio with Austria.
		4	"XYZ" affair.
		17	Peace of Campo Formio.
	December	5	Bonaparte arrives in Paris.
		16	Peace conference to arrange terms between France and the Holy Roman Empire opens at Rastatt.
1798	January	22	Batavian Republic established in Holland.
		24	Lemanic Republic proclaimed in Geneva.
		28	France invades Switzerland.
	February	11	French take Rome.
		15	Roman republic proclaimed and Pope Pius VI leaves Rome for Valence.

	March	5	France occupies Berne.
		29	Switzerland reorganized as the Helvetic Republic.
	May	19	Expedition to Egypt sails from Toulon.
	June	12	French take Malta.
	July		Bonaparte's victory at the battle of the Pyramids.
		1-3	French take Alexandria.
		21	Battle of the Pyramids.
	August	22	French force lands in Ireland but invasion fails on 28.
	September	5	Military conscription made compulsory.
		9	Turkey declares war on France.
	November	29	Ferdinand IV of Naples declares war against France and enters Rome.
	December	4	France declares war on Naples.
		6	Naples and Sardinia declare war on France.
		10	French occupy Turin.
		15	French recapture Rome, and overrun the Kingdom of Naples.
		23	Russo-Turkish treaty against France.
		24	Anglo-Russian alliance.
1799	January	2	Britian joins the Russo-Turkish alliance.
		23	Parthenopean Republic established in Piedmont.
	March	12	War of the Second Coalition.
	April	5	French defeated by Austrians at Magnono.
		8	Conference of Rastatt is dissolved.
		27	Cisalpine Republic ends.
	July	20	Talleyrand retires but reappointed November 10.
		24	Bonaparte defeats Turks at Aboukir.
	August	22	Bonaparte leaves Egypt.
	October	9	Bonaparte lands at Fréjus.
		22	Russia leaves the Coalition.

	November	9-10	The coup d'état of Brumaire. Directory overthrown, Bonaparte made first consul.
		10	Bonaparte appoints Talleyrand foreign minister.
	December	24	Constitution of the Year III proclaimed in Paris; first consul assisted by 2 consultative consuls, Senate of 60, Tribune of 100, and legislative body of 300 members.
1800	February	11	Bank of France established.
	March	20	Kléber defeats Turks and Mamelukes at Heliopolis.
	May	15-20	Bonaparte's army crosses the Great St. Bernard Pass.
	May-June		France renews hostilities against the Coalition.
	June	2	French occupy Milan; Cisalpine Republic reestablished.
		14	Kléber assassinated at Cairo.
	December	16	Paul I of Russia leaves the Coalition, and allies with Denmark, Prussia and Sweden against England.
1801	March	28	Peace between France and Turkey; Egypt restored to Turkey. Peace of Florence between France and Naples, by which British vessels to be excluded from Neapolitan ports.
	July	15	Concordat improves relations with the Vatican and Catholic church fully restored.
	September	3	French evacuate Egypt.
		29	Treaty of Badajoz between France and Spain.
	October	1	Peace preliminaries between Britain and France.
		8	Peace treaty between Russia and France; and between Russia and Britain.
1802	January	26	Bonaparte president of Italian Republic (the former Cisalpine Republic).
	March	27	Peace of Amiens between France and Britain, which achieves the complete pacification of Europe.

	April	26	General amnesty proclaimed in France for all émigrés.
	May	1	Education reforms and *lycées* created.
		19	Order of Legion of Honor established.
	August	2	Bonaparte First Consul for life.
		4	Introduction of Fifth Constitution in France.
1803	April	30	U.S. purchases Louisiana Territory and New Orleans from the French.
	May		France occupies Hanover.
		18	Renewal of hostilities between Britain and France.
	December	2	French forces muster at Boulogne with a view to invading England.
1804	February	15	Arrest of Georges Cadoudal, and generals Pichegru and Moreau, for conspiring against Bonaparte.
	March	20	Duc d'Enghien, implicated in February plot (against Bonaparte), is executed.
	May	7	The Code Civile (or Code Napoléon) promulgated.
		16	Napoleon Bonaparte proclaimed emperor by Senate and Tribune.
	December	2	Coronation of Napoleon and Joséphine in Notre Dame.

SELECT BIBLIOGRAPHY

The list of publications, in French, on the Revolution is enormous, indeed, its an industry in itself. I have listed here books in the French and English languages that I have found useful in the compilation of this *Companion*. Additional titles are given at the end of many of the entries.

General

IN FRENCH

Boursin, E., and Challamel, Augustin, *Dictionnaire de la Révolution Française*, 1893.
Del Vecchio, Giorgio, *La Déclaration des Droits de l'Homme et du Citoyen dans la Révolution Française*, 1979.
Gaxotte, Pierre, *La Révolution Française*, 1975.
Godechot, Jacques, *Les Institutions de la France sous la Révolution et l'Empire*, 1951.
———. *Regards sur l'Époque Révolutionnaire*, 1980.
———. *La Grande Nation*, 1983.
Lefebvre, Georges, *Études sur la Révolution Française*, 1954.
Robinet, Jean Francois August, Robert, Adolphe and Le Chaplain, J., *Dictionnaire Historique et Biographique de la Révolution et de l'Empire, 1789-1815*. Two vols, 1889.
Walter, Gerard, *La Révolution Française vue par ses Journaux*, 1948.

IN ENGLISH

Aulard, F. V. A., *The French Revolution, A Political History, 1789-1804*. trans. 4 vols. 1910.
Brinton, Crane. *A Decade of Revolution 1789-1799*. 1934.
Bryant, Arthur. *The Years of Endurance*. 1942.
Cambridge Modern History. Vol. VIII, The French Revolution. 1934.
Campbell, Peter. *French Electoral Systems*. 1958.
Caute, David. *The Left in Europe since 1789*. 1966.
Cobban, Alfred. *The Social Interpretation of the French Revolution*. 1964.
Forrest, Alan I. *The French Revolution and the Poor*. 1981.
Hampson, Norman. *A Social History of the French Revolution*. 1963.

———. *The First European Revolution 1776-1815*. 1969.
———. *The French Revolution: A Concise History*. 1975.
Hibbert, Christopher. *The French Revolution*. 1980.
Hunt, Lynn. *Politics, Culture and Class in the French Revolution*. 1984.
Johnson, Douglas. (ed.). *French Society and the Revolution*. 1976.
Jones, R. Ben. *The French Revolution*. 1974.
Lefebvre, Georges. *The French Revolution*. trans. 2 vols. 1962.
Roberts, John M. *The French Revolution*. 1978.
Rudé, George. *The Crowd in the French Revolution*. 1959.
Stuart, John Hall. *A Documentary Survey of the French Revolution*. 1951.
Sydenham, Michael John. *The French Revolution*. new ed. 1969.
Thompson, James M. *The French Revolution*. 1944.
Weiner, Margery. *The French Exiles, 1789-1815*. 1960.
Williams, Alan. *The Police of Paris, 1718-89*. 1979.
Williams, Gwyn A. *Artisans and Sans-Culottes: Popular Movements in France and Britain during the French Revolution*. 1968.

Ancien Régime

Barnave, A. P. J. M. *Introduction to the French Revolution*. 1971.
Behrens, Catherine B. A. *The Ancien Régime*. 1967.
Blum, Jerome. *The End of the Old Order in Rural Europe*. 1978.
Chaussinand-Nogaret, Guy. *The French Nobility in the Eighteenth Century: From Feudalism to Enlightenment*. 1985.
Cobban, Alfred. *History of Modern France, 1755-1799*. 3rd ed. 1963.
Cowie, Leonard W. *Eighteenth-Century Europe*. 1974.
Dakin, Douglas. *Turgot and the Ancien Régime in France*. 1939.
Darnton, Robert C. *The Literary Underground of the Old Regime*. 1982.
de Tocqueville, A. *The Ancien Régime and the French Revolution*. 1976.
Doyle, William. *The Parliament of Bordeaux and the End of the Old Régime, 1771-90*. 1974.
———. *The Old European Order, 1660-1800*. 1978.
———. *Origins of the French Revolution*. 1980.
Égret, Jean. *The French Prerevolution, 1787-88*. 1977.
Gillespie, Charles C. *Science and Polity at the End of the Old Régime*. 1980.
Goodwin, A. (ed.). *The European Nobility in the Eighteenth Century*. 1953.
Harris, Robert D. *Necker: Reform Statesman of the Ancien Régime*. 1979.
Herr, R. *Tocqueville and the Old Régime*. 1962.
Hufton, Olwen. *The Poor of Eighteenth-Century France, 1750-89*. 1974.
Lefebvre, Georges. *The Coming of the French Revolution*. trans. 1967.
Lough, J. *Introduction to Eighteenth-Century France*. 1960.
Mathews, G. T. *The Royal General Farms in Eighteenth-Century France*. 1958.
Sorel, Albert. *Europe and the French Revolution: The Political Traditions of the Old Régime*. 1969.
Williams, E. N. *The Ancien Régime in Europe*. 1970.
Young, Arthur. *Travels in France and Italy*. 1792.

Biographies

Beach, Vincent. *Charles X of France: His Life and Times*. 1971.
Bernard, Jack F. *Talleyrand: A Biography*. 1973.

Besterman, Theodore. *Voltaire.* 1969.
Boylan, Henry. *Theobald Wolfe Tone.* 1981.
Bradby, E. D. *The Life of Barnave.* 2 vols. 1915.
Brailsford, H. N. *Voltaire.* 1963.
Buckman, Peter. *Lafayette: A Biography.* 1977.
Clapham, J. H. *Abbé Sieyès.* 1912.
Cole, Hubert. *Fouché: The Unprincipled Patriot.* 1972.
Cooper, Duff. *Talleyrand.* 1947.
Cronin, Vincent. *Napoleon.* 1971.
———. *Louis and Antoinette.* 1974.
Crankshaw, Edward. *Maria Theresa.* 1969.
Curtis, E. N. *St. Just: Colleague of Robespierre.* 1935.
Égret, Jean. *Necker.* 1975.
Fay, B. *Louis XVI, or, the End of a World.* 1968.
Garnier, Jean-Paul. *Barras.* 1970.
Gazley, John G. *The Life of Arthur Young.* 1973.
Gershoy, Leo. *Bertrand Barère, A Reluctant Terrorist.* 1962.
Gottschalk, L. *Jean Paul Marat.* 1927.
Grimsley, Ronald. *Jean Jacques Rousseau.* 1983.
Hampson, Norman. *Danton.* 1978.
———. *The Life and Opinions of Maximilien Robespierre.* 1974.
Hearsey, J. E. N. *Marie Antoinette.* 1972.
Macpherson, Crawford B. *Burke.* 1980.
Madelin, Louis. *Fouché 1759-1820.* 2 vols. 1930.
———. *Talleyrand.* 1948.
Mason, Haydn. T. *Voltaire: A Biography.* 1981.
Nicolson, Harold. *Benjamin Constant.* 1949.
Rose, Robert B. *Gracchus Babeuf: The First Revolutionary Communist.* 1979.
Rude, George. *Robespierre: Portrait of a Revolutionary Democrat.* 1975.
Scarfe, André. *Chénier: His Life and Work.* 1965.
Taylor, I. A. *Life of Madame Roland.* 1911.
Thompson, James M. *Robespierre.* 2 vols. 1935.
Thrasher, Peter Adam. *Pasquale Paoli: An Enlightened Hero, 1725-1807.* 1970.
Tulard, Jean. *Napoleon, the Myth of the Saviour.* 1984.
Watson, S. J. *Carnot.* 1954.
Welch, O. J. G. *Mirabeau.* 1951.
Wolf, J. B. *Louis XIV.* 1968.

National Convention and the Constitutional Monarchy

Gooch, R. K. *Parliamentary Government in France, 1789-91.* 1960.
Palmer, R. R. *Twelve Who Ruled.* 1941.
Patrick, A. *The Men of the First French Republic.* 1972.
Soboul, A. *The Parisian Sans-Culottes in the French Revolution.* 1964.
Sydenham, Michael John. *The Girondins.* 1961.
Thompson, E. *Popular Sovereignty and the French Constituent Assembly, 1785-91.* 1952.
Vovelle, Michel. *The Fall of the French Monarchy 1787-1792.* trans. 1984.

Terror, the Reaction, the Directory

Bouloiseau, Marc. *The Jacobin Republic. 1792-94.* trans. 1983.
Brinton, Crane. *The Jacobins.* 1961.
Kennedy, Michael L. *The Jacobin Club of Marseilles, 1790-94.* 1973.
———. *The Jacobin Clubs in the French Revolution: The First Years.* 1982.
Kerr, Wilfred B. *Reign of Terror 1793-4.* 1927.
Lefebvre, Georges. *The Thermidorians.* trans. 1965.
———. *The Directory.* trans. 1965.
Lenotre, G. *The Tribunal of the Terror: A Study of Paris in 1793-1795.* trans. 1909.
Loomis, Stanley. *Paris in the Terror, June 1793–July 1794.* 1965.
Lyons, M. *The Directory.* 1975.
Lyons, Martyn A. *France under the Directory.* 1975.
Macdonald, J. *Rousseau and the French Revolution, 1762-91.* 1965.
Palmer, R. R. *Twelve Who Ruled: The Year of the Terror in the French Revolution.* 1941.
Scott, William. *Terror and Repression in Revolutionary Marseilles.* 1973.
Soboul, A. *The Sans-Culottes: The Popular Movement and Revolutionary Government, 1793-1794.* 1981.
Sydenham, Michael John. *The Girondins.* 1960.
———. *The First French Republic, 1792-1804.* 1974.
Thompson, D. *The Baboeuf Plot.* 1947.
Thompson, James M. *Robespierre and the French Revolution.* 1952.
Woloch, Isser. *Jacobin Legacy: The Democratic Movement under the Directory.* 1970
Woronoff, Denis. *The Thermidorean Regime and the Directory, 1794-99.* trans. 1984
Wright, D. G. *Revolution and Terror in France, 1789-1795.* 1974.

Wars, the Army and Napoleon

Blanning, T. C. W., *The Origins of the French Revolutionary Wars,* 1986.
Clapham, J. H. *The Causes of the War of 1792.* 1899.
Connelly, O. *Napoleon's Satellite Kingdoms.* 1965.
Geyl, P. *Napoleon—For and Against.* trans. 1947.
Glover, Michael A. *Warfare in the Age of Bonaparte.* 1980.
Lynn, John A. *The Bayonets of the Republic: Motivation and Tactics in the Army of Revolutionary France 1791-94.* 1986.
Phipps, R. W. *The Armies of the First French Revolution.* 4 vols. 1926-39.
Roger, A. B. *The War of the Second Coalition: 1798-1800. A Strategic Commentary.* 1964.
Ross, Michael C. *Banners of the King: The War of the Vendée, 1793-4.* 1975.
Ross, Steven T. *Quest for Victory: French Military Strategy, 1792-99.* 1973.
Rothenberg, Gunther E. *The Art of Warfare in the Age of Napoleon.* 1977.
Thompson, James M. *Napoleon Bonaparte, His Rise and Fall.* 1952.
Wilkinson, S. *The French Army before Napoleon.* 1915.

Church and Education

Aulard, A. *Christianity and the French Revolution.* 1927.
Barnard, Howard C. *Education and the French Revolution.* 1969.
Hales, E. E. Y. *Revolution and the Papacy, 1769-1849.* 1960.
McManners, John. *The French Revolution and the Church.* 1969.
Vidler, A. R. *The Church in an Age of Revolution: 1789 to the Present Day.* 1961.
Walsh, H. H. *The Concordat of 1801.* 1933.

France in 1789

showing provinces and principal centers of administration

Pays d'états: lands claiming preserved privileges

⊙ Sièges des parlements ⎫ centers of legal
■ Conseils souverains ⎭ administration

● Other centers of royal administration

Departments of France in 1790

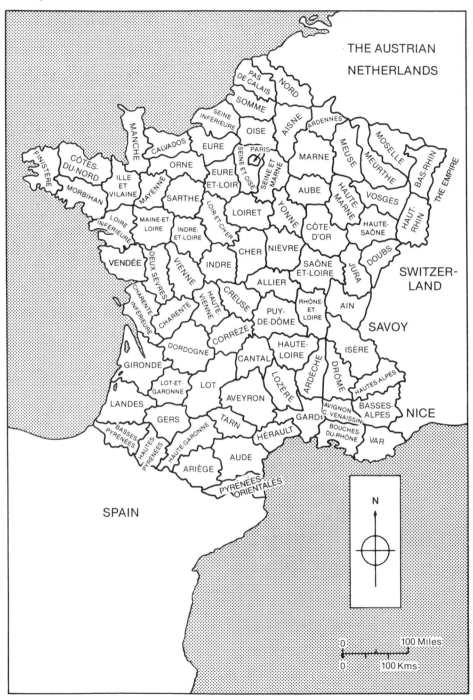

THE AUSTRIAN
NETHERLANDS

PAS DE CALAIS
NORD
SOMME
SEINE INFÉRIEURE
OISE
AISNE
ARDENNES
MANCHE
CALVADOS
EURE
PARIS
MARNE
MEUSE
MOSELLE
MEURTHE
BAS-RHIN
THE EMPIRE
FINISTÈRE
CÔTES-DU-NORD
ORNE
EURE-ET-LOIR
SEINE-ET-OISE
SEINE-ET-MARNE
AUBE
HAUTE-MARNE
VOSGES
HAUT-RHIN
ILLE ET VILAINE
MORBIHAN
MAYENNE
SARTHE
LOIR-ET-CHER
LOIRET
YONNE
CÔTE-D'OR
HAUTE-SAÔNE
LOIRE INFÉRIEURE
MAINE-ET-LOIRE
INDRE-ET-LOIRE
CHER
NIÈVRE
SAÔNE-ET-LOIRE
DOUBS
JURA
SWITZER-LAND
VENDÉE
DEUX SÈVRES
VIENNE
INDRE
ALLIER
RHÔNE-ET-LOIRE
AIN
SAVOY
CHARENTE INFÉRIEURE
CHARENTE
HAUTE-VIENNE
CREUSE
PUY-DE-DÔME
DORDOGNE
CORRÈZE
HAUTE-LOIRE
ISÈRE
GIRONDE
CANTAL
ARDÈCHE
DRÔME
LOT-ET-GARONNE
LOT
AVEYRON
LOZÈRE
HAUTES-ALPES
LANDES
GERS
TARN
GARD
AVIGNON C. VENAISSIN
BASSES-ALPES
NICE
BASSES-PYRÉNÉES
HAUTES-PYRÉNÉES
HAUTE-GARONNE
HÉRAULT
BOUCHES-DU-RHÔNE
VAR
ARIÉGE
AUDE
PYRÉNÉES-ORIENTALES
SPAIN

N

0 |———| 100 Miles
0 |———| 100 Kms

Paris at the Time
of the Revolution

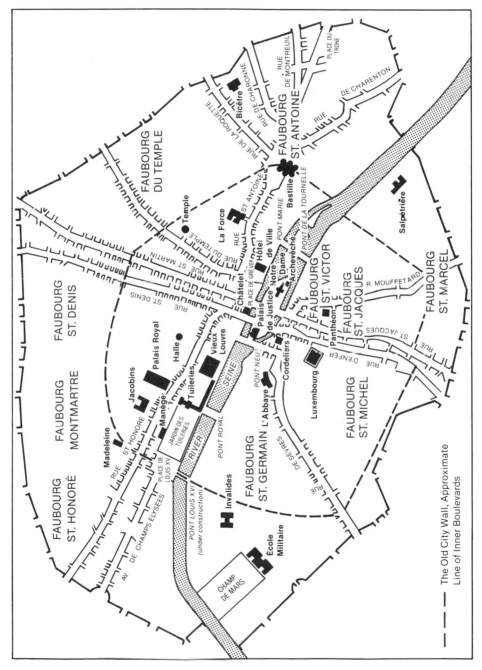

FAUBOURG
DU TEMPLE

FAUBOURG
ST. ANTOINE

PLACE DU
TRONE

DE CHARENTON

RUE DE MONTREUIL

RUE
DE CHARONNE

RUE DE CHARONNE

RUE DE LA ROQUETTE

Bicêtre

RUE

Salpétrière

Bastille

RUE ST. ANTOINE

PONT MARIE

PONT DE LA TOURNELLE

Temple

La Force

RUE DU TEMPLE

Hôtel
de Ville

PLACE DE GRÈVE

Notre
Dame

Archevêché

FAUBOURG
ST. VICTOR

FAUBOURG
ST. JACQUES

FAUBOURG
ST. MARCEL

RUE ST. MARTIN

Châtelet

Palais
de Justice

Panthéon

R. MOUFFETARD

RUE ST. DENIS

RUE ST. MARTIN

FAUBOURG
ST. DENIS

RUE ST. JACQUES

RUE DENIS

Palais Royal

Jacobins

Halle

Vieux
Louvre

Tuileries

Cordeliers

Luxembourg

RUE D'ENFER

FAUBOURG
ST. MICHEL

FAUBOURG
MONTMARTRE

Madeleine

RUE ST. HONORÉ

Manège

JARDIN DES
TUILERIES

SEINE

PONT NEUF

L'Abbaye

FAUBOURG
ST. GERMAIN

RUE

DE SÈVRES

RIVER

PONT ROYAL

FAUBOURG
ST. HONORÉ

RUE ST. HONORÉ

PLACE DE
LOUIS XVI

PONT LOUIS XVI
(under construction)

Invalides

Écoles
Militaire

CHAMP
DE MARS

AV. DE CHAMPS ELYSÉES

—— The Old City Wall, Approximate

- - - Line of Inner Boulevards

The Sections of Paris